Praise for *ONE OF A KIND*

"Stuey was a little bit of a gangster, genius, madman, tragic hero, and cardsharp. Add it all up, as Dalla and Alson have done in captivating style, and you get one of the most unusual characters to ever appear on the Vegas scene."

—Andy Bellin, author of *Poker Nation*

"Writers Nolan Dalla and Peter Alson have sprinkled gambling tales told in Mr. Ungar's own words into a largely nonjudgmental recounting of the many highs and lows of his life."

—*The Wall Street Journal*

"I knew Stuey Ungar well and played with him many, many times. He was one of the most remarkable characters to ever sit down at a poker table. Reading *One of a Kind* not only brought him back to life for me, it vividly re-created a time and place that we'll likely never see again. For anyone interested in understanding and unraveling the legend of poker's most creative thinker and tortured soul, this is the real deal!"

—Doyle Brunson, two-time world poker champion and author of the legendary bestseller *Doyle Brunson's SuperSystem: A Course in Power Poker*

"A heartfelt, respectful and accepting biography."

—*Publishers Weekly*

"A well-written and well-researched study of the most naturally gifted and emotionally stunted card genius in the history of poker."

—A. Alvarez, author of *The Biggest Game in Town*

"This book is the real deal about Stu Ungar's life . . . . [it] is powerful . . . it doesn't sugarcoat anything, and it shows you the genius and the demons in Stuey's life."

—*Cardplayer* magazine

"A stunningly detailed book."

—*Las Vegas Review-Journal*

"Dalla and Alson do an admirable job of not attempting to minimize Ungar's many faults . . . without resorting to the kind of hyperbole that dooms many sports biographies, *One of a Kind* shows what made Ungar so special to so many."

—*The Associated Press*

Also by Peter Alson

CONFESSIONS OF AN IVY LEAGUE BOOKIE:
A TRUE TALE OF LOVE AND THE VIG

ONE OF A KIND

THE RISE AND FALL OF STUEY "THE KID" UNGAR, THE WORLD'S GREATEST POKER PLAYER

NOLAN DALLA *and* **PETER ALSON**

FOREWORD BY MIKE SEXTON

ATRIA BOOKS

NEW YORK   LONDON   TORONTO   SYDNEY

ATRIA BOOKS

1230 Avenue of the Americas
New York, NY 10020

The Library of Congress has cataloged the hardcover edition as follows:

Dalla, Nolan.
    One of a kind : the rise and fall of Stuey "the Kid" Ungar, the world's greatest
poker player / Nolan Dalla and Peter Alson ; foreword by Mike Sexton.
        p.   cm.
Includes bibliographical references and index.
    1. Ungar, Stuey, 1953–1998.   2. Poker players—United States—Biography.
I. Alson, Peter.   II. Title.
GV1250.2.U53D35   2005
795.412'092 B—dc22   2005045334
[B]
ISBN-13: 978-0-7434-7658-4
ISBN-10:   0-7434-7658-1
ISBN-13: 978-0-7434-7659-1 (Pbk)
ISBN-10:   0-7434-7659-X (Pbk)

First Atria Books trade paperback edition May 2006

10   9   8   7   6   5   4

ATRIA BOOKS is a trademark of Simon & Schuster, Inc.

Manufactured in the United States of America

For information about special discounts for bulk purchases,
please contact Simon & Schuster Special Sales:
1-800-456-6798 or business@simonandschuster.com.

Credits for photographs in insert: p. 1 (top) courtesy of Ulvis Alberts;
p. 1 (bottom) courtesy of Pamela Shandel; p. 2 (top) courtesy of Caesars Palace;
p. 2 (middle), p. 3 (all), p. 5 (top left and top right), and p. 8 (top right) courtesy of
Madeline and Stefanie Ungar; p. 4 (top) courtesy of Imagemasters Photography;
p. 4 (bottom right) courtesy of Billy Baxter; p. 6 (middle) courtesy of Dr. Ray
Warchaizer; p. 7 (bottom) courtesy of Sian Kennedy. All other photographs are
courtesy of Nolan Dalla.

To Marietta
—NOLAN DALLA ♠ *To Alice*
—PETER ALSON

CONTENTS

CONTENTS

FOREWORD

I first met Stuey Ungar in 1978, at the Dunes Hotel in Las Vegas. Sadly, twenty years later, I was a pallbearer and speaker at his funeral. During my eulogy, I said, "Let's forgive Stuey for his weaknesses and drug problems and remember him for what he was—the greatest player to ever grace the green felt."

Forgive, but don't forget.

Stu Ungar was a legend in the gambling world. He had an aura and mystique about him that turned heads in every room he entered. Ungar craved action and bet on everything. Whatever he gambled on, whether it was poker, gin, blackjack (if they let him play—he was barred from just about every casino on the planet because he was too good), horses, sports, or golf, he was the highest of high rollers. Stu Ungar stories are legendary.

Physically, Ungar was small; but mentally, he was a giant. He had the quickest mind of anyone I've ever known. When it came to cards, Ungar had no equal. He was a genius and had a photographic memory. His raw talent was overwhelming. I still smile when I think of some of the plays he made in big tournaments, with hundreds of thousands of dollars on the line. And I have tears in my eyes thinking about what could have been.

Ungar was known for being fearless and aggressive—two traits that are very easy to talk about but almost impossible to display on a daily basis. Simply put, Stuey Ungar was the greatest gladiator in poker history. He took command of every table he played at and dominated his opponents heads-up (the final phase of every tournament comes down to two players facing off mano a mano).

For years, the second-largest poker tournament in the world (behind the World Series of Poker) was Amarillo Slim's Super Bowl of Poker. Only one player in history has captured the $10,000 championship event in both the World Series of Poker and the Super Bowl of Poker. That man was Stu Ungar. And he won each three times.

Remarkably, as great as he was at it, poker wasn't even his best game. Gin rummy was. He originally came to Las Vegas to play gin, not poker. Soon, however, after beating everyone, he couldn't get any games.

Unless you had seen Ungar play gin rummy, or talked to those who played against him, it would be difficult to imagine his artistry at that game. I've never met or talked to any people who played him who didn't consider Stuey to be far and away the best player they had ever seen. After one or two discards, he could place virtually every card in your hand. As the Poker Hall-of-Famer Doyle Brunson once said about Ungar's expertise at gin rummy, "It's scary to watch him."

Not long before he died, Ungar said to me, "Fifty years from now, I suppose it's possible that a better poker player may come around, but I can't see how there will ever be a better gin player. I really mean it. Michael Jordan won—what—four or five MVPs? If they gave an MVP for gin rummy, I would have won it every year since I was sixteen years old."

I spent a lot of time with Stu Ungar and Nolan Dalla the summer before Stuey died. Ungar wanted to write One of a Kind for several reasons. He was hoping there was a chance that someone would read it and it might change that person's life by leading him away from the self-destructive path that he had taken. He could also see the possibility that this book might become a movie, and he liked to picture himself at the Hollywood premiere and the Academy Awards. But mostly he wanted to write it for his daughter, Stefanie, whom he worshipped. Stefanie never really got to see the beautiful person that was her father in his prime— brilliant, daring, generous, kind, compassionate, and mesmerizing. Yes, Stuey was an addict, but he loved life and loved the people around him. And most of all, he loved and respected the game.

Stuey never got to finish his autobiography. But what you find here is the official biography of "the Kid." It's a powerful and remarkable re-creation of one of the most fascinating lives ever lived. Enjoy.

—MIKE SEXTON, LAS VEGAS,
APRIL 15, 2004

A NOTE TO THE READER

*O*ne of a Kind was originally intended to be Stuey Ungar's autobiography. Before Peter Alson got involved in this project with me, I spent many sessions interviewing Stuey face-to-face, often under the most trying physical and emotional circumstances. Most of the interviews took place in various hotel rooms scattered throughout Las Vegas in the summer and fall of 1998. At times, Stuey was remarkably cooperative and was able to recount details of his life that had occurred decades earlier. At other times, he was aloof and unable to remember even the simplest of details. At still other times Stuey was nearly incapable of functioning in normal human ways.

Many of Stuey's closest friends and supporters hoped this book project would be a catharsis for him, a purifying emotional exercise, which would allow him to come to grips with his drug problem. Stuey himself seemed to take great pride in reflecting back on his life and discussing the early influences that eventually made him an icon in the gambling world. Unfortunately, the temptations of that world and Stuey's own self-destructive tendencies doomed him to his tragic and in many ways predictable fate.

His untimely death produced an ethical dilemma for me as an author as to how to tell his story. I decided that it was important to tell parts of the story in Stuey's own words so that readers could grasp his streetwise vocabulary, his incessant vulgarity, his rough humor, and his deep passion for taking risks. I also realized that in shifting from a memoir to a biography I needed a coauthor who could help me tell a deeper story.

Peter Alson, a native New Yorker and acclaimed author, understood immediately both the significance of Stuey's story and what was needed to bring it fully to life. Not only did Peter know the terrain from having written about poker and gambling for magazines like *Esquire, Details,* and *Playboy,* but he is a poker player himself, who has competed in the final event of the World Series of Poker. He also had a personal brush with Stuey in 1988, while covering the Super Bowl of Poker at Caesars Palace, an event that Stuey Ungar won.

Together, Peter and I conducted extensive interviews of the people in Stuey's life, and we hope that the accompanying narrative will serve to give some insight into a man who was by equal turns fascinating and infuriating, inspiring and frustrating, generous to a fault and selfish beyond all reason.

—NOLAN DALLA

ONE OF A KIND

1.

THE KID

No one noticed him at first.

It was May 1997, fifteen hours before the start of the $10,000 buy-in at the World Series of Poker (WSOP) championship event, and in the satellite area, a low-lit collection of baize-topped hold'em tables in the back of Binion's Horseshoe casino, most of the players were too caught up in the business at hand to pay attention right away.

When one player did at last recognize the diminutive man wandering around the periphery of the room, he muttered something to the fellows at his table, and a couple of them turned to look. Then a couple more looked.

Stu Ungar, the two-time world champion of poker, was not unaccustomed to drawing stares in a poker room. The man they called "the Kid" was the most feared tournament player in poker history. Yet here it was, the eve of the championship, and this was the first time he'd been sighted during the more than three weeks that poker's greatest stars had been gathered at the Horseshoe in Las Vegas for their annual shoot-out.

As Stuey continued to navigate his way through the room, the whispers grew louder. He tried to ignore the eyes that widened at the sight of him. It wasn't easy. He had once been dubbed in print the "Keith Richards of poker," both for his rock-star aura and for his spindly little-boy body and mop-topped boyish good looks, and he had always loved the attention. But this was different. This was not the kind of attention he was used to. Starstruck awe had been replaced by morbid fascination. Those who knew him were appalled by what they saw. Up close, the boy-ishness was gone. Stuey's face was sickly white, ravaged by years of hard, careless living and drug abuse. One side of his nose was collapsed from snorting too much cocaine. His skin was papery and looked as if it might rip at the slightest touch. More disturbing, in a way, was how he'd let himself go. He was unshaven. His fingernails were long and dirty. His clothes looked slept-in. And he smelled.

For a man who had won millions of dollars playing in the highest-stakes games in Las Vegas, it was humbling to have to walk into this room this way—and worse still because the millions were gone, squan-dered on drugs and outrageous sports wagers. In a matter of hours, Jack McClelland, the tournament director, would utter his famous com-mand "Shuffle up and deal," and the twenty-eighth annual champi-onship would commence. Unless Stuey could persuade someone to back him, he'd be watching the action from the rail with the rest of the poker world's unwashed masses.

The night before the main event was a time of feverish desperation in the satellite area. Players who hadn't yet won an entry were taking last-gasp shots at scoring a seat in an event that happened only once a year. Most of the players who had already won seats, or who had the lux-ury of buying in for the full ten grand, were upstairs in their rooms, or across the street at the Golden Nugget. They were resting up, getting a good night's sleep, taking baths, getting massages. They knew that they were going to need every ounce of energy they could muster if they wanted to make it through the grueling four-day marathon.

Those still playing satellites were the luckless losers who hadn't been able to catch a break for three weeks but didn't want to admit defeat. They were stubbornly pursuing the dream—a dream that, even if they achieved it, would put them at a huge disadvantage relative to the rest of the field. Imagine a runner needing to win a three-mile race in order to qualify for a thirty-mile race later the same day against opponents who had qualified weeks ago and were fully rested. That was the uphill task facing most of the men (and the few women) now in the room.

Better in than out, though, despite the disadvantage—especially for a two-time world champion. Stuey saw Billy Baxter getting up from a table across the room and made a beeline for him. Baxter, a large, cheerful southerner, was a great lowball player who had won so many gold bracelets in deuce-to-seven lowball draw at the WSOP that one player jokingly began calling it the "Billy Baxter benefit tournament." Oddly enough, Baxter had never played in the $10,000 event, but after entering a $1,050 buy-in satellite (essentially, a one-table mini-tournament to get into the tournament) on a whim, he had managed just moments before to win it. He was now the proud owner of a slip of paper entitling him to a seat in the Big One; not surprisingly, he was in a good mood.

"Hey, Billy," Stuey said, drawing near. "Lyle turned me loose. I'm giving you the first shot at backing me tomorrow." Stuey's voice was pure Lower East Side New York—a guttural, rapid-fire, wiseguy mumble that recalled Mugsy from the old *Bowery Boys* shorts. Stuey was referring to Lyle Berman, a multimillionaire businessman, who would be inducted into the Poker Hall of Fame in 2002 and would become a driving force behind the Travel Channel's World Poker Tour. Berman had backed Stuey selectively in the past, but his timing had always been lousy, even when the Kid was on top of his game. Berman had wanted no part of Stuey in his current condition and had already told him so.

Baxter's luck with Stuey had been a bit better through the years, though on at least one occasion, in 1990, he experienced the downside of backing a drug abuser when Stuey failed to show up for the final two days of the WSOP. A sharp businessman and professional sports bettor, Baxter considered himself Stuey's friend. Their friendship complicated matters. "I liked Stuey," Baxter said. "I always wanted to help him out when I could."

In this case, however, even flushed with victory, Baxter did not feel comfortable. Stuey looked horrible. It was hard to imagine him finishing the four-day event, much less winning it. Baxter wasn't the type to throw away ten grand on a gesture.

"Stuey, I haven't been going all that great in sports lately," he said. "Try to get it from someone else. I mean, I'm sure you can get a hundred people in this room to back you."

At one point that had certainly been true, but no longer. A quick look around the room forced Stuey to face the truth: he was no more than an object of pity here, maybe even a butt of jokes. He turned and slunk out of the casino. No one knows exactly where he went, but somehow he managed to scrape together a few bucks and buy a vial of crack. Midnight found him in a den in the worst part of town, sucking on a crack pipe, trying to forget about the depths to which he had sunk and all that he had lost.

It seemed almost impossible to believe that four days later he would be back at the Horseshoe, a phoenix risen from the ashes, celebrating one of the greatest comebacks of all time.

2.

Bookmaker's Boy

In New York during the 1950s, nearly every neighborhood bar (or corner candy store or deli) had a bookie in residence. This was before the advent of the state lottery, legalized casinos in nearby Atlantic City, and offtrack betting parlors: illegal outlets were pretty much a gambling man's only recourse.

Most bar owners or store owners would allow a bookie to set up shop in their establishment for a cut of the profits. Often, the mob took a cut as well. But at Fox's Corner, a bar and restaurant in Manhattan's East Village, the owner—Isidore Ungar—had a different idea.

Isidore—or "Ido," as some of his friends and associates called him— was a stout middle-aged Hungarian Jew with a fondness for well-tailored suits and curvaceous blondes (having a wife and child did little to deter him from his extracurricular pursuits). Ido had dropped out of grade school and had never learned to read or write, but he was nevertheless smart, energetic, and ambitious. By the time he was in his thirties, he had made enough money selling housewares and clothing to the lower-middle-class Italian and Jewish immigrants on the Lower East Side to expand his horizons. Using several connections he had made along the way, Ido was able to secure a liquor license, and in 1949 he opened the doors to Fox's Corner, on Second Avenue and Seventh Street.

Rather than allow a local bookie to use his bar as a base, Ido decided to book bets himself. The idea seems obvious now, but in the early 1950s Ido Ungar was among the first to realize the synergy of combining a bar and a bookmaking operation. He installed a television set (still a relatively new technology) above the walnut-stained bar in the front room, essentially creating a sportsbook that kept his betting customers around, continuing to drink and eat, so that they could watch ball games or fights they had wagered on.

With Ido serving the liquor, controlling the gambling, and making up the daily menu for several hundred regulars, one patron suggested that Ido had the "vig on living." The vig, which is the 10 percent commission that bookies take on all losing bets, amounted to a bundle—thousands of dollars a week.

In a mob-infested city like New York, where all the rackets were controlled by the five major crime families, operating as an independent bookie was not the safest way to make a living. But Ido's social graces and well-considered payoffs managed to keep the right people happy and allowed him to stay in operation.

The joint with the neon-lit fox outside quickly became a favorite haunt of wiseguys and gamblers. Men with names like Nicko and Farny used it as a clubhouse, talking loudly and openly about their affairs, swinging deals, and doing business together. These were men who had come up the hard way on the mean streets of New York City; they were bookies and racketeers who talked like longshoremen and dressed like movie stars.

Ido himself looked down on gambling. He was a businessman. He had no interest in taking crazy chances. Every day, he dealt with broken-down, busted-out gamblers and heard their stories of misery. He saw their desperation; he saw how, even when deep in the hole and pleading for more time to pay off their debts, they still craved action. Ido came to realize that gambling made honest men dishonest and dishonest men ruthless. Not that his conscience ever prevented him from taking or collecting bets. Few bookies conducted business the way it's portrayed in the movies. Customers who failed to pay didn't wind up with a broken arm or leg. They suffered a far worse fate: they were cut off from further betting. A gambler whose word couldn't be trusted became an outcast, a pariah, and would not dare show his face in the bar—this was one reason that most gamblers paid Ido before they paid the rent or bought groceries.

Unlike some bookmakers, who liked to gamble on games themselves, Ido always did his best to keep his book balanced, aiming for equal action on both sides, so that he could be sure of collecting the straight 10 percent vig, guaranteeing himself a steady income. Between the on-the-square revenue he made from alcohol and food and the added income from the illegal gambling, as well as loan-sharking (which was a natural extension of bookmaking), Ido soon became a wealthy man.

Although he may have been a good and disciplined businessman, Ido was not a good husband. In the summer of 1951, while his wife and teenage son were vacationing for the season in the Catskills, Ido began an affair with a sexy thirty-seven-year-old bleached blonde named Fay Altman, whom he had met in a dance hall on the Upper East Side. Fay was a five-foot-one package of dynamite, with an easy infectious laugh, a lust for action, and curves in all the right places. Ido, although seven years her senior, managed to impress Fay with his charm, dapper suits, and free-spending nights on the town.

Afraid that the truth might scare her off, Ido told Fay that he was separated from his wife. He had access to apartments all over the city, thanks to his many friends and wiseguy connections, so this deception worked for a while. But as the summer passed, and he had to leave town to spend several weekends with his wife, Fay began to wise up. Eventually, Ido confessed the truth to her, and the night before his wife and son were scheduled to return to the city, Fay issued him an ultimatum: either he tell his wife about her, or she was through with him.

The day after his family returned to the city, Ido, terrified that Fay was serious about leaving him, told his wife that he was in love with another woman. Devastated and enraged, his wife told him that she'd never grant him a divorce. Despite Ido's assurances that he would "take care of her," she said that no amount of money could buy her off and release him to marry "that tramp."

Ido moved out anyway, and not long after, Fay announced that she was pregnant. On April 19, 1952, Fay gave birth to a girl, Judith.

Seven months later, she was pregnant again. On September 8, 1953, Stuart Errol Ungar was born at Gouvernor Hospital in lower Manhattan.

Ido's wife was true to her word—at least for a while. It would take four more years—years of bickering, threats, and legal hassles—before Ido's marriage to her was dissolved and his two children by Fay could be legitimized. By then Ido had purchased an apartment for his new family in a middle-income housing project called the East River Houses. It was one of 4,500 apartments in an eleven-building complex overlooking the East River, down by the Williamsburg Bridge, on the Lower East Side.

The two-bedroom apartment on the fourteenth floor overlooked Corlears Hook Park and the East River. While the new apartment was fairly close to Fox's Corner—ten minutes or so by cab, depending on traffic—Ido preferred to drive himself, so he bought a new Pontiac Bonneville, a rite of fall that he would repeat every year after that for the rest of his life; Ido just liked the smell of a new car.

For Fay, the initial champagne fizz and sparkle of the relationship, the gifts of jewelry and nights at the Copa, quickly turned into the less glamorous chores of changing diapers and breast-feeding that went along with being a mother and housewife. At the same time, the children did help cement the bond between Ido and Fay—or at least made it harder to dissolve. By the time Judy and Stuey were ready to begin school, those who knew the Ungars regarded them as a fairly stable upper-middle-class family—perhaps not typical, but a family nevertheless.

Ido, like most men in the buttoned-down 1950s, viewed his role as husband in a very traditional way. His job was that of breadwinner, with no responsibilities beyond providing food, comfort, and shelter. Raising the children and keeping house were Fay's domain.

That Ido also felt entitled to continue philandering probably would have come as no surprise to Fay, who knew firsthand how susceptible Ido was to being led astray. To keep closer tabs on him, she came up with the idea of working alongside him at Fox's Corner. The kids were old enough to attend school by then. Public School 122 was just three blocks from the bar; the children could walk there after school. Ido hated the idea of Fay's working at the bar and told her so. They fought about it for a week, but in the end she got her way.

During Stuey's first year of elementary school, Fay took the kids to school each morning in a taxi, then went to the bar to open up. After several months, however, she got tired of waking up early every morning, making breakfast for them, and then having to rush out of the house. Instead, she made an arrangement with a Yellow Cab driver: every morning at 7:45, he'd be out front waiting when she brought the kids down. It was like having a personal limo to shuttle them to school. Afterward, Fay could go back upstairs and catch a little extra sleep before taking a cab to the bar in midmorning.

Each day when school ended at 2:45, Stuey and Judy would head straight to the bar, where their real education would begin. When little Stuey and the tomboyish Judy weren't outside the bar roller-skating or playing handball in the street, they were inside Fox's Corner playing board games like Scrabble, Monopoly, and checkers and absorbing the gamblers' world.

It was there, in the bar, that young Stuey met the characters who would serve as models for the person he would become. He was fascinated by their hard-edged patter and attitude. Only suckers, he learned early on, worked at straight jobs. You had to figure your edge, get your advantage somehow. Otherwise you were just a fish.

I always tried to make excuses to hustle up to the bar where all the guys were talking. I wanted to see what was going on. The first thing I can remember, the first conscious memory that I have, was learning how to work the soda gun. I musta drank ten Cokes a day trying to weasel my way up to the bar to hear their conversations. I just wanted to be a part of it.

Stuey quickly learned about point spreads and money lines, heard the laments of the losers—"The fuckin' Giants cost me my lungs. I never shoulda laid that much wood"—and the even more intoxicating wisdom of the winners: "You know what they say, baby, money won is twice as sweet as money earned!"

Before he was out of second grade, Stuey was speaking in the same machine-gun wiseguy rhythms as the men who frequented his father's bar. Whereas most kids his age still believed in the tooth fairy and Santa Claus, Stuey's pragmatic worldview involved not allowing anyone to get over on you.

There was this guy called Joey Ripp. Let me tell ya, Joey was a real prick. He loved to see my father lose. I don't know what started it, but Joey and my father hated each other. That didn't stop my father from booking Joey's action, though. Hey, when it came to gambling, business was business.

When one of them won money, the other used to make the payoff in the most insulting way possible. Like one week my father paid off a thousand-dollar bet with Joey in one-dollar bills. The next week Joey lost something like nine hundred dollars and he walked into the bar and dumped out a big bag of quarters that spilled all over the place with this ringing clatter. Another time, I saw Joey drop his pants and take out the money he owed and wipe his ass with it before he handed it over.

But I really got him good once. I think I was eight years old at the time. Joey always used to come in late, right before the ball games would start. He'd ask me, "Who does your father need today? What team does he like?"

I had started following sports because we watched all the games in the bar. I even started doing the parlays and keeping the books straight for my father, so I usually knew what was going on. If everyone was betting on the Yankees or the Red Sox or whatever, I knew my father needed the other side to make money. After a while, I figured out what Joey was doing. I knew he was asking me first, so he could bet the other way. So I started double-dicking him. Let's say my father needed the Yankees bad; I'd tell Joey that my old man needed the Red Sox. That way Joey would make a big bet on the Yankees and even out the books, which was just what my father wanted. But that's not all. Since he always took the other side, I'd tell my father which side Joey was going to bet and he'd shave the money line the other way. Man, we fucked him good.

Ido took Stuey to see all the New York sports teams—the Yankees, the Giants, the Knicks—as well as the Golden Gloves and professional prizefights. He'd get cheap seats way up in the rafters at Madison Square Garden for all the Knicks' home games. Then, once the action started, the two would sneak down to the good seats after tipping an usher five bucks to look the other way. Whatever Ido did, he was always working an angle—a fact that wasn't lost on his son.

Most kids who follow sports develop loyalty to a specific team. But as a bookmaker's boy, Stuey was fickle, shifting with the prevailing wind. One night he would cheer for the Yankees; the next night, if his dad needed the Red Sox, he would switch his allegiance to the other side. One loyalty Stuey did maintain, however, was to the Yankees' Mickey Mantle. Stuey worshipped him.

In the late 1950s and early 1960s, Mantle was a cultural icon in New York City. His hard-living, full-out gusto for baseball and life won him millions of admirers. Every time the Mick stepped up to the plate, you knew he was going to either crush the baseball into the upper deck of Yankee Stadium or break every bone in his body trying. He played for keeps, all-out, leaving nothing behind. This was an approach to life and sports that Stuey himself favored, and it was not surprising, therefore, that he would be enamored of Mantle, the embodiment of that ideal.

Many city kids, even those whose fathers have straight jobs, flirt with minor juvenile delinquency as a way of testing both society's and their own boundaries—setting off firecrackers, shoplifting, breaking windows, pushing the limits to see how far they can go before they meet resistance. Stuey was no different. Interestingly, his father, whose moral authority might have seemed compromised by his illegal occupation, was furious when the cashier at the nearby Cozy Corner luncheonette informed him that Stuey had stolen a pack of Bazooka bubble gum from the counter.

"He came home that night," Stuey remembered, "and slapped me out of a deep sleep, then continued beating on me, telling Mom that I was a little thief."

It was ironic that Ido the bookie was so enraged by his son's petty thievery, but in fact it was the very pettiness of the act that hit a nerve. Ido took tremendous pride in showing the world that he was providing well for his children. The idea that Stuey would need to steal a pack of gum when Ido was providing nice clothes for his kids, a ride to school in a taxi every morning, long vacations, and tickets to ball games was irritating mostly because it might reflect badly on him.

My father had a hell of a temper. All he had to do was bite down on his lip and I was terrified. I guess you could say that was the first "tell" I ever discovered. It wasn't that he was abusive; he was mostly just strict. All the same, he really made it hurt when he hit me.

The thing with the bubble gum—it wasn't because I didn't have money. I just stole it for the thrill. I always liked the idea of getting something for nothing. I guess the worst thing I ever did in that vein was break into an office. There were three of us. We broke a window on the roof of the St. Mark's Theater and climbed inside. We turned the whole place upside down and found $75 in a desk drawer. Somebody must have heard us break the window or seen us and called the cops. Anyway, we heard something downstairs and got the hell out of there. Later on, we split up the money. But like I said, it wasn't about the $25. It was the thrill—the way it got my adrenaline flowing.

As much as Stuey enjoyed hanging out at his father's bar after school, restlessness began to set in during the cold winter months, when he and Judy were trapped indoors. Playing hearts and old maid and the standard board games—Monopoly, Scrabble, and checkers—became boring. To make the games interesting, to get that adrenaline thrill he loved, he and Judy began putting money on the outcome. Soon, it became unthinkable to play with no money at stake. "Whenever we played, it absolutely had to be for money," Judy said. "We'd play checkers for fifty cents a game. We'd play Monopoly for a dollar. I once said, 'Stuey, can't you play anything without betting money on it?' He said, 'No, it's just to make it interesting. Let's make it interesting.' "

It's not surprising that Ido Ungar's two children would get the idea that betting made life more interesting. How—looking around their father's bar—could they possibly think otherwise? The two kids were highly competitive, but Stuey sometimes went to extremes in his need to win. "I didn't mind playing against my brother for money," Judy said. "But it bothered me when I caught him moving pieces around the board—or when we played Monopoly and he'd steal money right out of the bank. Mom always had to separate us because we'd wind up having fistfights. He didn't care what it took to win the game. He would do anything. He just hated to lose."

Ido did not fail to notice his boy's aptitude for games and numbers, and by the time Stuey was in sixth grade, his father had assigned him the task of jotting down the previous day's sports scores and then marking the winners and losers on Ido's betting sheets. Since Ido could neither read nor write, he devised a system for his son in which each gambler was assigned a number rather than a name, and the sheets were organized accordingly.

Fay Ungar had little interest in her husband's bookmaking operation (other than the obvious financial comforts it provided), but unlike Ido, who did not like taking risks, she loved to gamble. Sports didn't appeal to her, but she was crazy about gin and poker and any other card games she could wager on. Unfortunately, her skill at these games did not match her passion. She was a particularly bad poker player. Twice a week, Fay would play with neighbors or at church socials. Sometimes she'd go to one of the illegal poker clubs scattered around Manhattan; Ido's connections hipped him to the locations of all the poker and dice parlors in town, and he indulged his wife's addiction by telling her where they were.

When summer came along, Ido chauffeured Fay and the kids to the Catskill Mountains in upstate New York—just as he had taken his former family. Fay, Judy, and Stuey stayed at the Raleigh Hotel, a grand manor-style all-inclusive resort nestled in a pine forest. After dropping them off to enjoy the cool breezes, Ido would climb back into his brand-new Bonneville and return to the muggy city to take care of business. The bookmaking operation required him to do pays and collects on Monday and Tuesday and be around to take bets during the week. He didn't trust anyone to fill in for him, but a number of times during the course of the summer, after the Friday ball games were over, he would drive up to the resort in the middle of the night and stay until Sunday morning.

In the 1950s and 1960s, the Catskill resorts were a hugely popular destination for vacationing American Jews. More than a million people inhabited the summer world of bungalow colonies, summer camps, and hotels, in what came to be known as the "borscht belt." The Raleigh Hotel was one of many resort hotels—along with Kutsher's, Brown's, the Pines, the Windsor, and the Del Mar—that served as a training ground for comedians, musicians, and other performers. In addition to the three meals served daily in a large dining hall, nightly entertainment was an integral part of the Catskill experience. There were comedy shows, Broadway musicals, and dances. Favorite Jewish tunes like "Tzena, Tzena," "Belz," and "Bei Mir Bist Du Schön" were performed on the same stage as numbers from *Camelot, Guys and Dolls,* and *Fiddler on the Roof.*

Fay would lounge at the pool by day, reading and socializing; at night, when not taking in a show, she would alternate between playing penny-a-point gin and $1–$2 poker, often losing more than $100 in an evening. If gambling was out in the open back in New York City, it was epidemic in the Catskills. Bridge, bingo, poker, canasta, and pinochle were the most popular games.

Even the staff gambled. The resort's summer employees—busboys, bellboys, valets, groundskeepers, lifeguards, waiters, camp workers, and dance instructors—would make as much as $1,500 to $2,000 for a season, money that helped put them through college or get a start in business. The ready cash also gave them a way, during their idle hours, to pass the time. Sunday night became "poker night," since tips were paid in a lump sum at the end of the week.

I used to sit behind my mother and watch her play seven-card stud. She was terrible. She played every single hand—and I do mean every single hand. It didn't matter what her first three cards were; she was in.

I watched my mother lose, saw the faces of the other players, how smug they were, the way they'd laugh at her behind her back and make wisecracks. They really thought they were hot shit. But they weren't any good, either. Even back then I could see that they were horrible. The only reason that they won her money was that she played even worse than they did. I didn't like to see that. I guess it affected me. It made me want to beat them. It made me want to get back at them for the way they treated my mother.

I have no idea how I developed card sense. It just came naturally to me. I mean, I could watch my mother play for hours and it was just so fucking obvious she was doing everything wrong. Apart from playing every hand, she was a calling station. She'd never raise. She'd never do anything deceptive. By the time I was ten, I was telling her how to play and pointing out her mistakes. She'd have an ace showing and two bad cards in the hole. She'd call the first bet, then she'd get a king. The bet was to her, but because she didn't have anything, she'd say, "Check."

I told her, "Mom, you've got to bet there."

"How can I bet? I don't even have a pair."

"Yeah, but they don't know that."

The waiters and busboys had a big poker game every Sunday after they got paid, and I started playing in that. I used to tell my mother to tip 'em good because I was going to get all the money back anyway. I'd win $60 or $70 every time I played. Mom said she wouldn't tell Dad I was gambling as *long as I didn't tell on her about how much she lost. I guess you could say we had a deal.*

Besides playing poker, I also shot dice with the waiters and busboys. Once, after I thought my father had driven back to the city, we started a craps game in the back of the kitchen, near the restroom. I was fading this guy who was shooting to make a point. He rolled his number but it didn't hit the wall.

"I'm not paying you! It didn't hit the wall!" I yelled.

Right as I was arguing with the guy, my father came down the hall to the restroom. He heard me and grabbed me by the arm. He gave me the worst beating of my life.

My father really hated me gambling. He couldn't stand it. And I was afraid of him—although not so afraid that I stopped. The following Sunday, I was back shooting dice again. This time, however, I made absolutely certain that he had gotten in his car and was headed back to New York.

At summer's end, Fay and the kids would return to New York, where the crisp September air had an edge of excitement that went along with the beginning of the school year. Stuey liked it; he didn't mind coming back to the city. He was an excellent student. His brain worked fast—if anything, too fast for his own good. His fourth-grade teacher noticed that he always finished his classroom assignments early. And it was true; he zipped through them, then got bored, wanting more stimulation. "I would read the sports page cover to cover beneath my desk by the end of my first class," he said.

Stuey rarely did homework or studied. He could remember lessons from memory; his mind was a vacuum cleaner for facts and figures. His best subject was math. He was able to rapidly calculate strings of numbers in his head. By the time he reached sixth grade, his teachers at P.S. 122, impressed with his natural abilities, recommended him for advancement. He skipped seventh grade and started eighth grade at P.S. 60 on Eleventh Street. But Stuey was undersize for his age, and his promotion into a group of boys and girls who were older and physically far more mature proved to be challenging.

I may not have been very big, but I was smart. I always made friends right away with the tallest, biggest, toughest kids. That's one thing in life I learned early.

For the most part, Stuey got along well with the other kids at school. The New York public school system was even more of a melting pot than the city itself, with children from all ethnic and religious backgrounds. Unfortunately, Ido Ungar had some old-fashioned ideas and prejudices that would eventually rub off on his son. Ido might have been happy to do business with customers of every race and ethnicity, but his private life was another matter. When Judy brought home a friend from school who was black, Ido didn't hide his displeasure.

"Don't trust those people! They'll stab you in the back!"

The situation got worse when Judy told her parents that she was attracted to a Puerto Rican boy. Ido flat-out forbade her to see him. "They're all criminals," he told her. "I don't want you going out with anyone who isn't Jewish."

The irony was that the Ungar family did not observe traditional Jewish laws and customs. "The Orthodox Jews in our building," Stuey recalled, "looked down on us for the way we acted." The Ungars spent most holidays, including Passover, at the Raleigh Hotel.

"We weren't religious at all," Judy said. "We ate pork, bacon, everything. When we went to the Raleigh Hotel for Passover, my mother wouldn't eat matzoh. She used to drive into town to get us bagels because she wanted bagels every morning."

Despite this seeming indifference to traditional customs, Ido pushed his son into a bar mitzvah. He wasn't happy about Stuey's gambling and hoped that the study and discipline of Hebrew school would help steer Stuey toward a better path. Stuey was already twelve, however, making it too late to begin the traditional course of study. Ido went to a local synagogue and explained the problem to a rabbi, who made a special allowance. Stuey spent the next six months taking a crash course in Hebrew. Somehow, between doing his schoolwork and balancing the books for his father, he found the time to chant passages from the Torah.

Stuey's bar mitzvah took place one week after his thirteenth birthday, on September 15, 1966, in the grand ballroom of the Americana Hotel. Although it was a traditional Jewish ceremony, not all the guests kept kosher. The room was filled with gangsters—Nicko, Farny, and a member of the Genovese crime family named Victor Romano.

There were so many wiseguys there, the feds wanted to subpoena my bar mitzvah album. After it was over, I went up to the fifteenth floor, where my father had a suite. I started opening up all the envelopes I'd been given, even though I wasn't supposed to. At least half the envelopes had Treasury bonds. I was already seriously into gambling by then. What good was a fucking Treasury bond to me? Was I gonna be able to take that to a dice game? Give me the cash.

Of more interest to the authorities than Stuey's bar mitzvah were the daily goings-on at Fox's Corner. The bar was occasionally under surveillance by police officers and, later, by federal agents targeting any one of the dozens of gangsters who made Ido's establishment their second home. Initially the heat was minimal, mostly just harassment. Ido was cited and paid a couple of fines.

Then, one afternoon, the bar was raided. Five undercover cops ran off Ido's customers and searched the office. They didn't find anything, and they left without making any arrests. Ido figured that it was just further harassment, that the cops were just going through the motions to satisfy their superiors.

He was right, but what he didn't know was that the cops had not really been searching for evidence; they had been planting wiretaps for the FBI. A few weeks later, when business had returned to normal, the cops came back to retrieve the various eavesdropping devices. The pay phone near the restroom provided them with hours of incriminating tape—bets being phoned in and accepted in Ido's deep, distinctive voice. In the eyes of law enforcement, Ido wasn't a small-time bookie. He was running a big-time racket. The authorities had enough evidence to bring in the IRS and put him away for tax evasion.

Fortunately for Ido, the New York police department in the early 1960s, before the emergence of the Knapp Commission and Frank Serpico, was deeply corrupt. Everything and everyone had a price. Ido later said that the only people who "couldn't be bought" in the city were the statues. In many ways, the police were worse than the criminals. Sure, the wiseguys broke the law, but they had never taken an oath to protect and serve. Ido regarded the hypocrisy of corrupt cops as a disgrace. "I guess there are some who never took the money," he said. "But I never met one of them."

How many times had he gotten out of traffic violations by tucking a neatly folded $20 bill underneath his driver's license when he'd gotten pulled over? It was the way things worked.

The problems at the bar were no different. Through an intermediary, Ido paid off a police lieutenant with an envelope full of money. The wiretaps with the incriminating phone conversations conveniently "got lost" in inventory before the charges could be drawn up. Ido was never prosecuted.

His troubles, however, were far from over.

One night, Farny, who was one of the toughest regulars, had a problem with another man in the bar. The two men were watching Judy Ungar and Farny's girlfriend playfully dance the twist to a Chubby Checker song. Farny thought the other man was watching a little too closely.

"You like my girlfriend's ass?" he said, grabbing the man by the shirt collar. "How do you like this?" He punched the man in the face, dropping him to the floor. Not satisfied, Farny grabbed the man by the seat of the pants and threw him across a couple of tables and chairs. By the time he was finished, "the guy was beaten to a bloody pulp," according to Judy. "Farny split the guy's head open. He beat the living daylights out of the guy."

The cops showed up at Fox's Corner to investigate after the man ended up in the hospital. It was the last thing Ido needed: more heat. Ido argued that he wasn't liable, but the police used their leverage to shake him down again, pointing out numerous complaints that had been lodged against the bar. In the end, Ido wound up paying off the cops in cash, directly this time. As before, no charges were filed.

But the problems didn't stop, and neither did the shakedowns. Saint Stanislaus, a Catholic church on the next block, began filing noise complaints against the Fox. "It got to be a real hassle for my father," Stuey said, "between the complaints and paying off the cops all the time." The stress was beginning to wear Ido down.

One afternoon a few weeks after his sixtieth birthday, Ido was standing behind the bar when he felt a sharp, stinging pain in his chest followed by numbness on his left side. He was paralyzed, unable to move. Fay frantically called an ambulance. Ido was rushed to a nearby hospital, where doctors informed him that he had suffered a mild stroke. After a short hospital stay, Ido was sent home with instructions to cut back on his activities and relax a bit more. Fox's Corner at that point was little more than a front for his bookmaking and loan-sharking. He didn't need the stress that went along with maintaining the public face of his real business. So when the lease came up, Ido decided not to renew. Fox's Corner shut its doors permanently in the spring of 1966.

Stuey was saddened. In many ways, this was the end of an era. The bar had been an integral component of his childhood. He had no idea that in the following months, life was about to change even more dramatically.

3.

Gin Joints, Big Dogs, and Monkey's Business

In the summer of 1967, Fay and the kids went to the Catskills, as always. Ido might not have been tied down to Fox's Corner any longer, but his bookmaking and loan-sharking actually had him hustling harder than ever, keeping up with his customer base in other bars and nightclubs, and keeping him home in the city.

Late one July night, Fay received a phone call from Ido's brother, informing her that Ido, at age sixty, had suffered a massive, fatal heart attack.

Fay packed hastily and drove back to the city with the kids late that night. They arrived at Ido's brother's house in Brooklyn as the sun was coming up. Funeral arrangements were already being made.

Fay was told that Ido had suffered the heart attack two days earlier; his body had been found in a 1965 Plymouth parked on the street. Still in shock, Fay left Stuey and Judy at Ido's brother's house and took a taxi to the mortuary to view the body and take care of further arrangements.

The next day, Ido was buried. Afterward, at a reception at his brother's house, Fay found herself ambushed by her husband's former family, who still harbored ill will toward her for breaking up his first marriage. They exacted their revenge in the cruelest way possible: by setting her straight on the true circumstances of Ido's death.

He had died in the arms of his mistress, Suki, his heart giving out in flagrante delicto. Suki had panicked and called one of Ido's bookie associates for help. The associate had rushed to Suki's apartment, and with the help of a few friends, carried Ido's body outside and placed it in the front seat of a Plymouth they found parked on the street. A while later, Suki had called the police and reported that she'd found Ido unconscious, lying in someone else's car. The far-fetched tale did not convince the police, and under pressure from the investigators, Suki had finally broken down and told them what had really happened.

Fay was devastated. Despite the fact that her marriage was far from perfect, she had loved Ido, and the truth broke her heart. Judy remembered the cruel satisfaction on the faces of Ido's former in-laws as they imparted the news to the grieving widow. "Why did they have to tell her?" Judy wondered. "Why didn't they just leave it that he died of a heart attack in the car? It was vicious."

For Stuey and Judy, the truth about their father's death added to the hurt. "I wasn't really close to my father," Stuey said. "I didn't even cry at his funeral. He fucked around a lot, and everyone knew it. I don't know if there was a sense of shame, but I knew it wasn't right, and I lost a lot of respect for him in that way. After he died, I told myself I'd never be like him."

The spoils of Ido's life of bookmaking and loan-sharking amounted to hundreds of thousands of dollars in cash stashed throughout the city. He had been terrified that he would be busted for tax evasion and wind up serving jail time, and he had spread the money around to protect himself. For the heirs to his small fortune, his squirreling away of his assets presented serious difficulties. It was bad enough that bundles of cash were locked inside nearly a dozen safe-deposit boxes in different banks; what was worse was that many of the boxes were listed under assumed names, making them hard to locate. Fay knew a few of the aliases that Ido used—Bobby Shaw, Eli Ungar, and one or two others—but there were many she didn't know. Finding the boxes could be the difference for her and the kids between continuing to live a comfortable life and a slow but inevitable slide into poverty.

The day after Ido's funeral, which was made even more painful by the animosity between the two families, Fay taxied up and down the busy avenues of midtown Manhattan in a mood of grief mixed with desperation. Every bank she tried turned her away. Ido had been remiss in looking out for his family, perhaps in part because of his illiteracy. He had listed only Isidore Ungar or whatever alias he had chosen as the account holder—never his wife. Until she could obtain a court order, Fay would not have access to any of the boxes.

Hearing rumors of Ido's treasure chests, Irwin Ungar, Ido's son from his first marriage, went to court himself. A college professor, Irwin was nobody's fool, and he certainly had a legitimate claim to a percentage of the inheritance. In a civil lawsuit filed in the city court of New York, Irwin, as one of Ido's three surviving children, demanded one-third of his father's estate.

The dispute was contested in court for several months in late 1967, and the parties were motivated as much by personal bitterness as financial interest. Ultimately, the case was settled out of court, with Irwin receiving an undisclosed settlement and Stuey and Judy being awarded $50,000 each from the estate, with the money to be held in an escrow account that would be parceled out to Fay to feed, house, and clothe them while they were minors. Of the $50,000, $10,000 was earmarked specifically for their education.

"My father was a millionaire when a million dollars really meant something," Stuey later said about his father's wealth. "The trouble was, I never saw one-tenth of it. The government and the lawyers got most of it." How many undiscovered safe-deposit boxes Ido left behind was hard to say, but whatever went unclaimed probably wound up going to the State of New York.

With Ido gone, Fay would not or could not face up to the financial impact his death had on her and her kids' lives. Although she was not working and had no means of financial support beyond the kids' inheritance, she refused to modify their lifestyle. Over the next two years, they continued to spend the summer in the Catskills, and in most other ways they maintained the life to which they'd become accustomed. Looking back, Judy speculated that her mother didn't want her and Stuey to suffer after the loss of their father. In fact, in some ways, Fay indulged them (and herself) more extravagantly than ever before. During the summer, Stuey and Judy were sent to Camp Roosevelt, an expensive eight-week private camp in the Catskills. The $1,600 fee was an exorbitant expenditure for a family with dwindling financial resources.

Back in New York, depressed and lonely, Fay bought a Doberman pinscher puppy. She told herself that it was for the kids, but in fact it was to keep her company; she needed some way to fill the void in her own life. She named the puppy Hud after the title character played by Paul Newman in her favorite movie. "My mother was in love with Paul Newman," Judy said. Even so, it was an odd choice of name, and not just because the dog was female. Newman's character in *Hud* was an egotist whose bleak view of humanity was summed up thus: "You don't look out for yourself, the only helping hand you'll ever get is when they lower the box."

Hud the dog soon outgrew her cute puppyhood, and Fay's infatuation faded. A Doberman pinscher was not a good choice for a family of three living in a cramped New York apartment. Hud consumed large quantities of food and required at least three walks a day, rain or shine. Just as Fay had become weary of taking the kids to school years earlier, she soon tired of having to care for the dog. She would skip walks, Hud would crap on the floors, and then Fay or one of the kids would have to clean up. There were dog hairs all over the place, and the apartment smelled. Stuey found it embarrassing. He didn't like bringing friends home.

One afternoon, during a spring rainstorm, Stuey came home, and, in the dim light of the apartment, didn't see the big dog leap at him. Hud's enormous paws landed on Stuey's chest and knocked him to the parquet floor. There was an audible crack: the fall fractured Stuey's arm in two places. He wound up having to wear a full cast for two months, but instead of the truth, he told people that the arm had been broken in a fight. "You shoulda seen the other guy," he boasted.

Fay's neglectful attitude toward Hud paralleled her lack of attentiveness to her children. She did her best, but her best was not very good. There had always been in her a deep well of longing for attention—and, when that attention was lacking, her suffering consumed her. Some widowed mothers might have found solace in rising above their own needs and their grief for the sake of their children. Not Fay.

With parental supervision all but nonexistent in their daily lives, Stuey and Judy ran wild. Stuey gambled now whenever he could. Every hood and wiseguy from Battery Park to Harlem knew the smart-aleck kid from Fox's Corner who rattled off shtick like a vaudeville comedian. Stuey loved hanging out with gangsters. He called them by their first names and got away with it because he was Ido's kid and because he was small and quick-witted and they got a kick out of him.

There were dozens of illegal card clubs in New York City, a subculture that found shelter in church basements, Italian social clubs, Hungarian business clubs—or "goulash joints," as they were called. Entry to these clubs required secret knocks and being "a friend of a friend of Louie." At a more upscale place like the Mayfair Bridge Club on West Fifty-seventh Street, a uniformed doorman posted outside might even open the door for you once you'd presented your bona fides.

One afternoon eight months after his father had died, the fourteen-year-old Stuey scaled a narrow flight of stairs to a club on Ninth Street between Second and Third avenues. He had a few dollars in his pocket that he had borrowed from his mother, and he expected to get into a game. It should be pointed out that Stuey was perpetually short of money, and so he borrowed from people around him—particularly, in those days, from his mother and his sister. In Judy's memory he was like Wimpy in the cartoon *Popeye:* "For a hamburger today, I'll gladly repay you on Tuesday." In fact, Stuey's signature plea, as reported by his sister, was, "Let me borrow fifty today, and I'll pay you back a hundred tomorrow." Though he rarely made good on this promise, it became Stuey's trademark borrowing technique throughout his life.

Let into the club on this day, with money in his pocket, he was disappointed to find that the one poker game going was full. Frustrated, jangly with pent-up energy, Stuey noticed a wiseguy he'd never seen before sitting alone at another table playing solitaire. The man's name was Art Rubello.

"Wanna play, just you and me?" Stuey asked him.

Rubello looked at him, amused, going along with it. "What game, kid?"

"How about gin?"

"Sure. How much?"

"Twenty bucks," Stuey said. "That's all I have."

Rubello shrugged. "What the hell?" He was just killing time anyway.

They played on a square wooden table warmed by a bright, shaded light hanging overhead. Stuey didn't realize it, but he was playing against one of the club's best gin players—it should have been a total mismatch. The poker players, if they noticed at all, must have assumed that the much older Rubello was giving the young Stuey pointers. A few other players entered the club and, while they waited for a seat in the poker game to open up, began watching the two.

Gin is played with a standard fifty-two-card deck. The modern version of the game was invented in 1909 by Elwood T. Baker, according to most authorities, although it clearly has roots in an older Mexican card game called conquian, which was played in the nineteenth century. Gin became a favorite game in high society in the 1930s, and by the 1940s it had become extremely popular in New York City, particularly among the Jewish population.

It's an easy game to learn and fairly fast paced, so it is a great game for gambling. Most gin sessions involve multiple games, played up to a certain score (most commonly 500 points, with a designated dollar value for each point when it's being played for money). There are various forms of gin. Standard gin rummy is the most popular, but there are also other versions, such as Oklahoma gin rummy and Hollywood gin.

In standard gin rummy, each player is initially dealt ten cards from the deck. Then players alternately select from two piles to improve their hand. The two piles consist of the faceup discard pile and the facedown stock pile. Each time a player picks up a card from either pile, he must replace it by discarding a card from his hand into the faceup discard pile. The object of the game is to create "melds." A meld is a set of three or more cards constituting a set of the same rank, or a sequence of the same suit. For example, 4-4-4 constitutes a meld, as does 6-7-8 of diamonds. Since ten cards are generally dealt at the start, a completed gin hand— the point at which a player can declare "gin"—normally has one four-card meld and two three-card melds.

Knowing one or more of the opponent's melds has obvious advantages, especially in a version of the game called knock rummy, in which a player may hold a defensive card and play it as part of an opponent's hand.

As Stuey faced off against Rubello, the ten cards barely fit into his small hands. But he fanned out the cards each time he drew and then snapped the melds of cards back into a neat stack when it was Rubello's turn to draw. Stuey's level of concentration was frightening; he looked straight at Rubello, watching intensely when his opponent drew a card.

Five minutes into the game, against one of the best gin players in the city, Stuey calmly announced, "Gin."

"Look at that, the kid got lucky," one of the onlookers observed, amid murmurs of amusement. A couple of the waiting players slapped Stuey on the back and ribbed Rubello about losing to a kid.

The next game, Stuey beat Rubello again. Now the onlookers really started to needle Stuey's victim. When Rubello was vanquished in the third game, Stuey got to his feet and demanded that they settle up. A stunned Rubello counted out three crisp $20 bills. Stuey plucked them out of Rubello's hand, stuck the money into his pocket, and hustled out of the club. There was a horse he wanted to bet on at Roosevelt Raceway. If he hurried, he could make it to the track in time.

The thrashing he'd administered to Rubello took only thirty minutes, but it made quite an impression on all those who witnessed it. Word of the kid's conquest of Rubello spread quickly through the New York underground gambling world. Stuey later said that at the time he had no idea what he'd started. "To me, it was just another guy I was up against. I didn't think it was that big a deal to beat him. I was just better than him, that's all."

The following day, Stuey returned to the club on Ninth Street. The boss of the joint, impressed by what he had seen the previous day, asked if Stuey knew how to deal cards.

"Sure, I can deal," Stuey said.

"All right, show me." The boss handed him a deck of cards.

Stuey shuffled the cards four times, stripped the deck, and flicked out cards to the empty seats surrounding him with the precision and accuracy of a professional dealer.

"Can you manage a pot?" the boss asked.

"Yeah, I can manage the pot. Just tell me what I need to do," Stuey replied matter-of-factly.

He was hired on the spot. Three nights a week, starting immediately. With a guaranteed income of $80 a week, he wouldn't have to borrow from his mother or sister anymore. Unfortunately, dealing required more than dexterity. Stuey was so small that to reach the cards and chips across the expanse of the table, he had to place a wooden crate and a pillow on the seat of the chair, like the booster seats provided for small children in restaurants. More problematic than that, however, and less easily remedied, was Stuey's attitude. He found it nearly impossible to stay detached from the action, as a professional dealer was required to do. He analyzed and critiqued the play as it was happening, insulting players for stupid moves, calling out bluffs, and generally making himself obnoxious. Some of the regulars found his behavior amusing, but most—the losers in particular—did not.

When Stuey wasn't dealing at the club or playing, he was studying his chosen games, dealing out mock hands and formulating strategy, or poring over the *Daily Racing Form* trying to find winners. Less than a year after his father's death, gambling dominated his life. While other kids were in school or doing homework, Stuey was on the prowl for action. He frequently stayed up all night, first dealing, then playing with the money he'd made on tips. Weekends often turned into marathons of dealing and playing that stretched straight through to Monday-morning classes.

At the time, in 1967, Stuey was a ninth-grade student at Seward Park High School, a gloomy six-story redbrick building at 350 Grand Street, just a short walk from the Ungars' apartment. He was hardly the only truant in the New York City school system. Budget cutbacks along with poor administrative policies were responsible for an overwhelming dropout rate—Stuey was all but given a license to cut classes. His mother bore responsibility, too. When Fay received a phone call from a counselor at Seward informing her of her son's truancy, she was at a loss as to what to do. Certainly, she had been aware of all the mornings that her son's bed in the living room hadn't been slept in. But she was too absorbed in her own troubles to deal with the problem.

Judy was also cutting classes. Instead of gambling, like her brother, however, she was distracted by drugs. According to written reports from a counselor at Seward Park, Judy's behavioral problems were due to an "adjustment period" in the wake of her father's death. "Adjustment period" would have to be considered a dangerous understatement for what would eventually turn into a heroin addiction.

By the time he reached tenth grade, Stuey was barely attending high school at all. He was so far behind in his studies that almost all the academic advantages he had enjoyed when he was younger had been squandered. On an unseasonably warm autumn day in October 1968, Stuey made one last, halfhearted appearance at Seward Park. Whatever vestige of desire he had to follow a more normal path was trumped by his inability to see any point at all in what was being offered in the classroom. Gambling had so much more juice than a bunch of bored-ass defeated kids and teachers who seemed to be just going through the motions. Something closed off inside him. After that day, Stuey never entered Seward's doors again.

If my father would have lived, my entire life might have been different. He would have forced me to stay in school and go to college. Who knows what I would have done? I'm not saying that I didn't have gambling fever. From the time I was seven, I was watching my mother play poker and gin; I was helping my father out, balancing his books. I mean, before I could tie my fucking shoelaces, I could handicap a horse race.

• • •

Stuey's new classroom was a card club, where his desk was covered with green felt. He was learning, but he was schooling people, too. It was startling and slightly disconcerting for those in the underground scene to be contending with an upstart kid who looked as if he hadn't yet reached puberty. And Stuey did not exactly try to keep a low profile. He frequently wore a large cowboy hat that almost swallowed up his small head, and he was constantly badgering and belittling his opponents. Sometimes he would even stand up on his chair, daring people to call his bets, jumping with excitement after a win, storming out of the club in anger following a vicious defeat. As Steve Fishman described him in an article written for *New York* magazine in 1999:

> Stuey was always a freak. . . . He looked like he stopped maturing the day he left Seward Park High. He never weighed more than 100 pounds and never stood taller than about five-five. What's more, he had a long simian jaw, drawn-out arms, a narrow waist, and a tubercular chest, bony and stretched tight. His nose was like an infant's. Some called him "Monkey." Add to this his hyperactivity. Walking, he raced. Talking, he churned the words so quickly they sometimes emerged as one long stuttering word.

Stuey's ability to instantly pick up and master a new card game was exceeded only by his desire to beat people who had been playing the game for years. Klaberjass—"klab" for short—was a popular card game played in the coffeehouses of New York and Boston. The game had its origins among the eastern European Jews who immigrated to the United States at the turn of the century. By the mid- to late 1960s, klab was virtually never played by anyone under the age of fifty. Stuey didn't care; he swaggered in and out of coffeehouses, often facing off against elderly men who had learned the game forty years earlier.

Another game he quickly mastered was ziganet, which originated in Sicily and was played mostly by members of the Mafia. Stuey sat and listened one day as a couple of gangsters explained the basics to him. Within a week, after practicing by himself with a deck of cards, he was playing heads-up with the most dangerous wiseguys in the city. Whatever game he was taught—whether it was barbotte, played primarily in the Arab community; konkan; or Greek rummy—Stuey quickly grasped the subtleties and advanced strategies and was able to compete on even ground or at an advantage against far more experienced players.

His standbys, however, remained gin, poker, and pinochle, in that order. As his skill at playing improved, his interest in dealing waned. Beyond that, many of the players complained to the management about his rude, derisive comments. When Stuey was playing, the other participants had no choice but to put up with him; when he was dealing, it was another matter entirely. Stuey didn't fret about his tenuous status as a dealer; he quit before anyone could fire him. The $80 a week he'd been making was chump change compared with what he could make playing cards full-time.

Less than two years after his father's death, Stuey had transformed himself from a high school student with a gambling bug into a professional cardplayer. He now spent afternoons and evenings in one club or another, looking for gin games or poker games against stubborn adults who couldn't believe that they were being beaten by a kid. For that reason alone, Stuey often won far more in his rematches than he did the first time around, his opponents simply believing that they had been the victims of bad luck.

The most important lesson about gambling I ever learned happened when I was around fifteen. I beat this guy really bad playing pinochle. I beat him for like $600, which was a lot of money back in those days. I looked up at him and I could tell he was embarrassed about losing to me. I felt sorry for the guy, and I almost gave him back some of the money. It was so sad seeing the guy like that.

A week later, we played again. The second time, he beat me just as bad as I had beaten him the week before. He took something like $800 off me. I didn't have the money on me and had to borrow it to pay the debt. I didn't even have a quarter for bus fare to get home. I remember when I looked at him this time, he was laughing and giggling and making fun of me. The cocksucker was rubbing it in my face. That taught me a real lesson about feeling sorry for someone I beat. I never let that happen again. Ever.

They used to call me a freak. I guess it was like Bobby Fischer in chess. At fifteen I was massacring people who had mastered this stuff for thirty years. I made a shambles out of them. I guess you could say I was a freak of nature.

The games I played in went on around the clock. It didn't matter what time of day or night you walked in. There was always a game going. One time, I played for four days straight. Four days! I was winning, but finally I couldn't take it anymore. I told the people I was playing with to let me lay down for a second. So they brought a chair and put it over in the corner. I sat in the chair and fell asleep upright the instant I closed my eyes. I woke up a day later and the game was still going on. I pulled my money out of my pocket and started playing again.

I could play gin for three days straight easily. We'd usually go $20 a game. When I got older it was $50 a game, then $100. I'd sit there and not even take a piss for a day. After I got up $400 or $500, I'd quit and take the express to Yonkers or Roosevelt racetrack and go broke again.

I used to go up to the $50 windows at Monticello racetrack. I'd give the money to strangers to make a bet for me. I'd tell 'em my dad was in a wheel-chair or something and stand there and watch them while they placed the bet. They'd be betting $50 for me and $2 for themselves. I thought that was so funny. I mean, legally, I wasn't even supposed to be there.

• • •

Stuey's daily life was without structure. He wandered the city and did as he pleased. He took a cab or the subway from one game to another, sleeping and eating wherever and whenever he felt the need. Desperate for some sense of direction, he again came upon Victor Romano, a short, squat, 200-pound barrel of a man, a chain-smoking ex-con in his sixties who ran a group of small card clubs in midtown Manhattan, and who would ultimately become Stuey's mentor, friend, guardian, manager, and father figure.

One night, Romano saw the youngster playing at his Jovialite Social Club, at 306 East Seventy-second Street. It was unusual to see an underage kid inside the club. His curiosity piqued, Romano strolled over for a closer look, and when he was a couple of feet away suddenly recognized the skinny boy with the mop of dark hair—it was Ido Ungar's boy.

Romano, a foot soldier in the Genovese crime family, had been one of Ido's closest friends. He remembered afternoons spent hanging out at Fox's Corner, smoking his trademark filtered Winstons, while little Stuey barked out the tally from his dad's bookie sheets. Romano had also attended Stuey's bar mitzvah.

By his fiftieth birthday, Victor Romano had spent half of his life incarcerated. He had been born in 1907, in the Little Italy section of New York; and, as one of ten children, he came up hard, fighting for every inch of turf, both in his family and in his small corner of the city. He was always in trouble, taking part in fights, stabbings, and stickups; by age eighteen, he had been arrested numerous times and had done stints in juvenile detention ("juvie") and in jail. At twenty, he was sent away for a twenty-year stretch for taking part in an armed robbery in which a New York City cop had been shot. He did six of those years in Sing-Sing, from 1927 through 1933, and then was transferred to Attica, finally gaining his release in 1946.

Despite his years of incarceration and his violent past, Romano wasn't a typical thug. He used his two decades in prison constructively, developing some highly unusual talents. In Attica, Romano spent three years studying and committing to memory every word in Webster's dictionary of the English language, a feat that enabled him, after his release, to win numerous bets. The wager was simple: his pigeon could choose a random word out of the dictionary, which Romano would not only have to spell in all its variations but also define. He never failed.

Romano also taught himself to play bridge while in prison. He became so proficient that he was able to publish articles in the magazine *Bridge World* under an odd byline: "V. Romano, Attica, N.Y." Romano was one of very few bridge masters to win the "Master Solvents" contest, a mail-in competition that attracted replies from the best bridge minds in the country. In fact, Romano won this contest two years in a row, causing the bridge world to take notice, along with the organizers of the contest, who were somewhat chagrined and embarrassed to discover that they had crowned a convicted felon. The following year they changed the rules of the contest, making it a subjective award given by a vote of a committee. A convict did not win.

By the time Romano was released from prison, he had no marketable skills other than the few parlor tricks and games he'd taught himself. He was a hustler and a tough guy, so it wasn't a big shocker when he settled in Queens and began operating a numbers racket under the protection of the Genovese crime family. By 1956, ten years removed from the penitentiary, Romano was a bookmaker earning a good living and supporting a wife and children.

As a sideline, he hosted card games regularly, holding them at various apartments that he rented around town. Occasionally, the games were raided by police. But "Victor would pay off the cops and everything would be dropped," a source close to Romano explained. "The whole New York City police department was on the Mafia payroll."

Still, there was a more hassle-free way of operating a card room, so Romano looked into procuring the rights to a social club, which would provide him with a legitimate cover. He knew of a club on Seventy-second Street between First and Second avenues run by Jewish gangsters, and he decided to buy them out. The club already had a social charter granted by the city, so it operated as a private institution and had a special tax status and other dispensations. Furthermore, after a few payoffs to the right people, there was no heat from the police. Victor opened the Jovialite club in the early 1960s. Within five years, it was one of the most popular hangouts for cardplayers on Manhattan's East Side.

Of all the clubs in the city, the Jovialite attracted the toughest characters, a crowd that gambled high and fast. Players at the Jovialite weren't bored housewives or retirees. They were jewel thieves, hijackers, hit men, fences, bookmakers, and assorted shakedown artists. One wiseguy, "Big" Anthony DiMeglio, was a regular at the Jovialite. John "Jackie Nose" D'Amico, reputed to be connected to the Gambino crime family, also sat in games almost every night. Although a strict code of conduct was in effect—since this was a mob-run joint—arguments and fights occasionally broke out. The Jovialite seemed like a peculiar hangout for someone as young and small of stature as Stuey, but thanks to Romano's blessing, Stuey felt comfortable at the club and increasingly drawn to its colorful cast of characters.

Despite the club's association with the mob, Romano had a reputation for compassion and generosity. He fed the homeless; he lent money to deadbeats knowing very well he wouldn't be repaid; he hired dealers who had been fired from other clubs; he took in people even when he didn't need any more staff, often paying pensioners and hard-luck characters $30 a shift just to stand around and clean out the ashtrays. One of the regulars at the Jovialite remembered that no one ever saw a dirty ashtray in the club, because Romano had so many people on the payroll.

At least initially, Romano's motivation for taking Stuey under his wing was financial, since he clearly viewed the young prodigy as a business proposition. But as this "odd couple" spent more time together, Romano's attitude toward his protégé became increasingly paternal. Interestingly, the relationship was almost short-circuited before it ever had a chance to develop.

On Stuey's second visit to the Jovialite, he threw a temper tantrum, an occurrence of the sort that had become commonplace for him in other clubs around the city. Romano was so incensed by the outburst that he came close to eighty-sixing Stuey for good right then and there. What turned him around, beyond the fact that Stuey was Ido's son, was his realization, in the course of a tense private discussion between the two, that Stuey was the young kid people had been talking about—the one who'd beat up on Art Rubello at gin.

As the conversation continued, Romano found himself impressed by Stuey's single-minded, almost fanatical obsession with card games. As someone so compulsive himself that he had memorized the dictionary, Romano could relate to this. The two debated strategy and theory the rest of that night in what would become an ongoing conversation. In the weeks and months that followed, Stuey became a regular at the Jovialite. Amid the drifting clouds of cigarette smoke and the constant background noises of shuffling cards and splashing chips, Stuey and Romano could be found sitting together at a small table in the far corner of the Jovialite, hour after hour, night after night, dealing out hands of gin, discussing specific situations and various ways to play. Although Romano was an excellent player and far more experienced, before long it was not he but Stuey who was coming up with the optimal strategy—the mentee tutoring the mentor.

Out of these sessions grew a bond of friendship, trust, and genuine affection between the unlikely pair. Romano began to regard Stuey as a son, even stating as much to several people. The relationship gave Stuey standing in the underworld and made him close to untouchable. Anyone who tried to give him trouble had to answer to Romano, and, by association, to the Genovese crime family—arguably New York's most powerful mob syndicate. What all this meant was that Stuey essentially had a license to do as he pleased.

As the relationship between the two men expanded beyond the club, Stuey started visiting the Romano family home in Astoria, Queens. Concerned that Stuey's frail body was the result of poor eating habits, Romano vowed to do something about it. "You can't be a sandwich-eater your whole life," Romano would say. "You need some real meat!" The ritual of weekly meals chez Romano eventually led to holidays spent with the family.

"Most of the time when Stuey came over, he and Dad would talk about hands they played," said Larry Romano. "If there was a really tough problem, Dad would pull a book off the shelf, or a magazine article, and read the analysis of the problem in there."

Stuey was tireless, never bored by this kind of talk; he had a level of concentration and a hunger for knowledge about these games that Romano had never seen in anyone else. Though these visits might have been fulfilling other needs in Stuey, his social awkwardness made it difficult for him to connect with anyone whenever the subject strayed too far from gambling. "He was always moving around," said Larry Romano. "He couldn't sit still unless he was talking about gambling or playing cards. Even then, he jumped from subject to subject, where it was sometimes impossible to follow what he was saying."

A bizarre ritual during the weekly dinners with the Romanos was watching *The Lawrence Welk Show* on television every Sunday at 6:00. Victor loved the blue-coated bandleader. But except for Stuey, who was equally mesmerized by the corny patter and polka music, Romano couldn't get the rest of his family to share his enthusiasm. Sitting there with a man old enough to be his grandfather, Stuey seemed miles removed from the other kids of his generation, who were absorbed in the musical and cultural movements of the 1960s, listening to the Beatles and the Rolling Stones, wearing bell-bottoms and smoking dope. Stuey was a throwback to the old school, even as a teenager.

Victor introduced me to people. He gave me money to play whenever I needed it. At that point, since I was so young, I needed someone around me like that. I might win money and get robbed otherwise. Some of the places I went, if it weren't for Victor I never woulda been able to make it out the door.

In those days, most of the people I hung out with were Italians. I also met some Westies. Lemme tell you, those guys from Hell's Kitchen were the toughest fucking Irishmen you've ever seen. They were cold-blooded fucking killers, vicious bastards. I was only a teenager, but I was affiliated with mobsters that most people wouldn't even be allowed in the same room with. Just like when I was in school, I was the smallest kid in the class. But just like then, I always had the tallest, biggest, toughest friends. To survive you didn't have to be the biggest or meanest person. You just had to make sure that the biggest and meanest guys were on your side.

Stuey's obsession with cards and gambling left him little time for anything else. He missed out on most of the things that make up the life of a normal teenager. He didn't have friends his own age, he didn't go to parties, and he never dated. That's not to say that he didn't have the normal teenage urges or feelings. Victor Romano constantly teased Stuey about his not having a girlfriend. The problem was that Stuey was shy and awkward around girls, and he didn't like discussing the subject with anyone. Romano assured Stuey that hookers and massage parlors were acceptable substitutes, that it was all right to satisfy your needs this way. He introduced Stuey to his favorite massage parlor, an upscale place in the East Fifties called Plato's Retreat (a name that would later be used for a famous sex club of the 1970s). It quickly became a favorite haunt for Stuey. Nighttime racetrack jaunts were replaced by visits to Plato's Retreat, where every girl in the place soon knew Stuey by name.

Whenever he was short of cash, Stuey gravitated to even lower depths for satisfaction: the adult movie theaters and porno shops along Forty-second Street between Seventh and Eighth avenues—most of them operated by the rival Gambino crime family. There, Stuey's sexual fantasies were gratified in filthy semen-stained peep-show booths that reeked of Clorox and Lysol.

If Fay Ungar had gradually abdicated her parental responsibilities, she became even less capable of caring for her children following a minor stroke she suffered in 1968, at age fifty-four. The stroke was a devastating blow to a woman who had once been so gregarious and full of life. After a week in Mount Sinai Hospital, Fay returned home. The stroke, combined with a developing dependency on barbiturates, tranquilizers, and painkillers, hastened her downward spiral. She clung to the memory of her beauty, but the ravages of age, infirmity, and loneliness had taken a toll, and her efforts to hide that harsh reality with hair dye and excessive makeup only drew attention to what had been lost.

She took some small comfort in the knowledge that Stuey had found, in Victor Romano, a surrogate parent, but her children's lives, as always, seemed distant and detached from her own. Though Stuey was still living at home, using the apartment mostly as a crash pad, Judy, who was seventeen, had moved out and gotten married. Hud was gone, too. Fay, unable to care for her, had given her away.

Stuey felt bad for his mother—it was easier than feeling hurt and angry. He sometimes brought money home. "Look how great I did this week," he'd say proudly, as he tossed a roll of tens and twenties into her lap. He was still desperate for some sort of approval. Most of the time, though, there were no kind words. Fay was too out of it to react.

The sad fact was that Fay needed money desperately. There were no more trips to the Catskills in the summertime. Little money was left from Ido's stash. What money there was now went toward paying for medical needs—some of them real, others imaginary. Fay's doctor made house calls and prescribed medication, charging her $35 per visit. He had her on Valium and Nembutal, presumably to calm her nerves.

As the doctor's visits became more frequent—from biweekly to every ten days to once a week—the dosage of Fay's medication increased. By Stuey's sixteenth birthday, Fay was staying in bed most days. Often, she was so doped up that she instructed the doctor to take the fee directly from her pocketbook. Knowing that she was incapable of keeping track, he took what he wanted.

Stuey's visits home grew rare. Spending time with his mother depressed him. Most nights, he sacked out on sofas at the clubs. Occasionally, he spent a night with the Romanos. At other times, he stayed at one of the apartments rented by the married wiseguys, who kept empty pads on the side where they could bring their girlfriends.

During one of Stuey's visits home, in a rare moment of clarity, Fay noticed that a significant amount of money was missing from her pocketbook. She had cashed her monthly disability check that day, and she asked Stuey if he'd taken the money. He insisted he hadn't. "It must have been that quack doctor of yours," he said. Confused and upset, Fay accused him of lying.

That was more than he could take. He stormed out of the apartment in a huff.

Instantly remorseful, Fay got out of bed and went after him. When she opened the apartment door, Stuey was in the hall, waiting for the elevator.

"Honey, I'm sorry," she said.

Stuey ignored her. The elevator doors were opening. Without saying anything more, he got on and punched the button for the ground floor.

Later that day, Stuey told Romano about his problems at home, and Romano found him a furnished place to stay for a few weeks. Eventually, the rift between him and his mother was smoothed over, and things went back to the way they'd been, with Stuey crashing at her apartment when he needed to. But those occasions became more and more infrequent.

4.

A MADE MAN

In card clubs around New York City, Stuey "the Kid" Ungar had become an increasingly common topic of discussion. Rumors of his prodigious talent extended beyond the island of Manhattan to clubs in Queens and Brooklyn, and even across the Hudson to New Jersey: word was out that there was a wired-up pint-size sixteen-year-old kid who was busting all the best players in the Apple.

Stuey liked the fact that people were talking about him. It was an unexpected by-product of his obsession. Making money felt good, too, though again, it wasn't the point. If it had been, Stuey wouldn't have dumped all the dough he won at the tables by going to the track.

I was an action freak. Winning got boring if it was too easy. I needed the constant challenge. There wasn't any challenge in beating a bunch of losers at gin or pinochle. That just wasn't a thrill for me. But give me a Daily Racing Form *and let me try to pick the winner of the third race at Aqueduct. Hey, that got my juices flowing. I think that's why I always loved the challenge of mastering a new card game. They couldn't teach me new games fast enough.*

Victor Romano's relationship to Stuey was complex. He appreciated Stuey's genius with cards on the purest level. He understood how special the kid was. At the same time, Romano was a businessman who could see that there was money to be made by channeling and pointing his prodigy in certain directions. All this was complicated by his evolving personal attachment to Stuey.

I remember when Victor first taught me how to play hearts. He was going to teach me bridge, too, because Victor was an excellent bridge player. But we talked about it and there was no money to be made in bridge so I never wasted time with it.

Hearts was a game I really enjoyed playing. I think it was because it was a brutal game. It was very tough on you mentally, especially if you were playing for serious money. In all my days back in New York, I only got into two fights. Both times it was in a game of hearts. That game could make the worst enemies out of lifelong friends. I got so good at it—at the time you didn't have to get rid of the queen at the first opportunity—that I played just to piss the other guy off. There was this one guy I played against, Davey K. (we always called people by their first names and initials—Davey K., Frankie D., Jimmy Z., or whatever), and he got so mad at me that he grabbed a wooden chair and hit me with it. He could have killed me, but I was lucky and moved out of the way and he just hit me a glancing blow.

A couple of days later, Davey K. came back into the club and Victor brought him over.

"Shake his hand," Victor said.

"What?" I said. "Are you fucking crazy? That cocksucker hit me with a chair!"

"Just shake his hand," Victor insisted. So I shook his hand. I looked at Victor and he winked at me. I really didn't know what that meant at the time.

Well, two days later, Davey K. was found shot to death.

Now, I don't know if our fight had anything to do with it, and I never asked any questions. When a guy was hit, it was just something you didn't ask questions about. Davey K. had violated a house rule: You didn't raise your hand or commit a violent act inside a wiseguy joint. The wiseguys had enough heat on them as it was. They sure didn't need fights and the attention that might bring, people phoning in complaints and stuff. So the guys who got physical were taken care of.

Obviously, Victor must have known that Davey was gonna be hit, because when he winked at me like that, he was telling me to go along with it, that everything was going to be all right. Victor was protecting me that day by making me shake Davey K.'s hand in front of everybody. That way no one could connect me to his death or think we were still at odds. Maybe, too, Victor was giving the guy a false sense of security, that the fight was no big deal, when the reality was that he was going to get whacked.

See, back in New York, it was no big deal when a guy got killed. People got killed every day. Some guys would just disappear. I never asked any questions. I remember when there would be a newspaper lying on a chair or something, I'd check out the front page to see if anyone I knew got killed. Then I went straight to the sports section.

I knew all these guys were probably involved in things, including murders. I mean, it was just common knowledge. But they pretty much kept me out of it. Not once did any of them ask me if I wanted to get involved. I was talent to them. They protected talent. They safeguarded it. See, I made money for a lot of people. I made a lot of money for Victor.

• • •

Romano arranged a gin game between Stuey and a hotshot named Teddy Price. Then in his forties, Price was one of the best gin players of his era. Oddly, in the way of these things, he often had no idea who his next opponent would be until very close to the date of the match. The mystery was necessary because high-stakes games posed certain risks. If word of a big game leaked out, the vice squad might show up, bust it, and seize all the money. "Most heads-up matches were arranged in a five-minute phone call," explained George "Rummy" DelFranco, who knew all the best cardplayers and pool hustlers in New York. " 'Hi, I'm so-and-so, I hear you want a game. I've got a guy who wants to play for $25 a point. Where do you want to meet, and what time?' That's how it was done."

A match between Stuey and Teddy Price was arranged at the Beekman Tower Hotel on First Avenue and Forty-ninth Street. When Stuey arrived, Price was sitting and waiting for him, doing a crossword puzzle. Romano had sent a bodyguard along with Stuey, and Price assumed that the protector was his opponent and that he had brought his teenage son along to watch the game.

When Stuey stuck out his hand, Price appeared confused and startled. He looked from Stuey to the bigger man. "Aren't you—"

"No, I'm the one who's playing you," Stuey said. "How much would you like to play for?"

Price was still puzzled. Was this a joke? "How much would *you* like to play for?" he asked the Kid as others in the room started to laugh nervously.

"Whatever you want," Stuey said, brimming with confidence. "Name it."

They settled on a wager of $500 a game.

Three games later, down $1,500, Price quit.

In the beginning, when Stuey first came on the scene, there were plenty of takers, who were curious to catch a glimpse of the Kid for themselves and test his skill. Stuey occasionally lost some of the more esoteric games, but at gin he was unbeatable. "He's going to be a millionaire," Romano told anyone who would listen.

The time had come for a bigger score.

Word about the kid genius reached Nat Klein, known in gambling circles as "the Bronx Express" or just "the Bronx." Klein was widely acknowledged by those who frequented exclusive clubs like the Cavendish East and the Mayfair, where big money was at stake, as one of the two best cardplayers in the city. The other great talent at that time was a man known as "Leo the Jap." Both were nearly legendary, so good that they had difficulty finding opponents to play for serious money. Annoyed by the rumors about the young phenom and intensely curious to meet him, the two maestros agreed to play against Stuey in separate matches, if the stakes were high enough.

Two private games were arranged. In the first, Stuey destroyed the Bronx Express in less than an hour, netting just over $10,000. The match against Leo the Jap took a bit longer, but Leo, too, surrendered after complaining that someone should have warned him about how good the Kid was.

There were several factors in Stuey's dominance over these older, more experienced players. One was his memory: he could remember every card that was played and the sequence in which cards were picked up or discarded. He was also incredibly observant, able to pick up on tells and interpret them. In gin, one of the most elementary defensive strategies is noting where opponents place cards in their fan. Many amateurs place their cards in a row, from low to high. By observing where in the row a card is placed, the opponent can easily deduce its rank. Stuey was therefore able to construct in his head a picture of what cards his opponent had and what he was seeking. As a result, he became the greatest "defensive" gin player of all time, less intent on completing his own melds than on preventing his opponents from making gin and winning points. Frustrated opponents often claimed that playing against Stuey, it felt as if they were playing with their cards faceup.

I beat everyone by the time I was sixteen—guys I had heard about since I could barely walk. Everyone has a specialty—well, mine was gin. In those days, I really wasn't that great of a poker player. I won at poker mostly because the competition wasn't that strong. Most of the New York guys had more money than brains. They'd look across the table at me and think, "Who the fuck is this?"

Oddly, one of Stuey's biggest wins as a teenager came not from gin or poker but from the neighborhood numbers racket—a mob-run lottery very much like the daily numbers game that the state runs today, the difference being that the numbers are generated not from a drawing but from the last three or four numbers of the handle (the total sum of that day's wagers) at one of the local racetracks. Since the daily handles from Aqueduct, Belmont, and other racetracks were published in the *Daily News* and the *Post*, this was a legitimate way of generating a random number that everyone could see.

A few months shy of his seventeenth birthday, Stuey bet the numbers of his birthday, 9-8-5-3, and when he checked the paper the next day, he discovered to his astonishment and delight that the handle at Aqueduct the day before had been $1,319,853.

The score was worth a cool $20,000 to the Kid. Ecstatic and wanting to celebrate, he took a cab straight over to a backroom blackjack game on Thirty-sixth Street. By the time he arrived, word of his big hit had reached the owners of the club, who, when they were assured that a runner was on his way with Stuey's twenty grand, decided to let him play blackjack on credit—a courtesy usually extended only to those with jobs and legitimate incomes.

"Before the guy even showed up to pay me, I had lost it all," Stuey recalled. "I was sick. Absolutely sick. And the cocksucker who owned the joint didn't even let me keep playing. He cut off my credit the minute I hit $20,000 in losses. Can you believe that?"

The bitter experience inspired Stuey to read up on what was then a new method for beating blackjack—card counting—and to discuss strategy with Romano. It also focused Romano on keeping Stuey occupied doing what he did best: playing gin. After Stuey's victories over Leo the Jap and the Bronx Express, his burgeoning rep grew even bigger, spreading beyond New York to other parts of the country. One well-known gin player heard about Stuey and challenged him to a match. Even though the challenger was a known cheat, Stuey told Romano to accept.

As always, Stuey went to the arranged meeting place accompanied by a bodyguard supplied by Romano. During the course of the match, Stuey's protector noticed that his opponent was sneaking a look at the bottom card of the deck when he dealt, and also "accidentally" lifting two cards instead of one when drawing. During a break in the action, the protector took Stuey aside.

"That lousy son of a bitch is cheating you!" he said.

"I know he is," Stuey said, impatiently, "but I can beat him anyway."

Stuey walked out the door that evening with $16,000 in cash.

Having beaten all the best local gin players, Stuey now took on a new wave of challengers, who flew in from Florida, Chicago, and elsewhere wanting to test their skills against the young upstart. Probably the best-known of these was a Canadian player, Harry Stein, whom everyone knew as "Yonkie."

Yonkie was a professional gin player, and he looked and acted the part. He wore fine clothes, lived out of hotel rooms, and flew all over the world, taking on the best players. He wasn't one to jump on a plane on a lark, either; he chose his opponents carefully, taking a very businesslike approach. Although he was young himself at the time, Yonkie wasn't enthralled with the idea of playing against a sixteen-year-old. Unless the stakes were extremely high, there seemed little to gain from the match. It took several phone calls and a fair amount of dickering, but Yonkie finally decided that the stakes were too good to pass up. He made the trip to New York, giving his side of the bet to an agreed-upon third party, who would hold all the money.

The match generated a huge amount of interest and side action among the cognoscenti, with Stuey initially listed as a 5–2 underdog. Even though Yonkie was the best-known gin player of the day, Stuey perceived this line as a slight and couldn't wait to prove the oddsmakers wrong.

The day of the game, Stuey arrived at the Pennsylvania Hotel on Seventh Avenue, directly across the street from Madison Square Garden. His entourage included Romano and several of Romano's associates. As Stuey and crew entered the hotel suite, the two gin prodigies came face-to-face for the first time. Their entourages of half a dozen men and handlers in dapper suits gave the occasion the feel of two great prizefighters meeting for the first time in the ring. Yonkie extended his hand. Stuey shook it, but halfheartedly, failing to look the Canadian in the eye. This irked Stein. Stuey showed none of the deference one would expect an up-and-coming player to extend toward a champion—even an uncrowned one.

An awkward silence followed, born of both players' competitiveness and social ineptitude. Romano suggested that they get started before they were charged another day for the hotel room, and that seemed to break the tension—at least briefly.

Once the cards were dealt, it was clear that more than money was involved in the outcome. This match was ego-driven and personal.

"I'd never played that high before," Stuey said. "But the money wasn't an issue for me. All I had to do was concentrate on the cards."

Over the next four hours, Stuey and Yonkie played twenty-seven games of Hollywood gin.* In one of the most astonishing feats in the annals of high-level gin, Stuey won every game—eighty-one straight columns. Everyone watching in the hotel suite was stunned. The best player in the world had simply been destroyed. According to those who knew him, Harry Stein was never the same after that night. He returned to Canada a broken man, so humiliated that he never again showed his face in gin circles.

"After I beat Harry Stein, I was a marked man," Stuey said. "I couldn't get a game anywhere in New York. I was royally fucked."

Stuey's cut of the take from the match was $35,000. It was gone at the racetrack within two weeks.

The demolition of Yonkie Stein showed both Stuey's genius at the game and his complete lack of understanding of the art of the hustle. Once he started playing, his competitive instincts took over and overwhelmed common sense. His mission wasn't to win money—it was to destroy people and be the best ever. As a result, he killed off any chance for a rematch, and he also scared away potential opponents.

On Mother's Day, 1970, Stuey, persuaded by Victor, went to visit Fay. Armed with a heart-shaped box of chocolates, he entered the apartment. What he saw shocked him. The place was a disaster, dirty and unkempt, with a foul odor of human decay. Fay was out of it, zonked on

---

* In Hollywood gin, scoring is magnified because winning or losing streaks carry over to subsequent columns. In other words, being outplayed can be devastating, both emotionally and financially. The ultimate humiliation is being shut out or "schneidered."

painkillers, barely able to register his presence or sit up in bed. After Stuey left that day, he decided that he couldn't just sit by and not do anything. He hired a live-in nurse and paid her $150 a week to take care of his mother.

One thing I never got into back then was drinking or drugs. I saw what booze did to people when I was a kid hanging out at my father's bar. So I was never interested in it. As far as the drugs go, almost everybody my age was into drugs. I would see them sniffing glue out of a bag when I walked down the street; they'd be hunched down next to the stoops. It was a cheap high, but I never considered it because it just made people look stupid and desperate.

There were other reasons, too. I had other things to do—things that kept me busy. And Victor said he would kill anyone that did anything to hurt me, so no one really ever offered me any drugs. They were scared to. No, the only thing I was interested in was gambling. That's what got me high.

Stuey's eighteenth birthday saw him receive the last chunk of his trust-fund inheritance from his father's estate. With interest, it amounted to a lump sum of nearly $14,000. For most eighteen-year-olds, a sum like that might have gone toward college or might have been put into some sort of long-term investment. Stuey ran through the entire bundle in two days at the track. "Yeah," Stuey said to anyone who would listen, "I blew my father's inheritance. So what? Fuck it."

Turning eighteen in 1971 also posed some immediate difficulties with Uncle Sam. Stuey was now eligible for the draft. With 350,000 American soldiers fighting in the jungles of Vietnam and Cambodia, many young Americans were terrified of being called up. Since Stuey was a high school dropout with no option of taking a college deferment, he was a prime target for induction. While his small stature—five feet five and barely 110 pounds—might have exempted him from serving, Stuey and his backers wanted to leave nothing to chance. The money he was already making for the mob, combined with his potential future earnings, made him too valuable a commodity to be shipped off to Vietnam. Something would have to be done—and quickly.

Victor Romano shared at least one aspect of Ido Ungar's philosophy of life: everyone and everything had a price. The going rate for a draft deferment in 1971 ranged from $500 to $2,500, depending on the circumstances. Local draft boards were run by underpaid civil servants, who were ripe for payoffs. An $800-a-month paper pusher on a draft board could earn ten times his salary by selling deferments. A stroke of the pen was all it took.

When Romano had one of his associates, known as "the Fixer," deliver an envelope stuffed with cash to the right person, Stuey's problem disappeared. Officially, he was declared ineligible for military service on the basis of "health reasons."

While Romano was looking out for his own pocketbook when he helped Stuey get out of trouble or lectured him about the hopelessness of the racetrack, he also genuinely cared about his protégé. Victor actually tried to persuade Stuey to go back to school. He really believed that Stuey had enough talent and intelligence to do anything. In fact, Victor made an extraordinary offer: he would pay for Stuey to go back to school to get a G.E.D. and then enroll in college.

Stuey wasn't interested. As far as he was concerned, school was for suckers.

If that was the way he felt, Victor said, then Stuey was going to have to change his attitude about playing cards. He needed to get serious about it, treat it as a profession, and become more disciplined and profit-oriented. Victor thought that by bringing Stuey closer into the fold, he would make his protégé see the gravity and sense of such an approach. As a reward after the annihilation of Yonkie Stein, Stuey was invited to a sit-down with the boss of bosses, the Mafia captain Gus Frasca. Victor thought it was important to make his relationship with Stuey official, so that everyone would understand that the Kid belonged to him. The meeting with Frasca, in a restaurant on Mulberry Street, lasted no more than five minutes, but when Frasca shook Stuey's hand, it was as if the king's sword had been touched to the shoulders of a young knight.

"I'm a made man," Stuey bragged to everyone after the meeting. He loved his association with organized crime. Being connected carried enormous stature in the gambling underworld, and it was a virtual guarantee of personal protection, of having the ultimate older brother. In a sense, that is an appropriate metaphor: the wiseguys had become, for all intents and purposes, Stuey's family. They supported him, housed him, fed him, and gave him a close-knit group of people he could trust. Stuey's affectionate nickname in the mob world became "Meyer," after the Jewish mobster Meyer Lansky. Stuey loved the name—especially as a replacement for his childhood moniker "Monkey."

Following the meeting with Frasca, Victor Romano took control of all of Stuey's financial affairs. When Stuey earned money, Romano took a cut on behalf of the organization. When Stuey (rarely) suffered a loss, Romano paid the tab. When Stuey got into trouble because of other gambling debts, Romano bailed him out. The alliance freed Stuey of any personal obligations and allowed him to strut around town like the cock of the walk. As long as he continued to earn money for the mob playing cards, he was the golden boy.

Having reached the legal age of eighteen, Stuey decided that he wanted a driver's license. He was tired of hitching rides and taking subways and taxis back and forth from the racetrack. A car would give him independence. The trouble was that he didn't know how to drive, and he had no interest in studying a driver's manual or taking a written test. That was what squareballs did. So Stuey talked to Victor, and Romano bribed a clerk at the Department of Motor Vehicles, just as he had bribed the draft board. For $200 cash, Stuey was issued an official New York State driver's license. The only problem was that he still didn't know how to drive.

I got my first car when I was eighteen. It was a Ford, and it cost me $2,400. Sal the Albanian took me out and gave me a driving lesson. Thing was, in New York, there wasn't anyplace I could go and take it slow. I'd never even sat in the driver's seat before. We went out on the West Side Highway, and I was driving eighty-five miles per hour. My first time behind the wheel! I was having a blast, but poor Sal was terrified. I looked over at him and he was white, the color just drained from his face. He screamed at me to pull over. "If you don't pull over right now, I swear I'm gonna kill you!" I said, "What difference does it make, then? I'm gonna die either way!" He didn't think that was too funny.

Stuey's sense of his own invincibility was combined with a wiseguy's contempt for people who tried to play by the rules, who in his opinion just "didn't get it." One day his sister, Judy, phoned him and brought him up-to-date on the struggles in her life—she was desperately trying to kick her drug habit and looking for a job. He couldn't have helped her morale much when he snapped, "Working is for idiots. I can make more money in one pot than most people make in a year."

It was an insensitive remark, to be sure. It also illustrated how far removed he was from the rest of the world, and how hard it was for him to relate to the more ordinary concerns that most people had. In the context of his world, it was hard to argue that he should completely abandon what he was doing to pursue an education. Looking for work and starting a career would have been ludicrous—given that he was an eighteen-year-old high school dropout making a grand a week or more. And even if he had wanted a job, what skills did he possess? What employer would hire him?

When it came down to it, who could blame Stuey for thinking he was special? He was living by his own rules, and not only getting away with it but thriving. What more could an eighteen-year-old want?

5.

BEGINNINGS AND ENDINGS

On December 15, 1971, eighteen-year-old Stuey Ungar boarded an Eastern Airlines flight bound from New York's La Guardia Airport to Miami. He was bored with his routine in New York and sick of the cold weather. He needed a change.

The gin games in New York had mostly dried up. To take up the slack, Stuey was playing seven-card stud, with occasional one-on-one games of hearts and pinochle. But his daily routine—waking up, going to the track, playing all night, and crashing until noon—was getting tiresome.

Romano pushed for the trip to Florida. It was sunny and warm there, with plenty of high-limit action, and the promise of some good gin games against top-flight competition. "It's just what you need. It'll do you good," Victor said.

"I'll go," Stuey said, "but only if they have racetracks."

Miami's rich retirees, many of them Jewish, seemed like the perfect target for Stuey. Assisted by one of Romano's underworld contacts in south Florida, he rented a one-bedroom apartment on Collins Avenue in the heart of South Beach. Even though this seemed like an ideal situation, Stuey found it difficult to deal with Florida in large doses. During his initial few months there, he flew back and forth between New York and Miami eight times. "I was there on and off for six months," Stuey said. "Florida was nice in the beginning, but after I slaughtered all of the superstars, it was back to the same old thing. I got bored with it."

Miami's slower-paced lifestyle irritated the mile-a-minute native New Yorker. He complained that he couldn't get decent Chinese food at two in the morning or hail a cab or find a massage parlor like Plato's Retreat that was open 24/7. On one occasion, Stuey had a chance to go deep-sea fishing with a few men from the Genovese mob, but the entire concept of fishing seemed pointless to him. "Why should I go out and spend the whole day getting heatstroke, trying to catch a fish, when I can go to the market or get it at a restaurant? I see no point to it."

As he had in New York, Stuey spent most of his afternoons with the *Daily Racing Form* in hand—at Hialeah or Gulfstream Park. If no card games could be drummed up at night, Stuey hit the dog track. "I was bored out of my fucking mind," he said. "It got so bad, I moved away from the beach on Collins and rented a place right across the street from the racetrack."

After six months, he couldn't take it any longer. One day, he jumped into a taxi and said, "Take me to the airport." He left behind a closet full of clothes and other personal belongings. He didn't want to stay one extra minute, even to pack.

Victor was disappointed. Not only had Stuey failed to take full advantage of the economic opportunities down South—he had acted unprofessionally. Romano's frustration was compounded by worries about his own health, and what that might mean for his young charge in the future. At that point, Romano was suffering from diabetes, hardening of the arteries, and failing eyesight. Late one night, as he and Stuey were leaving the Jovialite, Romano froze in the middle of the sidewalk and looked at Stuey with an odd expression. "I don't feel good," he said.

Stuey, remembering his father's heart attack, recognized the warning signs. Romano's face was twisting up in a frightening way. Stuey got him into the passenger seat of Romano's mammoth Cadillac, and slid behind the wheel. They sped through the crowded streets to the nearest hospital, forcing pedestrians to jump out of their way. At the hospital, Romano was rushed into surgery, where he had a successful coronary bypass operation.

A week later, Romano was released. Despite his speedy recovery, he was more convinced than ever that his own situation was tenuous and that Stuey needed a stronger mentor. He introduced Stuey to his thirty-eight-year-old nephew, Phil Tartaglia, better known as "Philly Brush," a name he had earned for his abrupt style and penchant for giving people the brush-off. Tartaglia was a rock-solid five-foot-eleven, 200-pound street fighter, who trusted no one. His shiny bald head was framed by big, bushy sideburns that made him instantly recognizable, even from a distance. He was someone who radiated an aura of "don't fuck with me" so palpable as to give pause even to other wiseguys.

Victor thought that Stuey might respond more positively to someone closer to his own age. It was agreed that whenever Romano wasn't around, Philly was to be Stuey's designated protector. Additionally, Philly would join with Victor in backing Stuey against anyone who wanted to play him for any amount of money. Their share would be 50 percent of Stuey's take. If Stuey used his own money to play and the game was set up by Victor or Philly, Stuey's percentage would be higher. But since Stuey could never hold on to his own money long, he continually had to rely on Victor and Philly for financial support.

Upon his return from Florida, Stuey needed a new wardrobe to replace the clothes he'd left behind. He purchased his new duds through a fence. "Most of my shopping was done that way," Stuey said. "I bought an Ultrasuede coat for $60. At Macy's it was $450. At the club there was a guy who handled clothes. Another one handled jewelry, another

TVs. Everything I owned was hot. My entire apartment was like a microwave."

Like many gamblers, Stuey counted off $100 bills at the betting window as if he were printing them himself, but when it came to more mundane necessities, he loved to get a bargain. It was the gambler's gotta-get-an-edge mentality.

Besides his new wardrobe, Stuey also was in the market for a new car. The Ford Galaxie he'd bought himself on his eighteenth birthday was history. He'd run it into a gulley near the Aqueduct racetrack in Queens, and rather than deal with the police or tow trucks, and nervous because of his falsely obtained driver's license, he simply threw the keys into the front seat of the car and abandoned it. "Bad beat," he mumbled to himself as he walked away, looking for the nearest cab.

He'd heard about an interesting way to get a new car. The wiseguys had a racket going: they'd rent a car from Hertz or Avis, using a phony driver's license and a stolen credit card, and never return it. Between the bureaucracy of the rental company and the incompetency of the New York City police, it would take weeks, sometimes months, before a car was actually reported stolen.

There were guys who specialized in that field. That was their thing. You told the guy what you wanted and they would just bring you the car. You didn't have to do anything. All it cost was three hundred dollars, and you got a new car. I must have gone through at least a dozen cars that way over the course of several years. I usually held on to them for, like, three months. But the longer you kept one, the riskier it was, because if the police stopped you while you were driving it, you had a lot of explaining to do. Namely, why were you driving a stolen car? You couldn't park on one of the main avenues. It had to be on a side street. They had people that went around and looked for stolen cars on the main streets. When a few months had passed,

and the car got too hot, I just left it parked somewhere, paid three hundred
bucks, and got another one. Or if I got tired of driving a Mustang, I got a
Bonneville the next week. It was easy.

The longest I ever kept one of those stolen rentals was something like
eight months. One time, I walked up to the place where I usually parked it,
and it was gone. Somebody must have stolen it. Imagine, stealing a car that
was already hot. Man, that poor fuck was really in for a surprise.

With his new, post-Florida wardrobe and his virtually new, albeit hot,
car, Stuey was lacking only one thing: someone to impress.

Madeline Wheeler was a twenty-year-old cocktail waitress at the
card club on Seventy-second Street when she met the kid everyone was
talking about. "He came into the club with a friend of his, a guy I had
been dating for a few months. The guy I was seeing introduced him to
me. To tell you the truth, I didn't think much of him. He was a jumpy,
skinny little guy with long hair and bad clothes—all this polyester crap.
And he had this attitude. He seemed kind of cocky and arrogant."

Stuey, on the other hand, was immediately attracted to Madeline.
"She was a real looker," Larry Romano recalled. "Big ass, big tits, tight
jeans, bell-bottoms, and lots of hair." Stuey started going to Seventy-
second Street frequently after that first meeting. One night, he ordered
tea from Madeline, his usual drink of choice while playing, and his eyes
held hers a little longer than necessary. There was "a spark," as Stuey described it. He tossed her a $5 chip. She smiled, and he smiled back.

Still, nothing happened right away.

"After a while, I broke up with the guy who introduced us," Madeline said. "And Stuey kept coming around. I knew he liked me, but I still
wasn't sure about him. I mean, he really didn't have much of a rap. He
wasn't charming me or anything. But he kept coming around."

A full year passed before Madeline agreed to go on a date with Stuey.

They went to a place called the Skyline for dinner. "It was a funny date," Madeline recalled. "We were both very nervous. I didn't eat much. I never did when I was with him."

Bar girls in New York were a dime a dozen. But Madeline was different. Not only was she stunningly attractive, she was streetwise and independent, and she had things in common with Stuey. Her father was a postal worker in Queens and a part-time bookmaker, who had taken her with him to basketball games, baseball games, and prizefights just as Ido had taken Stuey. There was more: her father, like Stuey's father, had died when she was thirteen.

"We had that bond of being able to understand one another," Madeline said. "The more I got to know about his life, the stronger I felt that. And the sports and gambling—I had grown up around it. So that was part of it, too."

At eighteen, Madeline had married an exercise boy at Aqueduct. They had a son, named Richard, but almost immediately Madeline felt tied down, suffocated—not by the baby, but "by being married." So she left. "I planned it. I took half the money we had in the bank, found a place in Howard Beach, and ran away. When I called to tell my husband, he was devastated. But I just didn't want to be married anymore."

Stuey was very interested in hearing Madeline talk about her son, Richie. "With a lot of men," Madeline said, "it would be like, 'Oh, she has a kid. I'm running the other way.' So that was one of the things that drew me to Stuey. That he wasn't that way, that he was sensitive and receptive to my situation. Also, when he actually met Richie, who was four at the time, it was like an instant bond. It was like he had found a new friend. So what might have been a minus with some guys was a plus with him. He was able to put himself on the level of a four-year-old, almost as if he wanted to be that age himself. He was very comfortable."

• • •

Before Madeline, I never had any confidence with women—at least ones who weren't working in a massage parlor or an escort service. In the circles I ran around in, there just weren't many women I could meet. I never made out with a girl when I was a teenager like other kids did. My sister went to the movies and made out with her boyfriend, and she'd tell me about it later, but I never got a chance to do those kinds of things myself. I never even really kissed a girl seriously until Madeline.

What I liked about her best was that she was my equal when it came to conversation. Whatever I threw at her, she threw it back, just like a typical New Yorker. And she saw who I was. That I could be out all hours of the night. That I might go to the track. She didn't mind all that. I could just be myself with her.

The fact was, however, that dating Stuey required a huge amount of tolerance. He dressed like an old man. His grooming habits were sporadic. And his attitude toward eating was eccentric, to say the least. He hated to waste time in restaurants—and on a date, that could be a drawback. "He'd call up the restaurant ahead of time," Madeline said, "so that by the time we got there, our food was ready. Then he'd shovel it down." As Larry Romano put it, "Stu didn't eat his food. He inhaled it."

Despite these drawbacks, Madeline found qualities to admire in Stuey, none of them more appealing than his instant devotion to her son. When Richie was around, Stuey's impatience vanished. He took the boy everywhere, even to the card rooms. Richie was his little buddy. It was odd. Stuey had no experience dealing with young children. His entire life had been spent with people older than he, and his feeling for Richie was unexpected. He couldn't understand why Madeline's ex-husband, no matter how hurt he'd been, wouldn't pay child support.

"He had no respect for my ex-husband," Madeline said. "Helping out your family was a big thing for Stuey. You helped out your blood. That was just an ironclad rule."

Stuey's living situation at that point was still catch-as-catch-can. When he wasn't at Madeline's home, he was either at his mother's apartment or crashing on a couch in a card room. Fay, however, wasn't thrilled by her son's new girlfriend, at least initially.

"Fay didn't like me in the beginning," Madeline said. "I think she thought I was going to take whatever little time she had with him at that point. But she got over it, and then we just bonded. I thought she was a sweetheart."

When Stuey moved into Madeline's place on East Eighty-ninth Street (she had moved there from Howard Beach), Fay was actually pleased. "I think she felt relieved that he had a place to go," Madeline said.

While Stuey's involvement with Madeline and Richie was deepening, his mother's health was deteriorating. Fay was always in and out of hospitals, and increasingly irritable, screaming for pills in the middle of the night and making scenes. The part-time nurse quit, unable to take it anymore. One night, while visiting, Stuey refused to give his mother her medication. Fay threw a fit, screaming so loudly that the neighbors came to the door.

Stuey let them in so that they could see that he wasn't killing her. But when she complained to them that her own son was depriving her of her medication, Stuey felt compelled to give her the pills. After the neighbors left, he was so enraged at his mother that he stormed out, swearing that he would never ever allow himself to become screwed up on drugs the way she was.

It was over a month before he saw Fay again. He got a phone call at a card game one night from Roosevelt Hospital, telling him that his mother had suffered a stroke and was in intensive care.

Stuey dashed out of the club, leaving his chips on the table, and took a taxi to the hospital. Fay's second stroke was far more serious than the first. She was paralyzed on one side, unable to walk. Though she was released after a week, she now needed a wheelchair to get around, as well as constant care. Drastic changes were in order. Stuey clearly couldn't care for her, but without the money to pay for a live-in nurse, the options were limited. A social worker recommended that she be placed in a nursing home.

Though he wasn't happy about it, Stuey agreed, and Fay was placed in a nursing home on Avenue D and Fifth Street. Not too long after that, for various economic and logistical reasons, she had to be moved to another home, in Queens. The situation was obviously painful for Stuey, even more so because he found visiting her nearly unbearable. A self-described "mama's boy," he sympathized with her, yet he couldn't seem to help her, and his helplessness made him want not to be around her or deal with anything pertaining to her situation, including her financial obligations.

Stuey's negligence in paying Fay's rent for her apartment and his failure to respond to notices from the landlord led to a dispossess order that was issued by the city and tacked to the door. Unless the premises were vacated within seven days, the order read, everything in the apartment would be confiscated and removed.

Stuey's sister found out about the dispossess order and tracked him down by phone at one of the card clubs.

"We need to pay the rent or get all Mom's things put into storage by Friday. Otherwise she's going to lose everything, Stuey," Judy pleaded. "I don't have the money to do it, myself, or I would." Judy was living uptown with her husband, Nicky Suarez, and struggling to get by.

"I'll take care of it," Stuey said, eager to get back to his game. By the next morning, however, the conversation with his sister had been forgotten, obliterated from his consciousness by one of his worst losses of the year, a $2,500 disaster in an all-night marathon of seven-card stud.

Six days later, four men from a moving company contracted by the city—four men who never knew or met any of the Ungar family—broke open the door at 421 FDR Drive and entered the apartment. They rolled up the Persian rugs that Isidore had walked on when he was alive and that the kids had crawled over before they could walk. They stacked up furniture, piece by piece, on top of the cherrywood dining table where the Ungars had eaten thousands of meals. They threw into bags a closet-ful of clothes and shoes, articles Fay had worn with the change of dozens of seasons and fashions. Within an hour, the men had gathered up the remnants of two decades of a family's life, boxed it, carted it, and hoisted it into the back of a truck, leaving behind an empty apartment.

Much of the contents of the apartment—mink and chinchilla furs, brooches, necklaces, earrings, and the fine furniture and rugs—were subsequently auctioned at an estate sale. The rest—the keepsakes and bric-a-brac, and the hundreds of family photos, the baby pictures of Judy and Stuey, the snapshots of vacations in the Catskills and of the Ungars in happier times—was discarded, incinerated in a mountain of trash in the city dump, a sad and anonymous end to a family that was no more.

6.

RAISING THE STAKES

In December 1974, a few months after his twenty-first birthday, Stuey took his first trip to Las Vegas. He went on an express junket, arranged by Philly Tartaglia, to play gin against some of Vegas's big-time high rollers. Stuey's ties to gambling circles in New York, combined with Philly's connections in Las Vegas, landed them free room, food, and beverages (a comp known as "RFB" in the trade) at Caesars Palace. All Stuey had to do was give the house action.

Less than an hour after Stuey and Philly had landed at McCarran Airport, their limo pulled up to the main entrance of Caesars Palace, driving past the grand fountain that the daredevil motorcyclist Evel Knievel had nearly killed himself trying to jump over six years earlier. The ornate Italian porte cochere, flanked by reproductions of classical statues of soldiers in scalloped niches, was the essence of the visionary hotelier Jay Sarno's philosophy to elevate gambling into the realm of exotic fantasy.

In those days, most hotels on the Strip in Las Vegas had names like the Dunes, the Desert Inn, and the Sands, but Caesars was the forerunner of the conceptual palaces that would come to define modern

Vegas. It had cocktail waitresses clad in flowing tunics, security guards dressed like centurions, a restaurant called the Bacchanal where wine goddesses massaged gentlemen diners, and a floating indoor lounge called Cleopatra's Barge.

Within moments after setting foot in this palatial dreamworld, Stuey was worked up into a state of high agitation. He'd been sitting on an airplane for more than five hours, an eternity for him. While Philly took care of checking them in, Stuey wandered away, saying that he wanted to take a look around and he'd meet Philly up in the room in a few minutes. As he left the front desk area and entered the low-slung casino, it was not the Roman decor that intoxicated him so much as the ringing of slot machines, the whirring rattle of the roulette wheels, and the musical chatter of chips and coins. In some respects, he was like an alcoholic stumbling into a distillery.

After a lifetime of underground poker and back-alley dice, he'd entered an alternative universe where the thing he loved the most had been transformed—something secretive and dark was here a veritable shrine, where people could openly celebrate their lust for action. As Stuey looked around him, his feet sinking into the deep plush carpet, he knew he had found his paradise on earth, the place of his true destiny.

He had brought $30,000 in cash—three bulging $10,000 packets held together by a single large rubber band. Now he removed it from the zippered pocket of his windbreaker, marched up to the nearest craps table, and dropped one of the $10,000 packets on the area of the craps layout marked "Come."

"Change only," the dealer announced, briskly counting out the hundred $100 bills with the practiced fingers of a bank teller. "Nine thousand eight hundred, nine thousand nine hundred, ten thousand . . . How would you like that, sir?"

"Two thousand in black. The rest large," Stuey answered.

The dealer counted out a stack of twenty black chips, worth $100 each, then reached into the bank of multicolored chips and counted out sixteen purple chips, each worth $500. He then slid both stacks across the felt to Stuey's waiting hands.

"Good luck, sir," the dealer said.

Stuey knew that the last thing in the world the casino wanted was for him to get lucky. He made a small bet and lost. Then he made another small bet and won. He won, then lost, then lost again. Soon, his bets increased. Instead of betting $100 black chips, he was betting purple chips on every roll. His luck grew worse. Before twenty minutes had passed, he broke the seal around the second bundle of cash and dropped another $10,000 on the table.

"Give me all purple this time," Stuey said.

The dealer complied, again wishing him good luck.

Stuey placed two purple chips on the pass line. Across the table, the shooter tossed the dice along the felt from right to left, all the players watching as the white-spotted red cubes skittered off the jagged wall at the table's far end.

"Five is the point. The point is five," the stickman chirped.

Stuey backed up the five with double odds: $2,000 behind the wager. Then he reached across the felt and bet $1,000 on "Come."

The stickman pushed the dice back to the shooter, who cupped the two red cubes in his right hand, shook his loose fist, and again flung them toward the back wall with all the action he could muster.

"Eight, no harm done," the stickman crowed.

"What's the maximum odds I can take?" Stuey asked.

"You can lay up to $2,000 to win $2,400, sir."

Stuey removed four purple chips from the wooden rail and dropped them toward the felt. The dealer lifted them just in time, the dice shooting past his arm.

"Seven out! Line away!"

In an instant, the dealer reached out and whisked the chips off the layout into a large pile against the rail near him. He placed them neatly in stacks.

Stuey retrieved his remaining chips from the cutout on top of the rail and stormed away, ignoring the dealer's hollow farewell, his salt-in-the-wound "Thanks for playing, sir."

In the space of forty minutes, the casino's ambience of luxury and excess had gone from alluring to irksome. The sparkling darkness and glittering veneer of the place seemed almost to mock Stuey. He stopped in mid-stride at a lonely blackjack table and took a seat, the chips clenched in his fist. The dealer eyed him dubiously. "Sir, this is a $100 minimum table."

Stuey smacked his chips down on the felt, five purple $500s. The dealer's eyes widened. Stuey just looked at him with contempt.

"Are you going to bet, sir?"

"Yeah, I'm going to bet. Whatta ya think I walked over here for? Give me a hand—here, here, here, here, and here!" Stuey slammed single purple chips onto each of five empty spots.

The dealer thumbed the cards out of the shoe, sliding one to each chip, and then a second. Stuey was dealt a motley collection of hands that he was mostly forced to stand on in the face of the dealer's five. The dealer turned up another five to match the one he had showing, then peeled off a king for a total of twenty. Stuey lost all five bets, his $2,500 swept away in the blink of an eye.

He careened back to the craps table for more punishment, pulling out the last packet of $10,000. It was gone in less than ten minutes.

Stuey didn't even know his room number, and he was down three big dimes. He was about to stagger away from the table when the pit boss leaned over and touched his arm. "We'll take care of your room tonight, if you'd like."

"Are you kidding me?"

"Or if there's anything else we can do for you, sir?"

"Yeah, you can get me the hell outta here."

The pit boss smiled sympathetically. There wasn't much he could say to someone who in the space of an hour had just lost what most people made in a year.

Stuey found his way back to the front desk, but Philly was long gone. "I need to know my room number," he told the clerk. "Check under Tartaglia."

Minutes later, Stuey got off the elevator on the fourth floor and found their room down a long carpeted hall. He rapped on the door. It was opened by Philly Brush, wearing boxer shorts. He'd been stretched out on the bed, watching the tube. "Where were you?" he said. "I was looking for you."

Stuey walked into the room and took a seat on the edge of the bed without answering. On the television screen, Barbara Eden materialized out of thin air, wearing a skimpy genie outfit.

"They brought up some fruit and drinks," Philly said. "Help yourself."

"I'm not hungry," Stuey said, his head drooping down toward his knees.

Philly took one look at him and realized where he'd been. "I should have known you'd go right to the tables."

"I lost," Stuey groaned.

"How much?"

"All of it."

"The whole thirty?"

"Yeah."

"Fuck."

"Yeah, fuck."

There was an awkward silence—the kind familiar to those who mix money with friendship.

"What are you going to do?"

"I don't know."

Philly shook his head, trying to figure out how best to put a good spin on a bad situation. "Look, let's try to relax tonight. We'll have dinner and see the show downstairs, then we'll figure out what to do."

Stuey kept silent. He knew that his fate—and, more important, his ability to get back into action—was in Philly's hands. The whole purpose of flying 2,500 miles to Vegas had been to fleece a few gin suckers. Stuey's loss in the pit might have been a detour, but it didn't change the goal. The reality of the situation was that Philly Brush was bankrolled to the hilt, with almost unlimited capital between cash reserves and credit lines at all the major casinos. One phone call and they were back in business.

As they rode the elevator back down to the lobby, Philly lectured Stuey about his lack of discipline. "I know you want to gamble, but you gotta use your head. We're here on business."

When the elevator door slid open, Stuey said, "What am I supposed to do? I don't even have any walking-around money now."

Philly sighed. He knew Stuey had to have at least enough cash in his pocket for food and tips. He counted out $1,000, handing the money to his young charge with an admonitory look. "Let's go pick up those tickets," he said.

"I'll meet you back here in thirty minutes," Stuey said. "I gotta find a restroom."

Thirty minutes later, having picked up tickets for Sinatra, Philly returned to the lobby near the elevator where the two had parted ways. Stuey wasn't there. Philly headed into the casino, muttering to himself.

There were big crowds around the gaming tables. It was going to be murder finding the little bastard on the casino floor on a Saturday night. Philly made the rounds, peering over people's shoulders. It was like looking for a child in the middle of a parade.

Philly noticed that one craps table had a huge crowd around it, people packed at least three deep. Shouts and hollers roared up from the center. There were men in Ban-Lon shirts, gold chains, cowboy hats, and boots; women in tight dresses, diamonds, and furs. Philly wedged himself through the outer ranks of the crowd and caught a glimpse of the craps shooter just as he was about to fling another roll. Next to the shooter, hunched over, placing bets on the table as fast he could, was little Stuey. The rail in front of him was filled with chips—not just black chips but purple chips, and lots of them.

Stuey's mood had swung 180 degrees since forty-five minutes earlier when he was slumped on the edge of the bed.

We never made it to the show. I mean, how in the fuck was I going to sit there and watch a show after going through a sixty-thousand-dollar swing, from thirty-gee loser to thirty-gee winner in an hour? Philly would have had to tie me down and put me in a straitjacket. What he did instead was to arrange a gin game for me across the street at the Dunes. There was a guy there, Johnny Hawk, who had lots of money, so we went over there, and I whipped him good.

After I whipped him, he turned to me and said, "Now, you wanna play for some real money?"

I said, "Real money?"

"Yeah, I got a friend. Likes to play real high."

So Hawk picked up the phone and dialed up this guy I never even heard of. Name was Danny Robison. Hawk warned me that Robison was supposed to be the best gin player in Las Vegas.

I said, "Tell Robison he hasn't met the best gin player yet."

Robison heard me talking that way, and he was at the Dunes within an hour.

We played late into the night and I beat him for a hundred thousand dollars. I didn't just beat him. I humiliated him.

• • •

Stuey wasn't a con man or a hustler; he was an assassin. That was just who he was, and he couldn't control it. The downside was that by annihilating Robison the way he did, instead of hustling him, the pint-size prodigy might as well have put a neon sign on his head warning others away.

On only his first day in Vegas, Stuey had played the best guy in town, maybe the best guy in the world, and handed him his lunch. During the rest of the trip, Philly managed to find a few more players in Vegas for Stuey to thrash at gin—adding perhaps another ten grand to his winnings—but word had gotten out, and it was tough to rustle up action. It would be impossible to calculate how much money Stuey lost from blowing his cover so quickly and so completely, but it's safe to say that he must have sickened Victor and Philly and his other backers in New York.

His return to the city was hardly triumphant. He had made money in Vegas, but it was unclear what his next step would be. The truth was that New York now seemed slow-paced compared with the round-the-clock high-stakes insanity of Vegas. A number of the Manhattan card clubs had been shut down, and the city itself was in a bad way, teetering on the edge of bankruptcy.

Bored and antsy, Stuey made a return trip to Vegas in a matter of weeks, a journey he would repeat with increasing regularity over the next few years. Most of the money he made in Vegas, as in New York, came from gin, but he was also getting interested in the poker games there, which had the added advantage of introducing him to potential gin opponents.

"Amarillo Slim" Preston, a lanky six-foot-four-inch hustler and country cowboy with a southern drawl, who managed to wring a lifetime of publicity (including eleven appearances on *The Tonight Show*) out of a single world championship in the World Series of Poker in 1972, remembered the first time he met Stuey. "When he first surfaced in Las Vegas, he was a little smart-ass with the best mind for a kid in his twenties I've ever seen in my life. I had a friend in Las Vegas named Stan Silverman—everybody knew him better as Jimmy Black in gambling circles—and I thought he ruled the universe when it came to gin. Well, Stuey said he could deal to Jimmy and beat him, which is a big edge to overcome. So I decided to back Jimmy in a game, and I put up $25,000 cash. I want you to know Stuey won that $25,000 before you could tuck your shirt in your britches."

After beating Jimmy Black, Stuey set up a rematch with Danny Robison. Despite the earlier humiliation, Robison was eager to get another shot at the Kid, but only if he was spotted an edge. Stuey agreed to let Robison look at the bottom of the deck to see the last card, a huge advantage for a top gin player, enabling him to adjust his strategy so as to avoid melds around a key card that would come up only at the end. The spot didn't help Robison, however. He lost another $30,000. "He [Stuey] knows something everybody else doesn't. It's like a sixth sense," Robison told a writer for *New York* magazine years later.

To continue attracting competition, Stuey's enticements became increasingly outlandish. He began to offer rebates, something unheard-of in high-stakes gin, reducing his opponents' losses by as much as a third. As an added inducement, he offered to add a third of the wager as a bonus if his opponent was able to beat him. No one is known to have ever collected.

Billy Baxter, another top gin player and all-around gambler, who would later back Stuey in poker tournaments, summed up the general sentiment: "Stuey was a great poker player later, maybe the best ever. But when it came to gin, Stuey was hands down the greatest player that's ever lived or maybe that ever will live. He's the only player I ever saw that could give a world-class player a spot and still win virtually every time he sat down."

• • •

Gin is a lot different from any other card game. It's not like poker. You can't bluff or put moves on people. Gin is a game of control. I used to break my opponents down. They'd crumble right in front of my eyes. I got a lot of satisfaction from that—seeing the smirk disappear from their faces and turn into fear. They'd come in wearing ties, with their hair neat, and after five hours with me their tie would be undone and their hair would be all over the place. They'd have this look in their eyes like they realized they couldn't win. It was fucking beautiful.

As Stuey ran through the best of the gin world and his confidence grew, his sports gambling escalated. Back in New York, after a trip to Vegas, he would unwind at the racetrack and bet thousands on sports. Unfortunately, sports and horses were losing games for him, as they were for all but a few handicappers. Before the trips to Vegas, he had bet $200 to $300 a game—"fun bets," he called them. Now, with a hefty bankroll, he could—and did—bet thousands. It wasn't difficult to find bookmakers around the city willing to take his action, especially when word circulated that the Kid had made a big score.

Theoretically, Stuey was a bookie's dream. He bet the board daily (meaning he had money riding on every single game played that day), a sucker's strategy if there ever was one. As a consequence, his gin winnings didn't last long, and before long he was racking up debts he didn't have the cash to pay. He owed one bookie $3,000 and another $6,500; and like most money-chasers, he began finding new bookies to bet with so that when he won he could pay off the bookies he already owed. The problem was that he kept losing, and it got him into serious trouble.

Victor and Philly pleaded with Stuey. But they couldn't control him. By the summer of 1977, he was $65,000 in the hole and had pissed off a bunch of people who were not people you wanted to piss off. Aware that he was in a bad spot, Stuey decided to go into hiding, staying away from the card clubs and his other usual haunts. Several of the bookies Stuey owed money to were under the control of the crime boss Funzi Tieri, one of the toughest wiseguys in the city. Tieri was known to play hardball with people who crossed him.

In a meeting with Victor Romano and Philly Brush, Tieri let them know that he understood that Stuey was broke, but he didn't appreciate being taken advantage of. Stuey's two protectors had tried in vain to find their young prodigy. They'd called Madeline, only to learn that she and Stuey were on the outs and she hadn't seen him in weeks. Now, they tried to play to Tieri's sympathies, explaining that Stuey's mother was in a nursing home and that he had lived on his own since age fourteen.

"He's not a bad kid," Victor said. "He's just a little fucked up."

"That little cocksucker's got about as much respect for money as I got for a pissant," Tieri said. But despite his anger, he recognized that he would be better served by managing and controlling Stuey than by punishing him. Strong-arm tactics would serve no purpose. As long as Stuey could be found and he, Victor, and Philly could agree to work out a way to pay the debt, all would be forgiven.

But first they had to find him.

7.

BOTH ENDS AGAINST THE MIDDLE

Stuey arrived in Southern California in July 1978, scared and broke. To this day, there remains some mystery as to how he financed his journey westward, but there's no mystery about his reasons for leaving New York. He was terrified that some physical retribution would be meted out for his failure to make good on his debts, and California was as far away from New York as he could go. There was another reason he chose Los Angeles as a place to take it on the lam: he had heard talk of big-time gin action there, at the Cavendish West Bridge Club downtown and at the Friars Club in Beverly Hills. These two private establishments attracted movie moguls and wealthy socialites who liked playing for high stakes in a relaxed clubby atmosphere.

Stuey bought a cheap used car so that he could get around, and he found a place to stay in a weekly motel across the street from the Santa Anita racetrack, in Arcadia, twenty miles east of L.A. For the next few months, he bounced back and forth between the Cavendish, the Friars, and the local racetracks in a $300 shit box with a knocking engine. Southern California's elite social clubs were an odd venue for the wired-up bookie's son from the Lower East Side—he didn't exactly fit in with his well-heeled martini-sipping hosts—but one can presume that they viewed him as a novelty. Then, too, there were rumors that Stuey was the much-ballyhooed "Kid" from the east whom they'd heard about, and the notion that there was a card savant in their midst inspired a few high rollers to test their skill against him.

How Stuey financed himself is, again, a matter of speculation. It's likely that either Romano or Philly wired him the money to play. As always, whatever he managed to win at gin then vanished through the betting windows at Santa Anita. Given Stuey's background and obvious knowledge of the way things worked in the New York underworld, it's hard to imagine how and why he thought he could escape requital for his debts. It is probable that Victor or Philly impressed this point upon him.

Eventually, what they were telling him appeared to penetrate, and Stuey was reassured that as long as he agreed to work off his debt, no revenge would be taken. Not that he had much choice. It was either play the game according to their rules or be on the lam from Tieri for the rest of his life. Sixty-five grand was too big a number to forgive or forget. An arrangement was reached whereby he'd play cards and pay out all his winnings minus a strict weekly $450 allowance.

At the Cavendish West, Stuey had been introduced to the concept of the gin tournament, and when he learned that the tournaments with the biggest prizes were held in Las Vegas, he decided, now that he could emerge from hiding, to take another trip to the bright lights of Nevada. His very first gin tournament was at the Maxim Hotel, a nondescript mid-rise (since replaced by the Westin) just east of the Strip on Flamingo Boulevard. The entry fee was $1,500. First prize was $50,000. The tournament began with more than one hundred top gin players from all over the world. Three days later, Stuey was the champion.

He'd found the perfect setup, the one venue where he could compete in a game he ruled without giving away spots or handicaps. On a level playing field, Stuey was a man among boys. The problem was that he was reluctant to use his windfall to pay back his debt, which even the $50,000 first prize wouldn't completely cover.

Word of his victory got back to his chit holder, Tieri, who immediately dispatched one of his associates in Vegas to have a talk with the boy genius. Before Tieri's goon could catch up to him, however, Stuey had returned to Los Angeles and dropped out of sight again. Needless to say, such antics did not amuse the mobster.

Stuey next surfaced three months later, at another gin tournament in Las Vegas (this time at the Riviera Casino), and this time Tieri had his ear to the ground a bit sooner. After Stuey blitzed through the field and made it to the finals, he and his remaining adversary stopped for a dinner break. As Stuey made his way into the nearest restroom, two men followed him.*

One of the two men was Tony "the Ant" Spilotro, Las Vegas's most notorious mob killer, who had once placed a man's head in a vise and tightened it until the victim's eyeballs popped out of their sockets (a scene Martin Scorsese immortalized in the movie *Casino*). Though Spilotro would get his just deserts in the end (he was bludgeoned to death with baseball bats in an Iowa cornfield), it's safe to say that while he was alive, Spilotro was not someone you wanted to meet in a bathroom alone.

Spilotro demanded that Stuey pay the money he owed Tiero, and was not happy when Stuey explained that he didn't have any money left, that he had borrowed money to enter the tournament.

"How much is first prize?"

---

* This conversation was overheard by Glenn Abney, better known in card circles as "Mr. Gin," who happened to be in one of the restroom stalls during the encounter.

"Fifty thousand."

Spilotro's associate grabbed Stuey by the collar and shoved him up against the paper towel dispenser.

"Then you better fucking win."

The two men exited the restroom, leaving behind a very rattled Stuey staring at his ghost-white face in the mirror over the row of sinks.*

Stuey's opponent knew nothing of what had taken place in the men's room during the break. With Spilotro and his goon looking on, the final game of the tournament was played. It was a tense, unpleasant experience for Stuey, but somehow he managed to win.

Afterward, while he was shaking hands and getting his picture taken by photographers from the local papers, the two hoods stood off to the side, waiting with their arms folded.

Never one to accept a cashier's check or a bank draft, Stuey went to the cage to collect his winnings in cash. Spilotro and his sidekick stood right beside him as the cashier counted out the money.

"Aren't you going to let me have anything?" Stuey pleaded.

"This doesn't even cover the sixty-five you owe. You're lucky to be breathing." And with that, the two men pocketed the cash and left.

Despite this setback, Stuey's successive wins at the Maxim and the Riviera convinced him that he had a permanent home in Las Vegas. New York and Los Angeles simply couldn't compete in terms of gambling opportunities. For the next several months, he took up residence in different hotel rooms, a short elevator ride away from the action.

Philly flew out for a visit, determined to persuade Stuey to approach gin as a business. "If you take this seriously," he said, "you will be a millionaire."

A month later, Stuey entered another gin tournament, this time at

* When Glenn Abney left the restroom stall, he exchanged a knowing look with Stuey but said nothing.

the Aladdin. He made it down to the final two players, a point at which it was not uncommon for players to make a deal to hedge the difference between first- and second-place prize money—in this case $50,000 and $25,000. Stuey, however, was not interested in hedging. He wanted to win outright and take down the money.

There was this guy. His name was Gus. They said he had won six major gin tournaments. He leaned over and looked at me straight and said, "What kind of deal do you want to make?"

"What do I want to do?"

"Yeah. What do you want to do?"

"How's this: let's play the match winner take all. Let's put both first- and second-place money into the pot and let's play for the whole fucking thing!"

When I said that, it completely shattered him.

They would announce the scores—"Stu Ungar 112–0, Stu Ungar 114–37, Stu Ungar 105–81." Yeah, sure, right. I'm going to chop the prize money with a guy who ain't got a chance in hell of beating me. It was like a joke to me.

From early 1978 through the end of 1979, Stuey entered five gin tournaments and won three of them. At the two events he didn't win, he placed in the top four, and in one of those two, at the Union Plaza, his defeat did not come at the hands of another player; he simply failed to show up for the second day of the tournament. "I guess something better came along," Glenn Abney remarked.

When Stuey did show up at the Riviera to defend his title in the fall of 1979, as he was standing at the registration desk, waiting to pay his $1,500 entry fee, tournament officials pulled him aside.

. . .

They told me that they didn't want me to play. The excuse they used was that people were not entering the tournament because when I played they didn't have a chance. I could see that the other players didn't like having me there.

It certainly didn't help Stuey's cause that he was an obnoxious winner and a poor sport. He had proved to be too good and too irksome for the rest of the field to handle, so they took their ball and went home. The ban would be the last card off the deck in Stuey's career at gin. It was clear that if he planned on making a living as a professional gambler, he was going to have to find a new game. Poker seemed the most obvious choice.

In those days the poker rooms of Las Vegas were snake pits of hustlers and cheats. Players colluded, shot angles, kited chips from the pot, held out cards, and were constantly on the lookout for a mark.

The biggest games were played at the Silverbird, the Dunes, and the Golden Nugget—all of them hotbeds of cheating, among both the players and the management. By far the most corrupt room, however, was the Stardust. One newly hired dealer there noticed that the backs of some of the cards he was dealing were marked. Mindful not to upset the game on his very first day on the job, he approached a floor supervisor during a break.

"You're not going to believe this, but the deck on table four is shaded."

Without skipping a beat, the floor man shot back, "Don't worry about it. Just keep dealing. You'll get your share."

At poker tables nowadays, there is a clearly visible money-slot in the table so that the players can watch the dealer as he drops the rake (the standard house take is a maximum of 10 percent of each pot up to $5). But in the early days in Vegas, dealers pretty much took whatever they wanted, and any player who complained was instructed to read a small sign posted in every card room alerting players that the house could take up to 50 percent of each pot. Although few dealers actually took the 50 percent, some of them probably came close. As a result, the smaller games, in particular, were practically unbeatable. One dealer at the Stardust allegedly set the record for "snatching," as the practice was called. He snatched $800 in a single hour at a $3–$6 game—the equivalent of taking just about every chip off the table, based on the players' average buy-in.

High-limit players were exempt from these kinds of house shenanigans. Card room managers were well aware that pros wouldn't tolerate snatching. There was enough shady activity among the players without an additional cut for the house (beyond what it already got for looking the other way).

News that cheating was tolerated, if not tacitly encouraged, by the casino would have been devastating if the public knew the truth. The Nevada Gaming Board (NGB), which oversees all casino gambling in the state of Nevada, would have been none too pleased, either, if it had found out—although there have been suggestions that the NGB in its early days was nothing but a rubber stamp, approving whatever the casinos wanted.

Many poker pros figured that if a sucker got hustled, it was simply part of the edge he was giving away by sitting down with them. Some people were just too dense to see that they were being duped. The Las Vegas poker scene in the 1970s was an embodiment of Darwinism dressed in the silk shirts and gold chains of the disco age. The most successful pros in the biggest games lived off the Hollywood people, drug dealers, and criminals who wandered into the room from elsewhere in the casino looking for a little extra-special thrill.

One of the most notorious high-limit poker players of that era was the cocaine kingpin Jamiel "Jimmy" Chagra of Texas, who went through millions of dollars of illegal drug money at the tables. While awaiting trial for murder in Texas, Chagra came to Las Vegas for one last hurrah. On the trip, Chagra is reported to have played golf for half a million dollars a round. He once tipped a cocktail waitress $10,000 for bringing him a bottle of water. Although he beat the murder rap, he was still sentenced to thirty years at Leavenworth on related charges.

Other high rollers included Larry Flynt, founder and publisher of *Hustler* magazine, who had enough money to play in any poker game, no matter how high the stakes, and favored seven-card stud, a game at which he has since become formidable; Gabe Kaplan, star of what was then the hottest show on television, *Welcome Back, Kotter;* Ron Stanley, one of the stars of the hit movie *Deliverance* (1972); the Academy Award winner Richard Dreyfuss; and Telly Savalas of *Kojak.* It's safe to say that what attracted men like this to poker was partly its democratic nature, the fact that they were not afforded special privileges or rules—they were treated just like everyone else. What could get their competitive juices going more than having their celebrity status rendered superfluous?

There were high-stakes games at several casinos in Las Vegas, but no room had higher action than the Dunes, a mob-run casino at the corner of Flamingo and Las Vegas Boulevard, where the Bellagio now stands. The poker room at the Dunes was owned by Syd Wyman and run by the poker legend Johnny Moss, a three-time champion at the World Series of Poker, who was known as the "grand old man of poker." Casinos normally contracted out their poker room operation, which was primarily a loss leader—its profitability came from bringing high rollers into the casino, in the hope that they'd dump their poker winnings in the pits later on. The Dunes spread $300 to $600 or $400 to $800 almost every night, limits at which a single hand of stud could cost a player $3,000 to $5,000.

The regulars in these games, who waited patiently for the fish to come feed them, were men such as Sarge Ferris, Puggy Pearson, Bryan "Sailor" Roberts, Doyle Brunson, Amarillo Slim Preston, and Bobby Hoff. Most of them had been playing their entire lives and were then in their forties or fifties. Some were in their sixties and seventies. They viewed anyone under the age of forty as fresh meat. Beyond the generation gap, there was also a geographical gap. The old guard was made up mostly of southerners and Texans, who had transplanted themselves in Vegas because the games were better—and legal to boot. These old Texans played in the biggest games and always got all the money. In fact, during the first eight years of the World Series of Poker, from 1970 to 1977, a native Texan won the main event six times. The two exceptions were 1972, when it was won by Amarillo Slim, who had been born in Arkansas; and 1973, when Puggy Pearson, who was born in Kentucky, outlasted the Texans Johnny Moss and Jack "Treetop" Straus. It was a tightly knit circle that didn't embrace strangers warmly.

Danny Robison and Chip Reese were the first players to challenge the old guard. Natives of Dayton, Ohio, they stopped off in Vegas in 1974 for a weekend while on their way to California. Reese, a graduate of Dartmouth, was on his way to Stanford Law School. The first night, he turned the $200 in his pocket into $800, playing $10–$20 seven-card stud. By the end of the weekend he was up a couple of thousand and law school was on hold. Now, just a few years later, he was a millionaire, bumping heads with the best players in the world. Of course, most of those who were brave enough or dumb enough to try to beat the poker icons were fleeced and left busted—and there was always an empty chair in the big game waiting for the next guy who wanted to try his luck.

Reese and Robison had spent thousands of hours playing at the lower limits, honing their skills, before they stepped up to the big time, and it took many tough wins against the old guard before they were able to earn respect.

"At first we treated them like stepchildren," Amarillo Slim recalled. "I remember Doyle Brunson one night at the Horseshoe. He had Danny Robison on one table and would spin around in his chair and play Chip Reese on the other. He was playin' both of 'em heads-up at the same time! When I first saw them boys I thought they was soft as butter, but I come to find out they weren't. No, sir!"

While Robison and Reese were making names for themselves in poker, Stuey was finding it harder and harder to rustle up a gin game. His finances, however, took a dramatic turn for the better, as he went on a monster roll betting on sports in the latter half of 1979 that not only allowed him to pay off his debt to Tieri, but also swelled his bankroll to over $1 million. In his own classic fashion, he kept the money all in cash, in a safe-deposit box at the Dunes.

The fact was that Stuey didn't even know how a real bank worked. When a friend told him about interest-bearing accounts and banking hours (this was before the advent of ATMs), he remarked, "You've got to be kidding! What if I need fifty grand at midnight? What—I have to wait till they open up the next morning? What kind of person would put up with that, where they can't get their money when they need it?"

The money from betting on sports gave Stuey the kind of bankroll he needed to play in high-limit poker games. At the same time, he found a mentor: Chip Reese agreed to teach Stuey what he knew about seven-card stud if Stuey would teach him the finer points of gin. Reese had been intrigued by Stuey ever since Stuey had crushed Reese's pal Danny Robison for $100,000 playing gin during his first trip to Vegas five years earlier. Reese and Stuey, who were roughly the same age, developed an alliance and a friendship built on mutual respect. Stuey had played seven-card stud, of course—just as Reese had played gin—but each of them was eager to add to his knowledge, and who better to learn from than a master of the game?

In the beginning, Reese wanted Stuey to go to the Sahara and play $30–$60 stud to gain some experience. But Stuey wasn't interested in honing his skills at the lower limits. Grinding out $50 an hour seemed to him too much like work. Instead, he immediately sat down in the toughest $300–$600 stud games he could find, an approach that for even the most skilled gambler would usually mean financial suicide.

Under Reese's tutelage, Stuey picked up nuances of the game at lightning speed. He also learned from watching other players. Danny Robison, who reportedly won more money playing seven-card stud than any other player alive, had a deep impact on Stuey. Robison was always the biggest talker in the game. While other players were quietly contemplating big-money decisions, Robison would gab away nonstop, acting for all the world as if he were in a penny-ante coffee-klatch game. His ceaseless chatter unnerved many opponents and sometimes got them to call an extra bet or two in the vain hope that if they managed to put a bad beat on him he would shut up. This rarely worked.

One player recalled Robison playing a hand of stud while he was telling a joke. As Robison built up to the punch line, his opponent caught a miracle card at the end that resulted in a loss of several thousand dollars for Robison. Without flinching, Robison delivered the joke's payoff. And as the huge pot was pushed in the direction of his opponent, he smiled to acknowledge the laughter and guffaws.

Stuey was so impressed that he tried to model himself after Robison. Of course, Stuey himself had always been a talker at the table, but his style was much less ingratiating. He was a taunter and a braggart—a needler. That may have been an effective way of getting under people's skin, but more than anything else, it helped him to cope with one of his biggest problems at the poker table—boredom.

As Billy Baxter, one of Las Vegas's savviest gamblers, once said,

"Poker is a waiting game." Baxter, who wound up backing Stuey in many tournaments but whose biggest contribution to gambling was undoubtedly the landmark legal case he won against the Internal Revenue Service in 1985 that established gambling as a legitimate profession subject to the same tax statutes as other professions,* was so patient in his approach to the game that he'd "sometimes wait fifteen hours for the right moment to come up."

Stuey might have been able to control his impatience at the table, but his burning need to be at the heart of the action made it inevitable that he would ultimately find his way to the biggest game in town—the no-limit Texas Hold'em game at the Dunes. He had done well in the high-limit seven-card stud games, so it was really only a matter of time. But on the surface, at least, this jump—for a player of his inexperience—appeared to be suicidal. Any newcomer who took a seat in the no-limit game at the Dunes was basically asking for a severe beating.

"People showed up trying to play me in a game I had played all my life—no-limit hold'em!" said Amarillo Slim. "They were accustomed to playing limit poker and games like stud where you can bet a guy three

---

* The key argument in Baxter's suit against the U.S. government for the return of $180,000 that had been withheld from his tournament winnings was that poker should be considered a game of skill. As such, poker winnings should be regarded as earned income, subject to the same deductions as other earned income.

The U.S. government maintained that poker was a game of luck, in the same category as lotteries and sweepstakes, and therefore subject to the same tax requirements.

In the first filing in federal court in Reno, Nevada, the judge ruled in Baxter's favor, telling government lawyers that "if you think poker is luck, I invite your side to play Mr. Baxter in a poker game."

The U.S. government appealed the decision, and the case was retried in the Eighth Circuit Court of Appeals in Los Angeles. The judge there also ruled in Baxter's favor. Eventually, the case went all the way to the U.S. Supreme Court, but the U.S. government dropped the appeal before arguing in front of the highest court.

The $180,000 that the IRS had to return to Baxter in 1985 barely covered his legal fees. "But of course that was never the point," Baxter said. "It was a matter of principle."

hundred and he can call you, and then you get to the river and you can bet six hundred and he can call the six. Nobody's goin' to get whupped too bad. But with no-limit, they'd bet that same six hundred, then I'd raise 'em back ten thousand—and now you'd see 'em polish the seat of their britches. They'd get to wigglin' and squirmin' like jitterbugs. That's the difference between limit and no-limit."

Most of the gang at the Dunes knew Stuey Ungar or knew about him. They had figured the day would come when he would show up, and they were right. On a hot spring day in 1978, Stuey traipsed into the deep-freeze of the Dunes and was promptly carded by the security officer standing guard outside the poker room. Only after being waved in by Johnny Moss was Stuey allowed to enter.

As he approached the no-limit table, the players pretended not to notice him. They didn't want to scare him away by licking their chops.

"Wh-wh-what are you playing?" Stuey asked, stuttering slightly in his excitement.

"No-limit hold'em," answered a big fellow in western clothes, tipping back his hat to examine his cards more closely.

"Siddown, we have a seat for ya," said another.

"I never played no-limit before," Stuey replied honestly, aware that he was being coaxed into the game and that a remark like this would start a feeding frenzy.

He pulled $20,000 wrapped in a rubber band out of his pocket and plopped down in the empty seat.

Less than fifteen minutes later, he had to go to his cashbox to get more money. He'd lost the entire twenty grand. When he returned, he played more cautiously, though not timidly. The game went on through the night, into the next day, and then into the next night. Thirty-six hours after he sat down, Stuey took a break to get some sleep. He had won back the original $20,000 plus another $27,000.

"He had such a great mind," Amarillo Slim said. "I would be doing things that he would pick up on immediately. I mean, I'd have to explain my moves to most people, but little Stu intuitively knew why I did what I did. I've never seen anyone pick up on it so fast."

One thing that immediately struck all the legendary no-limit players in that game was how aggressively Stuey played. "To Stu," Slim said, "money wasn't worth the paper it was printed on. It was like water. It meant nothin' to that kid. Of course, that's what eventually made him a great player. He wasn't afraid to shove those chips into the pot. He could bet it all whether he had a hand or not."

Playing poker regularly with Billy Baxter, Slim, Treetop Straus, Chip Reese, and Johnny Moss was a tough way to break into the fast lane of no-limit hold'em. In that murderers' row of poker, perhaps no one was more formidable than Doyle "Texas Dolly" Brunson, who was the Babe Ruth of that lineup, both in the size of his accomplishments—he had won the final event at the World Series in both 1976 and 1977—and in his physical girth.

Whenever the big game was going at the Dunes, Brunson would travel from his ranch in West Texas to play in it. Though he preferred the slow pace of life away from the bright lights and neon of Vegas, a gambling man goes where the action is. Like a lot of the top poker pros, Brunson had been an athlete when he was younger, having earned a full basketball scholarship to Hardin-Simmons University in Abilene. He was scouted by what was then the Minneapolis Lakers, but just before the NBA draft, while working at a summer job, he shattered his knee as he unloaded a pile of Sheetrock. Pro basketball's loss was the poker world's gain.

Brunson went on to earn a master's degree in education, and he worked briefly as a salesman for business machines. At one of the first offices he called on, he got involved in a backroom poker game and won a month's salary in a single afternoon, at which point he reassessed his career path. Like many of his contemporaries, Brunson honed his poker game as a road gambler on the underground circuit in the South, winning hundreds of thousands of dollars while dodging the law and getting robbed at least a dozen times.

Beyond his accomplishments as a player, Brunson made perhaps his biggest contribution to poker with his book on poker theory and strategy, *Super/System,* first published in 1978 and originally titled *How I Won a Million Dollars Playing Poker.* This book was instrumental in educating a generation of no-limit players, and it prompted Brunson the player to wish that Brunson the author had kept some of his secrets to himself. "If I had to do it over again," he once said, "I wouldn't write that damn book."*

The first time Stuey encountered Brunson was at the Dunes. Stuey certainly knew who Brunson was—Brunson had won back-to-back world championships and was nearly legendary in the poker world—and perhaps the sense of familiarity that celebrity confers emboldened Stuey to approach him in the way he did. Brunson was an imposing figure in his large white Stetson hat and black horn-rims with custom-made tinted lenses designed just for poker. But that didn't stop Stuey from asking the big man straight out if Brunson might be able to get him tickets to that night's UNLV basketball game.

"Doyle looked at me like I was crazy," Stuey said. "The thing was, I had ten grand bet on the game, and I just wanted to be able to watch it. I'd heard Doyle had access to good seats."

When the awkwardness of the moment passed—a complete stranger had just asked him for the best seats to a sold-out game—Doyle was finally told that this was the Stuey everyone was talking about. That

---

* In fact, he has done it over again. *Super/System II,* a revamped and updated version of the original, was released in February 2004.

night, Stuey sat at courtside with Doyle and watched the Runnin' Rebels win, covering the point spread and earning Stuey a quick and easy ten grand. It was the beginning of a long friendship between the two men.

In only a year's time, Stuey had gone from being broke to living large as a professional gambler. The next thing to do was to get his personal life straightened out.

8.

The Second Time Around

"It takes a special kind of woman to be married to a gambler."
—Bobby Baldwin, winner of the World Series of Poker in 1978

While Stuey was still living in New York, he and Madeline fought and made up so often that it was hard for people who knew them to keep track.

"I was his first girlfriend," Madeline recalls, "and in the beginning he was more mesmerized by me than I was by him. I liked him, I cared about him plenty, but during that period he cared more about me. I had just left a man I was married to and had a child. I didn't want to be tied down again right away—not to Stuey or anybody. I had a lot of things to get out of my system. I left Stuey a lot while I was dating him."

During the breakups, especially when he was out of town, they'd start to miss each other. Then Stuey would start calling her, and things would heat up again. He'd fly back to New York, armed with gifts. It was the same way that Ido Ungar had wooed Fay. "He would always bring me jewelry," Madeline says. "Bracelets, rings, necklaces. Every time he came back he brought me a gift."

During the time Stuey was on the lam, hiding from the New York bookies, he stayed in touch with Madeline. Although he rarely spoke to her about his troubles, Madeline knew the reason for his abrupt departure. She realized, from the start, that life with Stuey would not be normal, and that it would require great patience and forbearance on her part to abide his eccentric lifestyle. As she put it, "I never knew if we were going to have turkey on Thanksgiving—or soup."

Stuey was fun to be with in short spurts, especially when he was winning, but the severe swings—both financial and emotional— required saintly tolerance. Madeline wasn't at all sure she wanted to sign on for the long haul; she had enough ambivalence about being in any relationship. So they were on and they were off, and during one of the off periods, while Stuey was away in Vegas, Madeline met someone else.

"He was an attorney," she says. "I thought he and I were going to make something good of it."

He was stable, kind, and considerate, and it must have seemed to Madeline, as a single mother, that for once she was making a sensible choice. When he asked her to marry him, she said yes. "I would have had a house," Madeline says. "I would have had a co-op in New York and a winter home in Florida."

As the wedding plans progressed, however, Madeline began to realize that she was not really in love with this sweet, decent man, no matter how much she might have wanted to be. It was always in the back of her mind, "Am I happy? Am I happy?" There was another thing, too— Richie. Despite the fact that the lawyer was never anything but nice to

Richie, the boy just didn't like him, not the way he liked Stuey. There was a special link between Stuey and Richie.

In 1978, right around the time Stuey was starting to play in the big no-limit game at the Dunes, Madeline's boss at the travel agency where she now worked told her that he needed her to bring a junket group to the Aladdin Hotel.

"What do I have to do?" she asked, already thinking: *Vegas. Stuey.*

"Just get them all settled into the hotel and get them tickets to a show and make sure they're all happy."

"All right."

So she flew out to Vegas. At the Aladdin, she ran into a mutual friend of her and Stuey's named Jerry Kurtz. She asked him not to tell Stuey she was in town. So what did he do? He told Stuey she was in town.

The Aladdin was across the street from the Dunes. As soon as Stuey heard that Madeline was there, he went running across the street to see her. "I had no clue what I was going to feel like," Madeline says. "I was thinking, 'I don't want to see him, I don't want to see him.' But as soon as I looked at him, I melted. And in that moment I made my decision. I went back to the Dunes with him. That trip changed my whole life."

Stuey asked Madeline to move to Vegas. When she went back to New York and told her fiancé, he was devastated. "It was awful," Madeline says. "I think he always knew in the back of his mind that he was competing with Stuey. But I'll never forget that day. He just looked like a ghost."

Madeline's boss also looked at her as if she were nuts when she told him she was quitting and moving to Vegas to be with Stuey.

"But you didn't want to be with him," he said.

"I am making a decision," Madeline said.

She packed up everything she could take, left what she couldn't take, and moved to Vegas with little Richie. Stuey was then living at the Jockey

Club, an eleven-story luxury apartment house right next to the Dunes, but he gave Madeline money to buy a condo—"I think it was about $32,000," she said—and she purchased a little place on Paradise off Harmon.

"We just—I don't know, that was how we did it; he was going to have his privacy, and we were just going to see how it was going to be," she said. "But once he saw where I was living, he didn't like it. He said, 'No, you aren't going to live here.' It was small and he didn't like it, and he said, 'You and Richie are not going to live here.'"

So mother and son moved into the Jockey Club with Stuey, into a 900-square-foot fully furnished unit overlooking the golf course at the back of the Dunes. Stuey told Madeline to buy a car for them. She went to the Fletcher Jones dealership and bought him a ten-year-old Mercedes, paying for it in cash he had given her. But when she drove it home, he took one look at it and said, "I'm not driving that." He wanted something newer and flashier. So she went back and exchanged it for a new Cadillac Biarritz. Meanwhile, after enrolling Richie in school, Madeline hired a taxi to take him there each day—just as Fay had done for Stuey and Judy.

With his girlfriend and her child living with him, Stuey no longer spent his entire day and night across the street at the casino. Now, he stayed home more often, hanging out with the two of them, watching sports and movies on television. One afternoon, in July 1979, he was at home watching a baseball game he had bet on. It had been a miserable day of betting—zero for six, one of his worst days since moving to Vegas. But the worst news of the day was yet to come.

Just after his sixth and final loss of the day, as he was cursing his bad luck, the phone rang. It was someone from the nursing home in New York. His mother had died. Stuey stood there without moving, holding the phone. Madeline came up behind him, and he turned. "My mother's gone," he said.

"He never really talked about it with me. It was just too hard for him," Madeline says. "We had told her that when we bought a house it would be a one-story house, wheelchair-accessible, so she could come out. That's what we were planning to do."

Stuey absolutely refused to go to New York, but he couldn't cope with making the funeral arrangements, so Madeline took care of everything. She called the nursing home and arranged to have the body transported to Las Vegas. She found a Jewish cemetery and a rabbi. Stuey wasn't observant, but he believed in God, and it was important to him to follow Jewish custom.

Madeline also made the other necessary phone calls, which included attempts to track down Stuey's sister, Judy, who was living in Puerto Rico with her husband. Stuey himself had no idea how to contact his sister. They had fallen out of touch. She was doing drugs and was married to a Puerto Rican, and Stuey disapproved. Madeline tried valiantly to reach Judy in time, but in the end, the funeral went ahead without her.

It was a modest affair. Aside from Stuey, Madeline, and Richie, there was only the rabbi in attendance. Fay was buried in a plain pine box, in accordance with Orthodox tradition, and all present threw a shovelful of earth onto the coffin.

"Stuey didn't show a lot," Madeline remembers. "That was just the way he was. He never showed a lot of emotion, except with children—with Richie, and then later with our daughter, Stefanie. But with his mother, even though he didn't talk to anybody about it, I could tell it was hard on him. There were things he missed. We used to call her up—she loved old movies—and we'd call her up in the nursing home and ask her the name of some movie, and she would tell him the name. They'd recite dialogue from it. There were movies where he knew every line. So they shared that. And, of course, she was the one who taught him to play cards."

Like a lot of young men who lose a parent—particularly a mother—Stuey now had a deeper need for someone important in his life. Madeline herself was now more eager than she had been for a more substantial relationship; she had decided that she wanted to get married and have another child. But Stuey wasn't interested in committing himself that deeply—at least not yet.

Nevertheless, within a year of arriving in Las Vegas, Madeline had persuaded Stuey to move out of the Jockey Club and buy a house. As with the Cadillac, he supplied the money for the house and she did the shopping. She found a two-story Tudor-style house on Coventry Lane in East Las Vegas that cost $175,000. Stuey put down $50,000 in cash and financed the rest under a no-qualifying loan. Getting the paperwork approved wasn't easy. Most gamblers don't qualify for a conventional loan. Even in a city full of gamblers, banks wanted collateral or the assurance of a steady income. But in the end, Stuey's willingness to pay nearly a third of the purchase price up front swayed the bank. Beyond the money, Stuey showed no interest in the details of the purchase, and in fact didn't even want to see the house until Madeline had decorated it. When the final papers were ready, the signing took place not at the title office but at the Dunes poker room while Stuey played in a $200–$400 game.

I had it pretty good with Madeline when we started out here. I could do whatever I wanted. We had money. We did things together. I guess, looking back on it, that was probably the best time of my life.

Madeline was really smart about how to control the money. She took care of all the bills and everything. I just asked her how much she needed and gave it to her. I knew that buying the house would make her happy. I know I was happy back then, and I think she was, too.

• • •

Stuey may have sincerely intended to be the man of Madeline's dreams, but he could never change who he was. He was a gambler. Sure, he'd take her out to dinner or out to the movies.

Unless there was a poker game going.

Or a sporting event that he had a bet on.

The call of the action would always pull him away.

In February 1979 Stuey learned that all the Vegas regulars were heading over to the Las Vegas Hilton to play in the inaugural Super Bowl of Poker. Hosted by Amarillo Slim (who was paid a handsome fee for lending his name), the Super Bowl of Poker—so named because it came at the end of January, right after the NFL's championship game—was positioned to compete with the World Series of Poker. For Stuey, it would be his first poker tournament.

Big events like the Super Bowl of Poker attracted two kinds of players: live-game players and tournament players. Live games and tournaments involved different skills, and rare was the player who was adept at both. Tournaments offered prestige and attention, but the biggest money was often to be found in the side games. For many of the high-limit players, the tournament was just an excuse to get together and play big, with the added enticement that there might be some rich amateurs around who'd been drawn by the tournament.

While at the Hilton, Stuey renewed an acquaintance with Mike Sexton, a fellow poker player who would eventually become his lifelong friend and, much later, a celebrity on television, as host of the World Poker Tour. Sexton, like Chip Reese, was originally from Dayton, Ohio. He had attended Ohio State University on a full athletic scholarship and excelled in gymnastics. Later, he joined the army and was assigned to the Eighty-second Airborne Division at Fort Bragg, North Carolina.

Like Doyle Brunson, Sexton began taking poker seriously when he could no longer take part in athletic competition—in Sexton's case, owing to his age. He began playing private games and soon discovered that he could make more money from poker than from his regular job coaching baseball. So he quit that job and started playing full-time. "I figured I had nothing to lose. If I went broke, I could always go back to work," he said.

Sexton went to the Hilton for Slim's tournament at a time when he was running bad and was nearly broke. In fact, he went completely broke while he was there and couldn't even get into the action. At that point, he found himself standing on the rail with a group of other people, watching Stuey, whom he'd first met a couple of years earlier at the Dunes.

Stuey was playing in a $100–$200 seven-card-stud game, talking a mile a minute and winning just about every pot. All of a sudden, he got up and said, "I need to take a piss."

He turned around and saw Sexton on the rail. "Sexton," he said, "get in here and pick up a hand for me."

Sexton was dumbfounded. "You want me to play for you?"

"Yeah, I'll be back in a few minutes."

Sexton stepped around the rail.

He sat down in Stuey's seat a bit sheepishly as the Kid rushed away. He felt seven pairs of eyes staring at him over Stuey's pyramid of black and green chips.

The very first hand, Sexton looked down at his two hole cards—the nine and ten of diamonds—that, together with his up card, the jack of diamonds, formed a three-card straight-flush draw. A powerful starting hand, but one that could be expensive, especially in a $100–$200 game, where playing a hand to conclusion could cost a couple of thousand dollars.

Playing with another man's money, Sexton found himself at an impasse. He and Stuey barely knew each other. Did he want to risk playing what could be a very costly hand? He decided to call the initial bet and see what happened. Four other players also called.

The fourth card brought Sexton the eight of clubs. Now he had an open-ended straight draw, meaning that he could make a straight if he drew a seven or a queen. He also still had three diamonds with three cards left to make his flush. Best of all, Sexton's cards were "live," meaning that none of the cards needed to complete his hand had been dealt. He was in a good spot.

The high card bet. The bet was raised, then raised again. By the time it got to Sexton, it was $300 to call. He craned his head around looking for Stuey.

The Kid was nowhere to be found. Starting to get nervous, Sexton stalled for time. With the other players growing impatient, he finally called.

On fifth street, Sexton caught a beautiful card—the queen of spades—giving him a straight to the queen. It was the perfect catch. "Nobody else had a pair on board, or a three-card flush, so I knew I had the best hand," Sexton said. That didn't stop the other players from jamming chips into the pot. The initial bettor bet again. He was raised and reraised before it got to Sexton, who made it four bets, cutting off $800 in black chips from Stuey's stack. As the dealer gathered in the chips, Stuey ran up to the table and became ecstatic at the sight of the huge pot. "All right!" he yelled, thrilled that Sexton was involved in a monster pot. "Whatta we got? Whatta we got?" He moved in behind Sexton, who obligingly peeled back the tips of his down cards, revealing the straight.

Stuey managed to keep a poker face as the sixth card and then the seventh and final card were dealt, with more chips going into the pot each round. There was now a mammoth pile of black tiger-striped chips in the center of the table. Two players had started out with three of a kind and never improved. Sexton's straight held up. It took the dealer three hearty shoves to get all the chips over to Sexton's corner of the table.

Standing behind Sexton like a proud father, Stuey was only too happy to salt the wounds of his pissed-off adversaries.

"You guys are so bad I can beat you while I'm in the shit house," he cackled.

No one else at the table smiled.

As Sexton got up to give him back his seat, Stuey glanced over at the neighboring table. "Hey, what are they playing over there?"

"It's $50–$100 eight-or-better stud," Sexton replied.

"How much do you need to get into that game?"

"I don't know. A thousand or two."

Stuey handed Sexton $1,500 in chips. "Go over there and play for us."

Sexton did as he was told and won another $4,000. He gave Stuey half.

"Because I picked up that one hand," he said, "I went from being broke to having a couple of thousand in my pocket. But more important, a friendship grew out of it."

It's been widely reported that the first no-limit Texas Hold'em tournament Stuey played in was the World Series of Poker of 1980. In actuality, his first tournament was at Slim's Super Bowl, where he finished thirty-fourth in a field of forty players. The World Series didn't come until two months later, in May, but it boasted a considerably bigger field of players, who came from all over the world, all vying for a little piece of immortality.

Binion's Horseshoe, the original home of the World Series, was, in 1980, before it bought the neighboring Mint Hotel, half the size it is today. Located on Fremont Street in downtown Las Vegas, in the area known as Glitter Gulch, the old Binion's was a throwback to the days when gangsters and gamblers ruled the town. It was dark, red-lit with stale red carpets and wood paneling, and with the feel of a whorehouse in New Orleans. While the tourists went to the Strip to watch circus acts and big-name lounge singers, the real gamblers went to the Horseshoe for the action.

Benny Binion, who bought the place in 1949, when it was called the Eldorado Club, knew what gamblers wanted. They didn't care for show-girls or fancy rooms or magic acts. They wanted a fair shake for their gambling dollar, and Benny gave it to them. He was an uneducated bootlegger and numbers racket man who had moved his family to Vegas from Dallas in the 1940s to get into the casino business. Benny's reputation as a cold-blooded killer back in Dallas followed him to the grave, but age and great wealth have a way of turning a tough character into a lovable one, and Benny—with his trademark white Stetson and gold-buttoned cowboy shirts—was regarded with enormous affection by his adopted city. In the 1970s, because of his own problems with the law, Benny placed his two sons, Jack and Ted, in charge of the casino's operations, but not before he had dreamed up the World Series of Poker, a brainstorm that would put Binion's on the map and change the course of poker forever.

The World Series of Poker, or WSOP, has evolved over the years. Since May 1970, when there were nine players and Johnny Moss was elected champion and awarded $30,000, the rules have changed and the number of contestants has increased. By 1980, there were twelve sepa-rate competitions beginning in April and stretching into the middle of May, a mix of different poker games that included seven-card stud, Texas Hold'em, Omaha high-low, razz, draw, and others, each winner earning a gold bracelet from Nieman-Marcus in addition to first-place prize money.

The crowning event of the WSOP has always been the $10,000 buy-in world championship, and the game played, except for that first year, has always been no-limit Texas Hold'em. Doyle Brunson has called no-limit Texas Hold'em the "Cadillac of poker games," and he devoted the bulk of *Super/System,* his treatise on advanced poker, to a discussion of this game.

Texas Hold'em is a variation of seven-card stud in which each player is dealt two concealed pocket cards. After the deal, there is round of betting. Next, the first three of an eventual five community cards are dealt faceup (the "flop"), and there is another round of betting. Then a fourth communal card (the "turn") is dealt, followed by another round of betting. Finally a fifth communal card (the "river") is dealt, followed by a last round of betting. Then, if there is still more than one player remaining, the hole cards are shown, and the player with the best five-card hand made up of any combination of his two cards and the five communal cards wins the hand.

Texas Hold'em originated more than a hundred years ago, but until the 1960s most poker players outside the South had never heard of it. According to legend, hold'em was first played on the open prairie by wranglers who needed a game that could accommodate as many players as possible. Even today, the game can be played with as many as twenty-three competitors, although most games limit a table to ten.

Texas Hold'em is a game of infinite and subtle variations—especially when it is played no-limit and a player betting all his chips at once can put a tremendous amount of pressure on his opponents. A pair of aces in the hole is the best possible starting hand, but after the flop anything is possible. A small pair in the hole can become three of a kind—or a "set," as it is called—and two suited connectors can become a straight or a flush. These possibilities, combined with the power of betting all of one's chips at any time, make it a game in which bluffing is a potent weapon, and players can win without having to show down the best hand. As Johnny Moss once said of no-limit hold'em, "it is to stud and draw what chess is to checkers." All this makes it the perfect game to determine the world champion of poker.

Stuey had returned to Vegas from Reno much richer from the side action at the Super Bowl of Poker. His cash reserve was now well over $1 million, most of it locked in a safe-deposit box at the Dunes. Just as his father had scattered loot around New York to avoid the tax man, Stuey was content to live and pay his bills out of the box, with Madeline taking care of the details.

When Stuey entered the poker room at Binion's Horseshoe on May 19, 1980, for the start of the big event, most of the competitors regarded him as little more than a curiosity. At twenty-six, he was by far the youngest player in the tournament (a far cry from today, when twenty-year-old players make up a significant part of the field). Not only was Stuey an entire generation removed from the top players in the game, he also lacked some of the essentials considered to be characteristic of a great player at that time.

This isn't to say that Stuey wasn't respected. Everyone who knew him understood his talent for cards, but he was still perceived as a cash player, and a reckless one at that. Tournament play required entirely different skills and strategies, since players could not reach back into their pocket for more money once they lost what they had on the table. Stuey was lacking in experience, and in the days before online poker and the wealth of information available now, the learning curve was much longer.

A record turnout of seventy-three players ponied up $10,000 for the final event of 1980. The previous year, Hal Fowler, an amateur, had won, besting fifty-three competitors, and that had given a lot of recreational players the idea that they, too, might be able to compete with the pros. Fowler, an advertising executive from Southern California who was in his late fifties, had shocked the gambling world with his victory. Heads-up against the seasoned pro Bobby Hoff, he filled several inside straights during a crazy rush of cards that left observers shaking their heads. He was not only the first amateur to win the title but the first amateur to win any money in the tournament's ten-year history. It would be twenty years before an amateur would win the title again.

Fowler let the lucky rush and the title go to his head, gambling away most of his winnings in the months that followed, including a $100,000 heads-up loss to Gabe Kaplan. Fowler kept playing, but he never came close to winning another tournament again, and he dropped out of sight a few years after that, never to be heard from again.

As Stuey took his seat with the seventy-two other players vying for the $365,000 first prize, he immediately launched into his go-for-broke style. He doubled through quickly, turning his $10,000 in chips into $20,000. Players who were able to get an early chip lead in tournament play were at a decided advantage. The extra chips allowed them to make aggressive plays and buy pots with raises and bluffs, without fear of being eliminated. Many players who bought in for $10,000 and a chance to play in the world's most prestigious poker event wanted to savor the experience as long as possible. Their fear of elimination played right into the hands of a player like Stuey, whose cutthroat style definitely served him well. He immediately sized up those players who were content to wait patiently for a good hand—and even then were loath to lose too many chips with it—and when he sensed any weakness in them, he put them to the test.

Gradually, players began to fall by the wayside. They included former champions like Bobby Baldwin, Amarillo Slim, Puggy Pearson, and Sailor Roberts. By the end of the first day, after thirteen grueling hours, fifty of the original seventy-three remained. Stuey was in fifteenth place, with $21,575 in chips.

The second day began at two in the afternoon. Seven hours later, the field was down to two tables and sixteen players. During a break, Stuey ran up to his hotel room at the Horseshoe and called his old mentor Victor Romano. During the previous eighteen months, he had maintained close contact with both Victor and Philly Tartaglia. Romano had serious health issues, and as a result had cut back on his gambling ventures to spend more time with his family. But he made sure that Philly was there to take his place in Stuey's life, and Philly had made numerous visits to Vegas to see Stuey.

"Yeah?" Victor said, picking up the phone.

"I'm doing good," Stuey stammered into the phone so fast that it was almost hard to understand him. "I'm going to win it."

Victor knew that "it" was the WSOP, but he asked Stuey to slow down and tell him all about it. As Stuey recounted the tale of his tournament, the moves he'd made, the hands where he'd gotten unlucky, and what lay ahead, Victor interrupted him.

"We're coming out."

"W-what?"

"Philly and me are gonna catch the next flight out."

Stuey was stunned and overjoyed. He got off the phone and returned to the tournament area, more determined than ever to win. The crowd squeezed in close, trying to follow the action at the final two tables as play resumed. Beneath framed photographs of Doyle Brunson, Johnny Moss, Slim, and other past champions, the contenders jousted with one another, betting and raising, laying their poker lives on the line. The crowd applauded each time a player was eliminated and was forced to stand up, shell-shocked, and stagger away from the table.

Stuey continued to play aggressively, accumulating chips. By the end of the day, the players were down to the final nine, and he was second, with $93,500. Gabe Kaplan was firmly in the lead with $203,100. Everyone realized that if Kaplan were to hold on and win, it would be a public relations coup. He was clearly a crowd favorite, and—not surprisingly—he loved the spotlight, playing to the audience at every opportunity. Kaplan had been into poker since childhood and was a regular at the Gardena card rooms in Los Angeles. Now, he was living out every player's fantasy.

On day three, a large crowd, which now included Victor Romano and Philly Brush, gathered around a well-lit table in the dark wood-paneled heart of the Horseshoe. It took six full hours to eliminate three of the nine finalists, a marathon by poker standards. Since only the top five were being paid, the next unlucky victim would walk away with nothing for his three days of work, while the rest would compete for escalating payouts, fifth through first, from a total of $730,000 in prize money.

To the disappointment of many, Gabe Kaplan, the crowd favorite, who had started the day with a massive chip lead, turned out to be the unfortunate bubble boy. A series of bad beats whittled him down, and after one final unlucky turn of the cards, he rose slowly from his seat and exited stage left.

That left five. There were no Hal Fowlers in this group, just a bunch of killers. Besides Stuey, the five were Johnny Moss, Doyle Brunson, Jay Heimowitz, and Charles Dunwoody. Heimowitz, who owned a beer distributorship in New York, and Dunwoody, though lesser known, were tough, respected players. As always, anyone watching who did not know Stuey would look at the table and wonder why a child was sitting there among the grown-ups.

As the day wore on, Stuey's youthful energy and aggression took their toll on his opponents. Even Brunson, who was usually the most aggressive player in any game he was playing, took a backseat to Stuey in that regard. Brunson found himself down to his last $44,000 late in the tournament, while Stuey was up over $300,000; but in a masterful performance, Brunson bet and bluffed his way back into contention. His comeback came at the expense of Dunwoody, Heimowitz, and Moss, all of whom were eliminated. Suddenly, all that stood between Brunson and his third world championship was the diminutive Kid.

Victor and Philly were watching, and they were among the few in the crowd who gave Stuey a chance against the poker behemoth Brunson. The two men began heads-up play with Stuey holding a slight advantage, $400,000 in chips to Brunson's roughly $300,000. Jackie Gaughan, a crusty former bookmaker who owned the nearby Union Plaza Casino, immediately set a line, making Brunson a 6–5 favorite, despite the difference in chips. During a break, Stuey announced to Gaughan that he wanted to bet $50,000 on himself. Brunson was so confident in his own chances that he told Stuey he'd fade the bet, himself, at 6–5.

During most of the tournament, the two players had been seated at the same table. Brunson knew Stuey well from the hours they had spent playing together in the poker room at the Dunes; and while he had respect for Stuey's abilities, he didn't consider them—at least at that point—to be equal to his own.

Later, Brunson would remark that if anyone had knocked Stuey out the first day, he would have, without question, won his third title. Stuey had still played very little no-limit and had virtually no tournament experience. But as each hour passed, he grew more clear-eyed, relaxed, and confident. By the third day, he was a monster. "In all the years I've played poker," Brunson said, "I don't think I've ever seen another player that actually improved as the tournament went along. He used the World Series and all of us as a training ground."

With the contest between them now personal—a $50,000 wager tends to have that effect—an interesting hand soon developed. The blinds and antes totaled nearly $10,000 in every pot before either player had acted. Brunson, on the button, called Stuey's big blind of $6,000, and Stuey, with 4-5 suited, checked. The flop came A-2-7, rainbow (three different suits).

Stuey checked his gut-shot straight draw.

Brunson peered at the board and fired $17,000 into the pot.

There's an old saying in poker that you should never draw to an inside straight. In limit poker that's mostly true, as you're rarely getting the proper pot odds to make it a correct play. In no-limit, however, with the huge implied odds—that is, if you make the hand, as you have a 1-in-11 chance of doing, and you think you will get paid off on the very large bet you make afterward—it can be a worthwhile gamble. In this case, Stuey reasoned that if he hit the miracle three, he might very well be able to bust Brunson. He called the $17,000.

The dealer knocked the table, then burned and turned a beautiful, unbelievable three of diamonds.

Stuey sat motionless, not even blinking. Inside, his heart was pinwheeling.

Most players in his spot would check, hoping to trap their opponent. But Stuey wanted all of Brunson's chips. The way to get them was by making him commit. A check-raise, and he would win the pot; but Brunson might get away from the reraise, losing only a small portion of his chips. Instead, Stuey, holding the nuts, reached for his chips. He had been superaggressive throughout the tournament, and he knew that Brunson might perceive a good-size bet as a bluff.

He counted out $40,000 and pushed the chips forward in a single motion.

Brunson reared back in his chair, hesitated about five seconds, then leaned forward and exclaimed "All-in!" pushing his chips, all $274,500 of them, into the pot.

The crowd drew an excited breath, then leaned closer, trying to see the cards and figure out what was happening.

For Stuey, it was the moment that every poker player dreams about—holding the stone-cold nuts and having your opponent bet all his chips into you. He leaped from his chair and said, "I call."

Now, there was an uproar in the room, as onlookers realized that this hand would in all likelihood decide the champion. As is customary at the WSOP when two players move all-in, they turned their hands faceup so that the audience could see.

Stuey flipped over his 4-5 for the wheel.

Brunson shook his head, then flipped over A-7 for top two pairs. He could still win the hand by hitting an ace or a seven. There were four cards that could help him, out of the forty-four left in the deck. He had a 1-in-11 chance. Oddly enough, Brunson had won his two world titles in 1976 and 1977 by hitting cards that paired the board and filled him up on the last card, each time holding what had become his trademark hand, 10-2. Could he do it again?

The dealer knocked the table, burned a card, then turned up the final card.

A harmless deuce of hearts.

It was all over. In the mayhem that ensued, dozens of reporters swarmed around the twenty-six-year-old in the brown-and-tan mesh cloth shirt. Stuey's long bangs fell almost to his eyes. He beamed as the reporters jabbed their microphones in his face, trying to get a reaction, but suddenly he seemed like nothing more than a shy, tongue-tied little boy.

"You were an underdog going into this," one reporter said. "Do you think you got lucky?"

"Lucky?" Stuey said.

Doyle Brunson graciously stepped forward. "He won this thing fair and square. He deserves to be the champion." He shook Stuey's hand and tried his best to hide the disappointment of not winning his third world title in five years.

One of the reporters asked Eric Drache, the tournament director, how Stuey stacked up against the best hold'em players.

"He's hardly ever played the game before. He's still learning."

Finally, Stuey stepped up and spoke for himself. "Oh, I've played it three or four times," he said. "I guess I've just got good card sense."

"What are you going to do with all the money?" another reporter wanted to know.

Stuey looked whimsical for a second, considering this.

"Gamble it," he said at last.

9.

WORLD CHAMP

Victor and Philly wanted to take Stuey and Madeline out to celebrate.

It was amazing: there was Stuey, surrounded by television people and reporters, and everyone was going up to him, wanting to touch him, ask him questions. Victor was puffed up with pride, watching. He was beaming. After all those years in New York's backroom card games, here was his boy on the big stage in Vegas—the world champion!

First things first, however. Stuey wanted to get paid, and that was turning out to be a problem. Eric Drache and Jack Binion walked him back to the cashier's cage, but they needed Stuey to supply them with a Social Security number, and he didn't have one. He had never worked at a conventional job, so he had never needed one. Even when he won gin tournaments, this hadn't been a problem, because those were private events—the organizers rented a ballroom in a casino and ran the tournaments themselves. In the 1970s, the Gaming Commission was fairly lax, particularly with independent contractors. But the Horseshoe, since it was the sponsor and host of the WSOP, had to follow all the gaming laws. There was no way around it.

"You're saying you can't pay me?"

"Stuey, I don't understand," Jack Binion said. "You've never needed a Social Security card before this?"

"Nope." The new champ was getting a rude introduction into the ways of the real world—where normal people filled out forms and paid income taxes.

Eric Drache picked up the phone and spoke to someone in the executive office at Binion's. He learned that Stuey could get a card issued at the Federal Building, a few blocks away. While Drache tried to get instructions on how to apply, Stuey kept interrupting.

"How long will it take? How long will it take? Ask 'em how long will it take." Stuey's impatience was almost comical. He seemed like a child tugging at his father's shirt.

Drache called for a limo, and Stuey was whisked off to the Federal Building. It was four o'clock, and the office closed at five. He had less than an hour to fill out the necessary forms and get processed.

Stuey rushed out of the limo and ran upstairs, bursting through the swinging doors into the second-floor office. Reaching the window, breathless, he asked a bored civil servant, "How do I get a Social Security card?"

"Fill out a form. It's over there," she said, pointing to a metal counter against the far wall.

Stuey filled out the form and brought it back.

"I need the card quick."

"It will take just a—"

"Here, honey, that's for you," Stuey said, slipping her a $100 bill across the countertop. "I need to get the card today."

The clerk was stunned. "Why do you need it in such a hurry?"

"You'll read about it on the front page of the papers tomorrow," Stuey said, his head cocked back, waiting for her to accept the hundred.

"I appreciate your generosity, but we issue the numbers right here, so it's not really necessary—"

"It's okay, honey, you keep that. It's for you."

Fifteen minutes later, Stuey had his temporary Social Security card in hand. He ran out the door and jumped back into the limo.

Drache was still in the cage with the money piled on a table when Stuey was brought back in by the guards. He slammed a small white card down on the metal desk.

"There! Now pay me my money!"

Drache counted out $365,000, consisting of thirty-six bundles of $10,000 each; then he added fifty $100 bills. The loot covered the desk, looking like nothing so much as the spoils of a bank robbery.

After deducting a sizable tip for the dealers and for Drache, Stuey took two bundles totaling $20,000 and put them in his pockets. The rest he instructed a clerk to put in a safe-deposit box for him. When the box was secured, he signed a slip and was issued a key.

That night, he and Madeline went out with Victor and Philly to an Italian restaurant off the Strip called Villa d'Este. The four of them were in high spirits, and for once Stuey didn't rush through the meal as if he had a train to catch. They drank a lot of wine, and Victor not only had a large plate of pasta like the rest of them but followed it with a veal dish and dessert and coffee (Victor liked to have his coffee served in a glass with a spoon in it so the glass wouldn't break). When the bill came, Stuey picked it up despite Victor's protests.

"I guess we can let the world champ take us out, huh, Philly?" Victor said at last.

Later that night, back at their hotel room at Caesars, Victor complained to Philly that he had indigestion from the meal. He took some antacid, but the pain persisted. Philly wanted to call a doctor, but Victor told him to wait.

Six hours later, Victor Romano died of a massive heart attack.

Stuey couldn't believe it. One minute he'd been on top of the world; the next he'd lost the man who had been like a second father to him.

"It meant so much to Stuey, having Victor come out here to see him in that moment of glory," Madeline said. "And then for it to turn out the way it did was just cruel."

Victor would have loved being able to go back to New York and tell the old crowd that I won. That would have been one of the highlights of his life. But he never had a chance to do that. After I heard what happened to him, suddenly the win didn't mean nothing to me no more. I'd have rather lost that tournament than to have what happened happen.

Stuey took it hard, grieving more for Victor than he had for the death of his own parents. Romano had been one of the few stabilizing elements in his life. When the loss was added to the change in the way people now perceived him, Stuey found himself struggling to maintain his balance. Gambling, as always, helped him stay centered—or at least kept him occupied. It was a good way to avoid thinking too much.

When Stuey flew up to Reno for Amarillo Slim's Super Bowl of Poker at the Sahara Reno on January 22, 1981, he was no longer a mysterious newcomer; he was the reigning world champion of poker. He was unaccustomed to the spotlight, and suddenly he felt as if he had a bull's-eye on his forehead. As he took his seat at the start of the $10,000 buy-in main event, other players kidded him or bemoaned their bad luck in having been seated at his table. If he was feeling the pressure, though, he didn't show it.

By the end of the first day of the $10,000 buy-in main event, Stuey was second in chips. Early on the second day, Stuey, holding the A-K of spades, ran into Tony Salinas, who had A-Q offsuit. The flop came A-K-Q with two hearts. Stuey moved all-in, and Salinas, with the top and bottom two pairs, called him. Stuey was a huge favorite to win. Only one of the two queens in the deck or running hearts could save Salinas. Incredibly, a queen came on the river, and Stuey was eliminated. Had he won, he would have been a huge favorite to go on and win the tournament. Instead, he stormed out of the Sahara and hailed a taxi back to the airport, leaving his clothes behind in his hotel room.

Even for a regular joe, life in Las Vegas can be a bit overwhelming. For the reigning poker champion, it was surreal. Wherever Stuey went he was regarded with curiosity and stares: "Is that really the poker champ? He looks like a high school kid." One wisecracking tourist reportedly asked him why he wasn't in class in the middle of a weekday afternoon. "Shut the fuck up," was Stuey's diplomatic reply.

In April, Stuey prepared to defend his WSOP title. He rarely played in any of the smaller events that led up to the championship, feeling that they weren't worth his time. But in 1981, on a whim, he decided to enter the Deuce-to-Seven Lowball event. Two days later, he took the $95,000 top prize, beating the champion of 1978, Bobby Baldwin, heads-up to win his second gold bracelet.

A week later, on May 19, 1981, the main event got under way. Bettors weren't enthralled with the defending champ's chances. Jackie Gaughan listed Stuey at 25–1, longer odds than Brunson, Baldwin, and eight others carried. When Stuey saw Gaughan's number, he was insulted. He let everyone know that it would only motivate him to prove that his victory the previous year hadn't been a fluke. When Gaughan walked onto the tournament floor, Stuey took the slight as an opportunity to make even more money by betting $5,000 on himself to win. Gaughan booked the bet and assured Stuey that he would pay $125,000 if Stuey won.

At the WSOP, the money bet by gamblers on one another was at times almost as exciting for them as the event itself. Telecasts of the WSOP from that era often refer to the excitement of the crowd, but that excitement was often fueled less by sentiment than by big bets they had riding on particular players. Hundreds of thousands of dollars routinely changed hands among those watching. Today, betting on the event is not permitted in Las Vegas—at least not out in the open as it was in the 1980s.

Amarillo Slim proposed at one point that he would be willing to take action on anyone who wanted to bet on "the Jews versus the Texans." Since most of the top players were Jewish (Stuey, Jay Heimowitz, and Mickey Appleman, to name three) or Texan (Slim, Brunson, Moss, and Jack Straus, to name four), it was a proposition that generated considerable interest. There was some debate about how to quantify both sides, and what to do in the case of a Jewish Texan, and so Slim was forced to modify his wager into the more readily visible "hats versus bareheads." Since the Texans usually wore hats and the Jews didn't, he was able to work a little bit of the spirit of his original proposition into the bet.

"Half the room had hats, so it really got some people to put up some bucks," Slim said. "Well, them boys with the hats usually ate everyone up like ginger cake. But things were changin'. The players with the hats had gotten older and then Doyle wrote that damn book of his. It got to where they could play good against us Texans."

The great secret of the WSOP of 1981 was that Stuey almost didn't get to play in it. A few days before the event, during a side game, Stuey, who had a well-deserved reputation for being tough on dealers, got disgusted after losing a huge pot and spit in the face of Harry Franks, a middle-aged part-time dealer at the Horseshoe. Dealing the high-stakes Vegas games was no easy job. With thousands of dollars at stake, tempers triggered easily. A slight mistake by a dealer could be tremendously expensive, and that fact, along with the need some players had to blame somebody for a loss or bad luck, meant that dealers were often in the line of fire. They had to be able to endure insults and grumbling without reacting (thus the dictum "Just dummy up and deal").

"Stuey never knew any of the dealers' names," one former dealer at the Dunes recalled. "He always called us the same thing, especially when he was losing. We were all known as 'motherfucker.' "

Stuey's insults weren't personal, although that didn't make them any less objectionable. Nor did his often generous tips excuse his behavior. But some of his defenders insist it was just his conditioning, what he was accustomed to seeing back in New York, and later in Vegas, where even the best poker players, legendary figures like Puggy Pearson and Johnny Moss, were notorious for their brutal treatment of dealers. Stuey's outbursts had gotten him into trouble before. On at least one occasion, he was invited to go outside and fight. Once at the Dunes, a female dealer named Darlene challenged Stuey to duke it out in the parking lot after her shift was over.

"Are you crazy?" he asked. "You think I'm going to fight a girl?"

"I get off in five minutes," Darlene shot back. "I'm gonna take you down."

Stuey didn't say another word. Her bravado had effectively shut him up, at least until the next bad beat rolled off the deck.

But spitting in a dealer's face was another matter. Stuey later explained that he had been simply shouting at Franks, when, in the excitement of the moment, some saliva managed to make its way across the table to Frank's face. Upon hearing of the incident, Benny Binion banned Stuey from the Horseshoe until further notice.

The idea that the world champion might not be able to defend his title was unfathomable. But it would have happened if Jack Binion hadn't intervened at the last minute and persuaded his father to take a less extreme stance. Although the Binions wanted to send a strong message to Stuey, they understood that the public's interest in seeing the champion defend his crown needed to be served as well.

In 1981, a fourth day was added to the main event to accommodate the ever-increasing size of the field. Seventy-five entrants put up the

$10,000 buy-in, for a total prize pool of $750,000, and first-place money of $375,000. Curt Gowdy and a crew from NBC Sports were on hand to film the event for a later telecast.

The first day of the tournament, in particular, was something of a fashion show, all the players wanting to bask in the moment and give the crowd and photographers and television crew something to gawk at. A. Alvarez, who chronicled the event in his superb book *The Biggest Game in Town*, described the scene.

One young cowboy was wearing a bright blue stetson and black shirt embroidered with black silk curlicues. Ken Smith, who is also a chess master and was Bobby Fischer's second in the Reykjavik marathon with Boris Spassky, wore what he always wears at competitions—a frock coat and a decrepit top hat, which he claims was found in the Ford Theater the night Lincoln was assassinated. Smith has a ragged beard, a squeaky voice, and a girth like that of Swinburne's giant slumbering boar: "the blind bulk of the immeasurable beast." Each time he wins a pot, he lumbers to his feet, doffs his topper to the audience, and pipes, "What a player!"

The others were less fashion-conscious, although, like the oysters in *Through the Looking-Glass,* "Their coats were brushed, their faces washed. / Their shoes were clean and neat." Brunson and Straus wore pale blue suede jackets over navy blue shirts and trousers. Chip Reese had abandoned his velour track suits and reverted to his Ivy League origins: gray flannel trousers and a gray shirt with blue pinstripes. Bobby Baldwin was dressed in gray trousers and a gray Lacoste tennis shirt, at once sporting and sober, to suit his image. Even Mickey Appleman was wearing a neat beige corduroy jacket over his black T-shirt, and Stu Ungar wore a clean bowling shirt.

Early in the tournament, it looked as though the oddsmakers who had made Stuey such an underdog were right. He couldn't seem to get any traction, and several times he came precipitously close to elimination, but somehow he survived—and in tournaments survival is everything. By the time the competition reached the final day, the eight other survivors included the chip leader, Bobby Baldwin, who had nearly $200,000 in chips; Jay Heimowitz, the formidable New Yorker; Perry Green, a roly-poly Alaskan fur trader; Ken Smith, the top-hatted chess master; and Bill Smith, a Texan, who confounded poker maxims about drunks by drinking straight whiskey throughout the tournament and continuing to win.

Stuey was hanging on with just over $50,000. He was fidgety, as he always was when sitting at a poker table, making faces, his eyes darting around with impatience. Dressed for the final day in a blue V-neck chemise, with a gold necklace draped across his concave, hairless chest and the gold championship bracelet weighing down his wrist, Stuey dextrously shuffled his small pile of chips with his chopstick-thin fingers.

By the time a couple of his fellow short stacks were eliminated, Stuey had been ground all the way down to $23,500. Meanwhile it appeared that Bobby Baldwin would run away from the field. He might well have done so but for one key hand. It began with Green raising pre-flop with a pair of pocket queens. Baldwin, holding a pair of nines, called. The nine-high flop gave him top set and looked for all the world like the end of Green and the beginning of Baldwin's coronation ceremony.

To Baldwin's further delight, Green bet $42,000 into him. Not wanting to get cute, Baldwin raised $85,000 more, setting Green—if he decided to call—in for all his money. The bearded, dumpling-shaped fur trader stared Baldwin down for a full two minutes, counting and recounting his chips. Finally, he pushed them forward. If Baldwin's set of nines held up, he would have more than half the chips on the table.

The turn brought a harmless jack. But the river spiked Baldwin in the heart with a killer third queen. Baldwin smiled weakly as Perry Green took off his hat in disbelief and rubbed his bald head. As the reality of the miracle catch sank in, Green smiled uncontrollably and did a little shimmy. Who could blame him for feeling giddy? The long shot river card not only had kept him alive but had vaulted him into the chip lead.

When Stuey, a few hands later, moved all-in for his last $23,050, with pocket fives, the still-giddy Green called with only a nine and a ten of clubs. Stuey's tournament life was on the line in what amounted to a coin-flip situation.*

Green would have liked nothing better than to eliminate a dangerous rival. But Stuey survived. The fives held up.

Fifteen minutes earlier, Baldwin had been on the verge of taking control of the tournament, but the bad beat against Green, despite the brave smile, tilted him briefly. He tried pushing a couple of ill-advised bluffs, including one against Stuey, that took his stack down even further. With pocket kings, he now moved all-in with the rest of his chips, and was called by Gene Fisher, a Texan, who—with his red, diagonally buttoned cavalry shirt, battered Stetson, silver hair, and full silver mustache—looked, as Alvarez described him, "like a reincarnation of Kit Carson." Fisher's pair of queens was drawing slim to the kings, but Lady Luck seemed to be against Bobby Baldwin on this day, and an unlucky lady on the river sent him packing in seventh place.

Jay Heimowitz had through much of the tournament worn a V-neck T-shirt that on his well-muscled torso made him look a little like an actor auditioning for the part of Stanley Kowalski. For the final day, however, he wore a pink-and-red-striped shirt that seemed more Ten-

---

* The precise odds favor Green's 9-10 suited by 52.43 to 47.56 over Ungar's fives.

nessee Williams than Marlon Brando. His preflop raise with the magical pocket queens was called by Stuey with jacks. The flop came king, jack, ten, giving him an open-ended straight draw to go with his queens, but giving Stuey a set of jacks. When Heimowitz moved in, Stuey called immediately. For once, the queens did not work their magic, and a fourth jack on the river brought a rueful smile to Heimowitz's lips.

From the brink, Stuey was now over the $100,000 mark for the first time in the tournament. A few hands later, starting to push people around, he vaulted into the chip lead. The hand began with the sodden Bill Smith—who looked, in his wide-lapel tan suit and big-collared brown shirt, like a refugee from the set of a John Holmes movie— betting $8,000 preflop with a 6-7 offsuit, and Stuey calling with K-5 of spades.

The flop came ace of spades, nine of clubs, five of clubs. Stuey checked, and Smith bet $10,000. Stuey quickly called. A six of spades came on the turn, giving Stuey a four-flush to go with his pair of fives. He led out for $40,000. Without hesitation, Smith reraised him all-in for $15,500 more.

Stuey obviously was not happy, but he was pot-committed and made the call.

"Whaddya got, Bill?"

"A straight," the soused Smith said, flipping over his cards. In fact, he had misread his hand. He had only a pair of sixes with a gut-shot straight draw. Nevertheless, he was in the lead.

Incredulous, Stuey got to his feet. He swung around, looking at Philly Brush, who was standing behind him along the rail. "He made a mistake," he exclaimed. "He misread it. Can you believe that?"

The dealer knuckled the table and dealt the final card. It took Smith fifteen seconds to figure out that the ten of spades that landed had given Stuey a flush and eliminated him. When he did comprehend it, he got up unsteadily and shook hands around the table. Stuey was now the tournament leader with $340,000. Green was in second place with $220,000, and Ken Smith and Gene Fisher had $95,000 each.

A short time later, the two chip leaders got involved in a hand. Green raised preflop with A-K. Stuey flat-called with A-Q. The flop revealed two more aces along with a three. Both players checked, each trying to set a trap for the other. The turn was another three. If it had been any other card but a queen, it is quite likely that Stuey would have lost most of his chips. As it was, the two players raised and reraised each other all-in, and then chopped the pot, each with the same hand, a full house, aces over threes.

Just after the dinner break, Perry Green eliminated Ken Smith and regained the chip lead, with $480,000 (to Stuey's $200,000 and Gene Fisher's $70,000). Another big pot then began to build between Stuey and Green. This time Stuey had pocket kings and Green had A-Q. When the flop came with an ace in it, Green bet $60,000, and Stuey called. It was a questionable call at best, but when the turn card produced a king, one of Stuey's two outs, the tables were suddenly turned. Stuey adjusted himself in his chair, shook his head impatiently, and pushed his remaining chips into the pot, $90,000. It was now Green's turn to shake his head. He squinted at the cards and then at Stuey, and slowly, painstakingly, he counted out $90,000 from his mountain of chips, shoving them in. When Stuey revealed his hand, Green nodded grimly, absorbing the sting of what was—no other way to put it—horrible luck. The harmless four of clubs that came on the river drew a cheer from the crowd. Ungar had retaken the lead with $400,000 in chips.

A quarter of an hour later, Gene Fisher got knocked out, unluckily, when Perry Green rivered a flush to beat his three kings. The world championship of 1981 had come down to Stuey and Perry Green, with Green holding a slight advantage, $420,000 to $330,000. Doyle Brunson, who was standing behind one of the cameramen, fished his bankroll out of his pocket and paid off Gabe Kaplan, who was standing next to him. "So much for the Texans," Kaplan said. "We got ourselves an all-Jewish final."

On the other side of the room, Johnny Moss, surveying the impregnable wall of chips in front of Green, was, according to Alvarez, "not impressed. 'I reckon Stuey's got it made,' he said. 'He may not look like no Buffalo Bill, but he's one tough poker player. That boy's got alligator blood in his veins.'"

As the two finalists squared off, Perry Green turned to Doyle Brunson, who was still up close to the rail, and revealed the secret of his success: "It's all because I read your book," Green said.

Doyle flashed a big smile and nodded.

The cards were dealt, and Green bet $16,000. Stuey, sitting with his elbow on the table and his chin held in the L formed by his index and middle finger, raised $40,000, and Green called. The flop came jack of diamonds, nine and eight of clubs. Stuey had the ace and jack of clubs. Top pair with the nut flush draw—a monster hand. He bet $60,000, and Green considered the bet momentarily before shoving all his chips in.

Stuey did not deliberate. "I call," he said. Green's $450,000 had him more than covered.

Green once again turned toward Brunson. "I've got your hand," he said.

Before Green could turn up his cards, Stuey sprang from his seat. "Ten-deuce of clubs?"

Incredibly, Brunson, while sitting on the sidelines, had influenced the outcome. Perry Green had made his remark to the poker icon about reading his book, and on the very next hand was dealt the master's trademark 10-2, the same hand Brunson had played to close out his two WSOP victories. How could the Alaskan furrier not play it? And when the flop gave him an up-and-down straight draw with a flush draw, what was he supposed to think? It was kismet.

But Stuey's hand cut off his flush at the knees. Green's only outs were the six cards that made him a straight without giving Stuey the higher flush.

The dealer turned up the final two cards. A jack on the turn, and a six on the river. No help for the 10-2.

Stuey was now well in front of his opponent, with $600,000 of the $750,000 chips in play. The end came after another hour of back-and-forth play. Green, with a 9-10 offsuit, made it $16,000. Stuey, holding an ace and queen of hearts, raised him $25,000. Looking a bit pained, Green called. The flop came 7-8-4, and two hearts.

The crowd leaned in closer, as if sensing the end. Stuey separated five stacks of red chips from his pile. "One hundred thousand dollars." Green only had $78,000 left. "I call," he said. When Green saw Stuey's hand, he sighed and said, "I got a draw." And as the dealer dealt the final two cards, he chanted "Nine, ten, six, jack," naming all the cards that could help him.

The dealer burned and turned fourth street, which was another four, then burned and turned the river. For a split second, it appeared that Green's prayer had been answered. It was definitely a face card. Could it be a jack, giving him the straight? Everyone's eyes were blurred, after hours under the hot television lights, but when the last card came into focus, it was not a jack, it was a queen, giving Stuey two pairs—queens and fours—and the championship. The spectators roared their approval.

Curt Gowdy interviewed Stuey directly afterward, amid the hub-bub, sticking a microphone under the champ's chin.

"Two years in a row," said Gowdy. "What are the odds on that?"

"Awful big," Stuey muttered. "It's very tough to win it. You've gotta get awful lucky in key situations."

He had won not only the first-place prize money, $375,000, but an additional $125,000 from his 25–1 bet on himself with Jackie Gaughan.

The money was great, but Stuey's real satisfaction was in proving the critics and oddsmakers wrong. Those who thought that his victory the previous year had just been a fluke, that he was a one-hit wonder, were forced to eat their words. At twenty-seven he was not only the youngest champion ever but a champion who had won it all twice.

10.

A Taste of Honey

Jack Binion was quick to recognize Stuey's marketability. The two-time champ was young and attractive, with the looks and aura of a rock star—a stark contrast to the older, leather-faced Texans who had reigned through the 1970s. Stuey might have been a little rough around the edges, but he had a natural charm. His tell-it-like-it-is style, conveyed in Lower East Side patois, was different from the homespun Texas witticisms of someone like Amarillo Slim but nevertheless engaging.

Binion and his brilliant public relations director, the Englishman Henri Bollinger, set up interviews for Stuey on television shows in Los Angeles, Houston, Kansas City, and New York. An interview with Merv Griffin for Griffin's afternoon television show was, to Binion's dismay and slight horror, scheduled at Caesars Palace. But the Horseshoe still reaped the rewards of all the publicity.

"Shortly after I appeared on the Griffin show, I got a check for three hundred dollars for my appearance," Stuey said later. "That was the only legitimate money I ever earned. The show was rerun again later in the year, and the next time I got a check for one hundred dollars. Just think, in my whole life, those were the only paychecks I ever received."

Stuey's short publicity tour further elevated poker and helped expand the popularity of the game. The public was fascinated by high rollers like the Kid. A regular poker tournament circuit grew out of the success of Binion's event, with other events scheduled throughout the year at casinos in Las Vegas, Reno, and Lake Tahoe, and later in California. Poker was changing from the days when the "men with the hats" were the best players, and Stuey Ungar was leading the way.

The New York *Daily News* did a feature story about Stuey—"Kid Ice"—in its Sunday magazine section. Eight million New Yorkers learned for the first time about the fast-talking, hard-gambling native son who'd made good. The publicity introduced Stuey to a whole new world beyond the smoke-filled back rooms of his youth.

After I won in 'eighty-one, I received all sorts of mail. I even got a letter from a guy who was locked up in prison. He sent a letter to Stu Ungar, and just wrote "The Horseshoe" on the envelope. It got to me anyway. The guy wrote, "I'm a relative, a long-lost cousin of yours." The letter asked me for money. So I sent him two hundred dollars. Of course, I never heard from him again after that. Some family, huh?

In fact, as a result of the national exposure, Stuey did actually reconnect with some members of his family with whom he'd lost touch. His half brother, Irwin Ungar, now a college professor in Ohio, sent Stuey a letter congratulating him on his win. It was the first time that Stuey had been in contact with his father's other family since the settlement of the estate. It would also be the last.

Judy Ungar, who was still living in Puerto Rico, happened to be visiting New York in May 1981 when Stuey won the championship and the

Daily News covered the story. She picked up the phone and called Binion's Horseshoe to try to find Stuey. A staff member gave her his address in East Las Vegas.

Judy wrote a letter to Stuey, but he ignored it. As far as he was concerned, Judy was no longer part of his life. He didn't approve of the choices she'd made—her Puerto Rican husband and her use of drugs. At least that was how he put it to himself. But Madeline and Judy struck up a dialogue of their own by phone, and Madeline finally succeeded in getting Stuey to talk to his sister. As it turned out, the phone call was a happy reunion. The two siblings had been out of touch for more than five years. They talked for an hour and a half. Near the end of the conversation, Stuey invited Judy to visit them in Las Vegas.

Judy was touched until Stuey nearly ruined it all by asking her if her kids were white.

"What!" Judy was flabbergasted and deeply offended. It hardly mattered that her husband had turned out to be a good provider and father, or that her kids had blond hair; she just couldn't believe her brother's crassness and insensitivity.

Stuey tried to talk his way out of it but just wound up making the situation worse. His attitude about race, most of which he had learned from his father, was so deeply ingrained that he wasn't even aware that there was anything wrong with it.

Despite her brother's blunders, Judy went to Vegas to visit him for three weeks in June 1981. The reunion went well. They talked and laughed and caught each other up on the past five years. When Judy was leaving, they promised to stay in touch. But they never did. Judy and her kids boarded a United Airlines flight and returned home to Puerto Rico. It was to be the last time the brother and sister would see each other.

The big payday, along with Stuey's more respectable and presumably more responsible station in life, got Madeline thinking about marriage. She desperately wanted another child, and began to broach the subject. She was in her thirties; her childbearing years were limited. But Stuey wasn't interested in marriage or a child.

When Madeline got pregnant in February, she was so fearful that Stuey might demand an abortion that she didn't tell him about her condition right away. At three months, she told him. But the way he looked at her made her realize that he didn't want her to keep the baby. Before he could say it, she said, "Stuey, I am not having an abortion. I am having this baby. But don't worry, we don't have to get married if you don't want to."

"Do you want to get married?"

"No. I don't want you doing me any favors."

Madeline was pregnant and there was nothing he could do about it, and this realization worked a number on Stuey. He was determined that no child of his was going to be born out of wedlock, a situation that was all too familiar to him because he had been born illegitimate himself. Still, he was resentful of the way it had come about. Twice, he and Madeline planned a trip to city hall to get married by a justice of the peace, but each time the modest civil ceremony was planned, a poker game or a sporting event came up, and Stuey postponed it. By late summer, Madeline was plainly showing signs of the pregnancy. Stuey realized that the clock was ticking down on him. One afternoon, he walked in the front door of the house, took a look at her ballooning belly, and said, "Let's go get married."

On September 24, 1982, Stuart Errol Ungar married Madeline Carol Wheeler at the Clark County courthouse in downtown Las Vegas. Since only Stuey and Madeline attended the ceremony, a lone witness, a deputy named George Johnson, signed the marriage certificate. It wasn't the fancy wedding most brides would have preferred. There was no white dress or wedding cake. But Madeline got what she wanted.

. . .

I really loved Madeline. But she trapped me into getting married and for that I could never forgive her. Still, I thank my lucky stars that she did, or we never would have had a kid. At the time, I didn't want a baby. We already had Richie to take care of. I couldn't be responsible for myself. How could I be responsible for another kid?

Like a lot of gifted individuals, Stuey had always been coddled and indulged, insulated from the mundane tasks of everyday life. He could recount in excruciating detail thousands of hands he had played, but according to the story in the *Daily News,* "he doesn't even know how to turn on the gas stove." Rather than wash his own hair, a few times a week, Stuey went to the Dunes, where a hairstylist washed it for him. He paid $30 and left a $20 tip. Madeline bought all his clothes, and he rarely changed them except when badgered by her. Even when he was buying a new car to celebrate his win in the WSOP, he had Madeline pick out the model (a Mercedes convertible) and color (yellow).

Stuey could be generous with money and gifts, but his thoughtlessness and self-involvement were at times staggering. On Madeline's birthday, he rarely bought her presents. Instead, he gave her money and told her to go out and buy herself a gift. Similarly, when Madeline told Stuey that Richie wanted a motorized dune buggy for Christmas, instead of going to the mall, he gave the ten-year-old the cash and told him to buy it himself. And when Madeline asked Stuey if he would take Lamaze classes with her, he simply told her he didn't want to.

The morning Madeline's water broke, she called her mother first before even waking Stuey up.

When she did wake him, she said, "I think my water broke. I think I'm going to have the baby."

Stuey groaned. "Are you sure?"

"Yeah, I'm pretty sure."

He was still half out of it, lying there in bed. "You're definitely sure?"

"Yes."

At the hospital, Madeline was wheeled into the delivery room and started having contractions almost right away. When she looked around, to her surprise, there was Stuey. He had made it clear that he had no interest in being there or coaching her, yet suddenly there he was, wearing blue scrubs and a mask. "It was one of those moments," Madeline said. "I was really moved, seeing him in there with me, giving me encouragement after he'd said he wouldn't be there. But I think it just touched him. He realized it was special and he wanted to be a part of it."

Stefanie Ungar was born on November 1, 1982. Billy Baxter's wife threw Madeline a baby shower, which was attended by an assortment of friends Madeline had met in the new neighborhood of Coventry Lane. Madeline was Catholic, not Jewish, and wanted Stefanie to be raised in her faith. With Stuey's approval, Stefanie was baptized in a Catholic church.

When his daughter was a newborn, Stuey was afraid of her. "He always thought Stefanie was going to break," Madeline said. "You know, that she was too fragile. If he saw her crying, he'd say, 'What is she doing? What's wrong? You better go check her.'" If Stefanie had a rash he would insist that Madeline take her to the doctor immediately. He was always very concerned about her. "He didn't have a lot of time," Madeline said, "but what time he had, he gave to the kids."

Any emotional impact his infant daughter had on Stuey, and on the state of his marriage, was short-lived, however. Like his father, Ido, Stuey was a rambling gambling man, and a philanderer. The fame and fortune from his victories in the WSOP put temptation constantly in his path and exacerbated these tendencies in him.

• • •

When I entered the limelight, women were at my disposal. I must have been with a hundred of them, and I mean the best, the cream of the fucking crop. Guys' wives, single chicks, models, it didn't matter who they were. To me, lust is just wanting to rip into a girl. I guess my gambling and my sex life are pretty similar, huh?

I picked up a floor girl at the Bicycle Club one time. She was working the floor and recognized me. We got to talking and half an hour later I was having sex with her. I got in the room with her and five minutes later we were going at it. Man, she was a screamer. I mean she was so fucking loud I thought I was hurting her. I thought I'd have to put a muzzle on her. I tried to put my hand across her mouth and she bit me, she was screaming so loud.

A couple of minutes later, I heard this knock at the door. It was hotel security. I opened the door and they said, "What's going on?" They looked inside and saw me and this naked girl. I said, "What do you think's going on?"

So they left us alone.

We got back at it and she started screaming again, screaming like a hyena in heat.

You like to think you're exceptional. I was saying to myself, "Jesus Christ—I am good, aren't I?" I thought I had some real talent in bed. Then later, I talked to this other guy who'd been with her, and he said she screamed with him, too. That was a real letdown, when I found out she screams with everybody. I was just one of a group.

I had a regular thing worked out where I would go with a girl. I'd have it arranged in advance to have someone call me up twenty minutes later with an emergency phone call. That way when I had to leave the house or leave the hotel room there wouldn't be any questions asked. I had my excuse for leaving.

The phone would ring like clockwork. I'd even let her answer it. They'd say, "Emergency call for Stuart Ungar." I'd pick up and say, "What? You've gotta be kidding!"

Then I'd put on my clothes and rush out the door. That way I'd be back playing or watching the ball game. Just like I used to call ahead to have my order ready when I got to a restaurant. I was thinking one step ahead when it came to sex, too.

Stuey's promiscuity resulted in several unplanned pregnancies. On six occasions, according to him, he agreed to pay for a woman's abortion. For Stuey, there was no shame or stigma attached to the decision. It was just the cost of having a good time. Tipping a doorman, bribing an usher, sex—everything had a price. And Stuey was willing to pay it. Whether the woman asking for money was really pregnant or just using a supposed pregnancy as an excuse to get money out of him remains open to speculation. But Stuey put himself in the line of fire with many reckless nights.

"Whatever they asked for, they got," he said. "I suspect not all of them were really pregnant. They were just coming to me for money. But what could I say?"

Once, Stuey confronted one of his girlfriends, asking her how she knew it had been he who had impregnated her.

"From the look on her face, I could tell it was mine. That's how I knew. I could just read her body language." Even away from the poker table, Stuey was picking up tells. "It didn't really matter, though. I was going to give her the money anyway."

Madeline knew what was going on to some extent, but tried not to really think about it. "Fame and money were overwhelming for Stuey," she said. "He got caught up in it and didn't want to just come home to one person and do the sit-down dinner thing or be entertained by one person. He liked other people to entertain him, preferably female people. I know that is basically what he wanted. And I was taking care of an infant; I wasn't even thinking about it. I was thinking, 'Okay, let's see what we can do for the little girl. What can we do for a first-birthday party?' All the things you do when you bring up a child. So our lives just always kind of crisscrossed. Here, I had made my commitment to be a mom and he had gotten to a point in his life where everybody was circling around him going, 'Oh, Stu! Oh, Stu!' And people were bringing women around and introducing them to him."

Sudden fame and wealth can unbalance even the most grounded of men; for Stuey, Las Vegas in the early 1980s became a carnival ride that wouldn't stop. "Las Vegas is a twenty-five-hour-a-day, 365-day-a-year town," he said. "Anything and everything is possible at all hours of the day and night. You might think that doesn't affect a person, but it does. You lose track of the day and night."

Even the party that wouldn't stop needed some kind of fuel. In the 1970s and 1980s, it was cocaine, the pricey white powder that became a status symbol of the elite.

When I first moved to Vegas, the city was buried in a snowstorm. Everywhere you turned people were doing cocaine. Everybody who had money, anyway.

The drug dealers were drawn to the high rollers. It didn't matter what time of day it was, blow was always easy to come by. I was just a casual, recreational user back then. It didn't affect my life. It sure didn't affect my play. Sometimes I could stay up longer with it, but I could play good with or without it. I know it destroyed some people. Some of the top poker players were killed by that stuff. You know that song "The Pusher" that Steppenwolf did? "People walking around with tombstones in their eyes?" Some people were like that.

NOLAN DALLA AND PETER ALSON

Stuey's introduction to drugs had actually taken place back in New York, in 1976. Before that, he'd always been vehemently antidrug, in part because of what he'd seen drugs do to his own family—his mother and her pill dependency, and his sister and her heroin addiction—and in part because of his association with organized crime, the wiseguys pounding it into his head that you just didn't do that stuff. "When I first met him, he had no tolerance for anyone who took drugs," said Madeline. "He was someone who was just focused on his work—the card playing. He didn't look at anyone who drank or did drugs. They were bad news to him."

That changed the day his mother went into the nursing home.

The day I put her in there, she was crying, and I couldn't take it. I went over to my friend Bernie's house because I had to escape. Bernie had some white powder spread out on the kitchen table. I asked him what it was. He said, "Go ahead. It will make you feel better." He snorted some, himself, using a small spoon. Then he handed me the spoon.

So I tried a little bit of it. I forgot my troubles just like Bernie said. I wasn't thinking about my mother in the nursing home no more. I was laughing and giggling. That's how it all started.

Stuey claimed that he used cocaine only occasionally in New York in the 1970s. Even after he first moved to Las Vegas, he was still primarily a recreational user. Madeline wasn't aware of his abusing the drug after they moved in together, but he was definitely using it when he "started hanging around all the card rooms with the poker guys."

Many of the big-name players like Brunson, Reese, and Baxter despised drugs. Some had a natural stamina that gave them an edge in the late-night sessions; but others, who lacked such stamina, indulged in a chemical pick-me-up.

"When we played poker back in those days, we'd sometimes sit in a game for two or three days at a time. Especially me and Chip. We'd just sit and play a few days, then pick it up and go home when the game busted. The secret is, the great players can hold their concentration. They can go for however long it takes and they'll get the money. Even in the 1980s, when I was in my fifties, I could hold my concentration for days. And so could Chip. We've just got great endurance. But Stuey was different. He could sit with us, but he always had to be involved in action. He wouldn't wait for a hand. He didn't have the patience. He didn't have that kind of endurance. After we played a long time, he would get tired. You could see it in his face. He could stay up for a day or two, but his game would drop off after that. Ours didn't."

Even so, Stuey said that before 1985, he rarely used cocaine while playing poker. He was just living in the fast lane, enjoying the spoils of success, and not thinking about the cost.

It would be a while yet before his lifestyle began to catch up to him.

11.

HIGH ROLLING

In the early 1980s, thanks to his back-to-back world poker titles, Stuey was probably the most famous gambler in the world. Everywhere he went, at least in gambling circles, people recognized him. Most of the time, he enjoyed the recognition, but not always.

Right after I won the second World Series of Poker, I went back to New York to see some of the old people in the neighborhood. While I was there I decided to make a visit to Atlantic City. It was the first time I'd been there since I was a kid, so it was the first time I saw what it was like with all the casinos on the boardwalk.

I was staying at Resorts when some security people came over to me while I was playing blackjack and arrested me. They accused me of being a cheater. They took me into the back and said they were detaining me for questioning. They said I had capped a bet. That means I added more chips to the wager after the cards were dealt. They said I doubled down and tried to put some more chips on the bet. It was all bullshit. Total harassment. I said, "I don't need to cheat to win." They asked me if that was true, then how was I winning all the time? I didn't answer. They were just testing me. Trying to keep the heat on. See, they knew about me. It was known in the industry that I was able to count.

I could have paid a five-hundred-dollar fine, which was nothing. It was just a misdemeanor. But I didn't want it on my record because they might use that to try and keep me out of other casinos. I mean, my whole livelihood would be threatened, ya know? To pay the fine would have been an admission of guilt. It wouldn't be good for a professional gambler to be accused of cheating and then admit to it by paying a fine. I heard later that they called some people in Las Vegas and told them I had been arrested. I guess they sent my name around to all those places. That really pissed me off. That's when I decided to fight the case.

The seeds of Stuey's problem in Atlantic City had been sown thirty years earlier, when Edward O. Thorp, a wonkish math professor from Los Angeles, proved that blackjack—the most popular casino game of all—could be beaten.

Thorp published his theories and findings in 1962, in a book called *Beat the Dealer,* which sold more than 200,000 copies and became the holy grail for an entire generation of blackjack experts who ventured to Las Vegas to strike it rich.

Thorp's system proved that, under ideal conditions, a player could overcome the inherent house advantage at the blackjack table. Thorp devised what he called a "basic strategy" for optimal blackjack play that, if followed precisely, would give a player nearly a fifty-fifty chance on every wager. But since close to even money wasn't good enough, he went further and developed an "advanced system" that didn't just neutralize the house advantage—it swung the edge in the player's favor.

Thorp's ideas were revolutionary. None more so than his breakthrough development of a technique called card counting. Thorp concluded that as cards were dealt from the deck, conditions for the player either improved or worsened. He reasoned that if a counting method could be devised that accurately measured the deck's composition at all times, players would be able to identify instances when conditions were favorable to them. At such times, they would be able to increase their advantage by increasing the size of their wager.

Thorp concluded that the composition of the deck would be in the player's favor when a disproportionate number of high-value cards were left in it. If, on the other hand, the deck was rich in low-value cards—particularly fives—the casino's advantage increased. Thus a card counter, by varying the amount of his bet depending upon whether the count was favorable or unfavorable to him, could seize control of the mathematical edge previously enjoyed by the house.

Thorp revised and perfected his methods over a period of years, and he recounted the process in his book. Oddly, he himself never made much money with his system, being less interested in the financial rewards than the academic and scientific satisfaction he derived from the exercise. Had he kept his discoveries secret, he might have made a fortune, but he made only a few visits to actual Las Vegas casinos to test his theories before going public with his findings at a conference of mathematicians in 1961.

The release of *Beat the Dealer* a short time later led to Thorp's being banned from the casinos in Las Vegas and sent a panic through the gaming industry. Casino owners feared that the book would inspire an invasion of card counters who, if unchecked, would cut deeply into their profits. As a result, they hurriedly changed the basic rules of blackjack, reducing the payouts for a blackjack from 3–2 to 6–5, and instituting other measures that effectively made it impossible to beat the games.

The results proved disastrous. Blackjack players stayed away in droves. Tables that had once been packed now stood empty. With the daily casino profits dwindling, rattled executives reversed field again, restoring the old rules. To their relief, the players came back. Obviously, the trade-off—putting up with a few card counters in exchange for the continued play of masses of relatively unenlightened gamblers who were mathematically guaranteed to lose—was one the casinos had to make.

But with hundreds of millions of dollars still at stake, the casino owners were not about to lie down for the counters. Thus, a game of cat and mouse evolved, each side trying to outsmart the other. The casino bosses felt they were entitled to kick out anyone they suspected of counting, and so, if they observed players who were watching a dealer's movements with undue concentration and then varying the size of their bets, they escorted those players out and told them in less than gentle terms not to come back.

In response, counters developed techniques for disguising what they were doing. Some acted out roles, feigning drunkenness at the table or pretending to be unfamiliar with the rules of the game. Others would make deliberately stupid plays like hitting on an 18, or standing on a soft 17—losing intentionally, in other words, to allay suspicion. Counters who had been banned by the casinos returned wearing disguises, including fake beards and mustaches. But over a period of years, these thespian performances began to wear thin, and the pit bosses started catching on.

The more sophisticated the players became at eluding detection, the more methods the casinos instituted to frustrate them. When a pit boss suspected someone of counting, he might instruct a dealer to shuffle the cards more often, thus destroying the count. Later, the casinos introduced six-deck shoes, then eight-deck shoes, all to minimize the effectiveness of card counting. They pushed the Nevada state legislature to ban the electronic devices used by some counters, and made operating one of these devices in a casino a crime punishable by imprisonment. Most effective of all, casinos began using hidden surveillance cameras above all gaming tables. The "eye in the sky" saw every movement, and security analysts would review the tapes if they suspected anything out of the ordinary. It wasn't just a game anymore. It was a war. And the methods used by the casinos rivaled the clandestine operations of law enforcement and espionage.

Certain that the future of their industry was at stake, executives pulled out all the stops in combating the threat. Eventually, their countermeasures—shuffling up, multiple-deck shoes, and constant surveillance, along with harassment—thwarted all but the most determined of Thorp's disciples.

And then someone new came along. Someone who was perhaps more dangerous to the casinos' interests than anyone since Thorp. His name was Ken Uston.

The first time I met Ken Uston was at Lake Tahoe in 1981. He came up to one of Slim's tournaments—not to play poker but to hang out. He immediately struck me with his charm. I mean, he was a fun guy to be around, and I could really talk to him. When he walked into a room, you could feel the electricity. I know that all the blackjack people thought he could walk on water.

The two of us made an instant connection. I guess it was because we had a lot of respect for each other. I knew who he was. And he knew about me—that I was the top person in my game. I guess you could say our reputations preceded each other. Gamblers are like that. We're a small, tight-knit group.

Ken Uston was a Phi Beta Kappa and magna cum laude graduate of Yale. In 1974, while working on the Pacific Stock Exchange, he received a phone call from a professional gambler who wanted to form a blackjack card-counting team. With the help of computers, Uston took Thorp's original ideas and retooled them to apply to the latest blackjack conditions created by the casinos. Years later, he told *Gambling Times:*

> I don't really consider myself a gambler. I'm more a mathematician and scientist. . . . I used to work in the stock exchange but I wouldn't put a dime in the goddamn stock market. No way in the world. . . . It's a gamble. And that's another irony. When I resigned from the stock exchange, I wrote a letter to the board explaining that, in my opinion, blackjack is a unique business. It's the only one that I know where you can actually assess the mathematical expectation of winning and losing in advance and know what those expectations are. When you open a laundromat or a brokerage house or a magazine, it's a gamble. You don't really know. But when I play blackjack, I know that in ten days I have about a ninety percent chance of doubling our bank and ten percent chance of being below that figure, and I know that if we keep going forever, we eventually have ninety-five percent chance of doubling. And I can assess one standard deviation, two standard deviations, four, and so forth. You can express it exactly mathematically. It's the only business I know of in the world where you can do that.

Uston was known for loving fast cars and pretty women. He drank the finest champagne, ate beluga caviar, and flew in Learjets all over the world. Many people, both in and out of the gambling world, confused Ken Uston with Stuey Ungar. The resemblance between the two men went beyond the similarity of their last names: they were both Jewish; they both had reputations as gambling prodigies with ferocious appetites for the high life; they had both left the East Coast to mine the neon desert's millions—and they had both succeeded beyond their wildest dreams. Not only that, but they looked alike—slender with brown curly hair.

One respect in which Uston differed from Stuey was that he always knew what he was doing. Every action was deliberate. Between his trips to Atlantic City and Monte Carlo, Uston was always on the lookout for an edge, any edge, however small.

His contribution to card-counting theory was an advance on previous methods, but his stroke of genius was the formation of a team, a group of trained counters willing to pool their money so they could withstand the inevitable swings of the big-bet technique that he was proposing.

The teams typically launched a hit-and-run approach, renting a room in a dive motel, then invading the floor of the target casino like a swarm of wasps. The hand spotters would play for small amounts, counting cards but not varying their bets or showing any of the other obvious signs of being a counter. When the count was favorable, they would signal the "big player," usually Uston in some sort of disguise, who would swoop in and make an enormous bet. Uston described their adventures in his book *The Big Player*, published in 1977. Several years later, his methods were copied and perfected by a group calling themselves the "M.I.T. Blackjack Team," whose exploits were chronicled in 2002 in a best-selling book, *Bringing Down the House*.

Uston's blackjack teams racked up astronomical wins. When casinos were legalized in Atlantic City in 1978, Uston's counters and other teams found a new and fertile territory in which to ply their trade. By the time Stuey showed up in 1982, card-counting paranoia had set in.

The first time I played blackjack, I was fourteen years old. It was back in New York. There were underground games all over town, mainly around lower Manhattan, where the law was greased in tight and there wasn't a chance in hell the place would get busted.

Back then I didn't know anything about counting. I'd never heard of Thorp. Uston was still in college. But the game fascinated me. It was fast. I mean, if I went to the track I had to wait twenty minutes till the next race. But with blackjack, you lose one hand and bam! Twenty seconds later they deal a new hand. Now that's action!

I have to admit that I usually lost at those places in New York. It wasn't until I moved to Las Vegas that I understood how much money could be made at blackjack. I started playing seriously a few years after I came into town. That was when I found out about card counting. For me, it was easy remembering cards. And it didn't take me very long to figure out one thing: What if a player didn't need to memorize a point count? What if I didn't need an electronic device in my shoe to count the cards? What if I could just remember how many cards were exposed and how many were left in the deck?

According to most psychologists, a "photographic" memory is more myth than reality, but some people do have an extraordinary ability to see, then remember, long strings of numbers or names after only a very brief exposure to them. Stuey was such a person.

He once sat down at a vacant poker table, surrounded by dozens of players, dealers, floor men, and a skeptical casino owner named Bob Stupak who had bet that Stuey couldn't count down two full decks. Counting down a deck essentially means watching the cards as they come off the deck and then, as you reach the last few cards, being able to determine which cards are left. As Stuey watched, a dealer turned over one card after another, a whirlwind of suits and ranks flashing before his eyes. When one card was left in the shoe, the dealer stopped. Stuey paused, closed his eyes, then said, "I'm pretty sure it's the ten of dia-monds." As everyone leaned forward, card number 104 was slid out of the shoe and turned over. It was the ten of diamonds.

I hired an attorney. Kenny Hance was his name. He was a brilliant lawyer, the best in the business. It wound up costing me $50,000 in legal fees to beat a $500 rap in the Resorts' case. Can you believe that? Not only that, but I had to fly back and forth from Vegas to New Jersey seven times because they had to take testimony from me.

In the end, I beat them, I beat the casino. They couldn't prove I was cheating. The judge laughed at their case, what they were trying to pin on me. They made fools out of themselves. The court decided that what I was doing, which was counting cards, wasn't a violation of the law; that is, it wasn't cheating. I think the casinos pushed it because they were trying to send a message—we can't ban you, but we're going to make life miserable for you if you try to play here. So it cost me $50,000 to play their game. In the end, the truth is, I lost. I lost and the casino lost. I guess the only ones who made out were the lawyers. Kenny wanted me to file a defamation of character suit against Resorts for what they did to me. But I didn't want to go through with it. I'd spent enough time on airplanes and inside court-rooms. There's no action there.

The experience was dispiriting to Stuey; he insisted that the legal battle had cost him a chance to win his third World Series of Poker in 1982. "I was so fucking tired from all the flying back and forth that I couldn't focus on anything else," he said.

Following the civil trial, Stuey's blackjack jaunts became increas-ingly rare. They were too much of a legal risk and not worth the hassle.

Besides, blackjack was a more methodical and mechanical game than poker. It wasn't gambling in the purest sense, which is what Stuey really wanted and enjoyed. It was a grinder's game.

Eventually, Uston's counting teams were worn down and disbanded. The heat from casino surveillance was constant. There were even reports that some casinos were resorting to physical violence against known counters. A few of the counters filed suit against the casinos for bodily injury. (Stuey was far from the only one who had legal problems.) Ken Uston wound up taking his case all the way to the New Jersey supreme court, where he won a landmark decision.

But Uston's legal triumph was just a fleeting moment. Although he established his reputation as the most dangerous blackjack player in the world, Ken Uston died a premature death in October 1987. It was a haunting omen for Stuey—Uston's body was found in a seedy hotel room in Paris, the cause of his death a mystery to this day.

Like a lot of gamblers, Stuey would bet on just about anything. Ask him which drop of water on a windowpane was going to make it to the bottom first, and more than likely he'd be willing to put some money on it. Bob Stupak, the man who bet that Stuey couldn't count down a two-deck shoe, challenged the reigning world champ to a heads-up freeze-out (winner-take-all) no-limit hold'em match for $10,000 apiece in cash. The $10,000 was chump change to both men, but when the cards were dealt, the game was about something more serious than money.

Stupak was one of Vegas's most colorful characters. Born in Pittsburgh in 1942, he came to Vegas with big dreams. He became a nightclub singer and cut several singles as "Bobby Star," then started a thriving business selling two-for-one coupon books to tourists. Eventually he made enough money to start his own casino, Bob Stupak's Vegas World, which quickly became a monument to his promotional genius.

What set "the Polish maverick" apart from other CEOs and gambling executives was that he was as action-crazy as the customers he coveted. He scheduled outrageous contests, tournaments, and special events; gave away prizes like Rolls-Royces at poker tournaments; and in his free time indulged in what he liked best: gambling and playing poker.

Stupak prided himself on his skill at poker, but while he did win some tournaments, he was probably better known for his wacky image and seemingly inexhaustible bankroll. Of his many feats, his proudest accomplishment was beating Mike Caro's ORAC, a poker-playing computer, in a $500,000 heads-up match in 1980. Stupak claimed that he was willing to face any player—even the world poker champion—for a bet of any size.

The heads-up match against Stuey took place on Stupak's home turf at Vegas World. Each player was given a full rack of black chips. In thirty minutes, Stuey had all of Stupak's chips, a $10,000 win. Stupak accompanied Stuey over to the cashier's cage, and as the two men waited in line for Stuey to cash out, they started pitching the black $100 chips against the wall—closest to the wall wins. Stuey was willing to fade Stupak's action on credit in a game that he had played in his youth for pennies. By the time the cage window was free, the two gamblers were so absorbed in the action that cashing out was forgotten.

"Let's make it five hundred a toss," Stupak said.

"Bet," Stuey said.

One of the chips hit the wall and bounded astray, rolling across the floor and under a nearby table. The two grown men scrambled around on the casino carpet like a couple of kids.

"Let's make it a thousand a toss," Stupak suggested.

"Bet," Stuey said.

Stuey had no idea that Stupak had hustled his schoolmates out of their lunch money pitching coins when he was a kid back in Pittsburgh—and that even in Vegas he still practiced regularly. It was a straight-up hustle. Within minutes, Stupak had won back the full rack from Stuey. "Fuck it," Stuey said, realizing that he'd been taken.

When it came to gambling purely for the sake of gambling, if Stuey had a rival, it was Jack "Treetop" Straus. Brunson and the rest of them wagered high, but they were always taking a calculated risk. Straus, like Stuey, gambled for the sheer joy of it. Legend has it that Straus needed to have 110 percent of his bankroll in action every single day. Betting his last $1,000 or $100,000, Straus gambled heroically. "Better to spend one day as a lion than a lifetime as a lamb," he was fond of saying.

Straus was truly an anomaly among the professionals. In a world of cutthroats, where suckers were never given an even break, Straus had a heart. He had been born in San Antonio, Texas, and he was nicknamed "Treetop" because he stood six feet seven inches and was a star basketball player at Texas A&M in the late 1950s. At sixteen, he won a car in a poker game. But it was his character more than anything else that came to define him. He was downright chivalrous. One recipient of his largesse, a young business owner who walked into the poker room at the Golden Nugget late one evening in 1982, described his encounter with Straus: "I walked to this table in the back of the room. There was a little guy; a big, heavy guy with horn-rimmed glasses; a Chinese guy; a chubby blond-haired guy; and this tall guy with a cowboy hat," the executive recalled. "At the time, I had no idea who they were. Later, I found out it was Stu Ungar, Doyle Brunson, Johnny Chan, Chip Reese, and Jack Straus. Anyway, I looked at the game and saw all these black chips flyin' and I just had to get in."

The young man, who had recently inherited his father's business, didn't know a thing about Texas Hold'em, but he went to the cashier's cage and bought $20,000 in chips.

"I went back to the table and asked, 'Is there a seat open?' They said,

'Yeah, come on in.' So I sat down in the game. In less than an hour, my whole twenty thousand was gone. I got up and walked back to the cage. Well, I was standing in line, getting ready to take another twenty thousand out of the box, and a strange thing happened. The big tall guy in the cowboy hat, who'd been in the game, was suddenly standing there next to me. I don't know where he came from. He must have followed me over. He tapped me on the shoulder and said, 'Hey, partner, I've got something to tell ya. But don't let anybody know, okay?'

" 'Okay,' I said. 'What is it?'

"He looked me straight in the eye and said, 'Don't buy back into that game. You can't beat it, because it's no-limit hold'em and those are the best five players in the world sitting right over there. You haven't got a chance, brother.'

"I later found out that the tall cowboy was Jack Straus. Most people in Las Vegas would have milked me for everything I had. But not Jack Straus. He wasn't that kind of man. He was a generous man with compassion and character."

In 1982, in the World Series of Poker, Stuey busted out early. He wasn't generally one to socialize in public at the big events. He liked to say that he wasn't there to make friends; he was there to get the money. And when he busted out of a tournament, he usually beat a hasty retreat. But on this occasion, he hung around because Jack Straus was a friend of his, and Straus ended up making it to the final table.

In those days, the crowd wasn't roped off the way it is today. There were no barriers between the players and the crowd. In fact, spectators were practically breathing down the players' necks. On the final day, Straus was dressed in a dapper suit and collared shirt. Directly behind him were Brunson and Stuey, his personal cheering section.

At one point, earlier in the tournament, Straus had moved all his chips into the pot and lost the hand. Thinking he was out, he got up from the table; but as he was leaving, the dealer noticed that he still had one green $25 chip left that had been covered up by a cocktail napkin. So Straus sat down again. The next hand he bet his single remaining chip and won the hand, the start of the most amazing comeback in the history of the WSOP. On the final day, as Stuey and Doyle rooted for him, Straus completed his remarkable journey, from which sprang the hoping-for-a-miracle refrain, "a chip and a chair," now commonly invoked by short-stacked tournament players the world over.

The win was a fitting reward for the bighearted giant, although how much money he won was purely academic. Most of the bundles of cash found their way to the sportsbook the next day, and the rest was lost on the golf course. Not many people could compete with the gambling theatrics of Straus, but Stuey would certainly give him a run for his money—especially on the golf course.

Nowhere in Las Vegas did the high rollers gamble higher than on the eighteen-hole emerald-green oases that looked so out of place in the bronze desert sand. Never mind poker and blackjack, golf was a betting man's dream. Benjamin "Bugsy" Siegel had planned to build Las Vegas's first golf course behind his crown jewel, the Flamingo, in the 1940s, but before he was able to realize his ambitions for it or the Flamingo, he was gunned down in a hail of bullets through the window of his mansion in Los Angeles. In 1952, the Las Vegas Country Club opened, and the course there was soon followed by golf courses at the Desert Inn and the Dunes.

Jack Straus took Stuey out to the Las Vegas Country Club one morning to teach him a few things about the game. Stuey had never held a golf club before, but he'd heard about the big-money games that Jack and Doyle and the rest of them were playing, and he was dying to get in on the action. In particular, his appetite had been whetted by stories about the drug lord Jimmy Chagra, aka "Dope Man," who showed up in Vegas ready to gamble his dirty millions. In one match against Puggy Pearson at the Las Vegas Country Club, Chagra lost $180,000. Stuey couldn't wait for his turn, but as was pointed out to him, it might be helpful if he knew how to play.

Straus showed Stuey the basic grip, and then watched him take a few ugly practice swings. He figured that maybe the best place to start was on the practice putting green, a small patch of close-shaven grass near the clubhouse. Straus tried to explain to Stuey the importance of putting and how critical a smooth touch was around the greens. Within minutes, his pupil had grown bored with the tutelage.

"How much if I sink this putt?" Stuey screamed across the putting green. Straus looked up, shaking his head at Stuey's egregious lack of etiquette. The hollering brought frowns from the other golfers.

"How much?" Stuey persisted.

"A hundred bucks says you miss it," Straus said in a stage whisper.

Before long, the two friends and rivals were betting $200 a putt, then $1,000, and then even more. As they putted for thousands, Stuey ripped the air with his putter when he missed and screamed profanities that carried all the way back to the clubhouse. In two hours, he lost $80,000.

"Do you think that anyone in history has ever lost $80,000 the first time he picked up a golf club?" Mike Sexton said later. "And he didn't even make it onto the golf course that day!"

When he did eventually make it onto the course, Stuey was a sight to behold. He always wore white golf gloves on both hands, pulled tightly over his wrists; double-knit polyester pants; and ridiculous shirts. Think of Rodney Dangerfield in *Caddyshack*. Whenever Stuey missed a shot—which was often—he jumped up and down and fell to the ground screaming. Though his playing partners may have been older and out of shape, they were skilled golfers. Brunson, for example, frequently shot in the high seventies. Pearson, Slim, and the rest also played well—especially with money on the line. Since they all knew that Stuey couldn't play, they gave him outrageous handicaps: dozens of strokes spread across eighteen holes in an attempt to give him a chance.

"We always had to spot Stuey a lot of strokes," Brunson said. "There were ways of making bets where you knew you were going to win even though you spotted a lot of strokes."

The advantages they gave Stuey included letting him hit more than one ball, letting him hit from the ladies' tees (which usually were twenty or thirty yards closer to the pin), and letting him tee up the ball from wherever it might land—the middle of the fairway, a sand trap, a dry creek bed. Stuey, in fact, concocted a whole collection of tees for different lies, some short and some with long spikes to prop up the ball for an easier shot. Never mind that he would still hack at it hopelessly, spraying it all over the place.

"If it was rainin' soup, Stuey'd be out in it with a fork," Amarillo Slim said of Stuey's ill-advised golf ventures.

Brunson remembered the first time he and a couple of other gamblers went out on a course with Stuey. Brunson was a longtime golfer, and he expected Stuey to have some sense of respect for what was a gentlemen's game.

On the first tee, Brunson coiled back and cracked the little white sphere with every ounce of strength in his mammoth frame. The ball rocketed through the dense morning haze, bouncing down the center of the fairway and coming to rest 250 yards away.

Next, it was Stuey's turn. He gripped his driver like he was holding on for dear life, jerked back the club, and slashed at the ball with all the grace of a mechanical toy. The ball whizzed off the tee, never going more than a few feet off the ground, sliced off to the right, and splashed into a muddy creek bed.

Normally, a shot like that would be forgotten and the player would take a penalty shot and drop a new ball off to the side. But Stuey couldn't stand losing a stroke. So he found his ball in the middle of the large mud puddle, reached into his bag, and pulled out a metal tee the length of a shish kebob skewer.

"You can't do that!" Brunson protested.

"Whaddya mean I can't?" Stuey replied, as he rolled up his pants and began wading through the foot-deep pond. He reached down and lifted his ball out, then placed it on his absurd extended tee. Stuey then took a hacking swing at the ball, topping it straight down into the mud. He teed up again, and took another hack. Before long, Stuey was covered head to toe in mud. By that time Brunson and the others were bent over double with laughter.

"Ah, fuck it," Stuey said, joining in the laughter.

Stuey had no conception of golf etiquette. There were no provisions in his world of golf for marking a ball or trying to avoid stepping on someone's line. "He'd walk right across your line and shoot whenever he wanted to," Sexton said. "But everybody had such a fun time with him and he was such an action player that nobody cared."

On one occasion, Straus and Stuey combined their bankrolls and played as a team. They agreed to a "best ball" match with Brunson at the Dunes golf course. The bet was that Straus and Stuey would each hit a shot, then play the better ball. Brunson, playing alone, would be permitted to hit only a single ball. Since Brunson was the better golfer, it seemed like a balanced wager. The bet was $50,000 for the entire eighteen-hole match.

"Jack wasn't much of a player and Stuey was just awful," Brunson said. "I wound up having to give them even more of a handicap. So on top of them getting to play best ball, they got to hit from the ladies' tees." Knowing Stuey's mischievous ways, Brunson always had to keep an eye on the pint-size duffer. There was no such worry with Jack, whose integrity was unquestioned. But Stuey was likely to do just about anything to win. He'd kick his ball down the fairway when Doyle wasn't looking, or magically find an errant ball on the edge of the fairway, announcing, "It must have bounced off a tree."

"Everybody knew he was lying, but how could you prove it?" Brunson said.

After a couple of holes, Stuey, Jack, and Doyle, arguably the three highest-stakes gamblers ever to inhabit one space, became bored with the stakes of $50,000 for the entire match. So they started betting $10,000 a hole, then $20,000. Straus played over his head that day, while Brunson had an off day. Meanwhile, Stuey occasionally cracked a lucky shot or sank a short putt. The match was tied as they drove up to the tee box on the final hole.

They agreed to double the bet. They would wager $40,000 on the hole, plus the $50,000 they already had riding on the match. The single hole was now worth $90,000 to Brunson and $45,000 apiece to Stuey and Straus.

By this time, word about the match had circulated throughout the clubhouse. The news had even hit the poker room at the Dunes. Several of the poker players had run over to the course to catch a glimpse of the big golf match and were sitting up on the edge of the green watching—and placing their own bets. There was also a caravan of golf carts following the threesome. One of the many witnesses that day was Phil "Doc" Earle, a high-stakes poker player from Houston who really was a doctor and was a close friend of Straus. Earle would later become an important person in Stuey's life.

"Stuey and Jack somehow got the ball on the green and made par," said Earle. "Doyle had to make par to tie. Now, let me tell you something. Doyle Brunson is the greatest money putter that ever lived. He's better than Nicklaus, Watson, and all the rest. When they're putting for money, I'll take Doyle over anybody. I'm serious. You could put all the money in the world on one putt, and I'll take Doyle over Jack Nicklaus in his prime. There isn't a nerve in that man's body."

Straus had made a long putt, forcing Brunson to two-putt for the tie. His ball was resting on the edge of the green, at least forty feet away from the hole. It was a long and difficult putt, down a slope and curving to the left. A two-putt would have been acceptable, even for a tournament professional. A three-putt would cost Brunson the match. He sized up the putt and calmly leaned over the ball. He practiced his stroke a couple of times, then backed off and studied the line again from behind the ball. Then he took his putting stance again, and stroked the ball smoothly and confidently. It took a slight curve to the left as it rolled over a hump in the green, then raced faster toward the hole, picking up speed with each rotation. Then it slowed down again as it neared the hole, and just as it appeared to be stopping, disappeared from sight with a soft *blup-blup* as it settled into the bottom of the cup.

"That putt was the most incredible thing I've ever seen," Earle said. "It traveled across a couple of time zones—and Doyle just hit it like he was killing time on the practice green. You would never have known there was all that money riding on it."

Stuey started jumping up and down like someone on a pogo stick, hurling his club far down the fairway. "He went off like a rocket," Earle said. "There was a profusion of elegant profanity that came out of his mouth, which is impossible to repeat but was beautiful to behold. He was just out of his mind, running around that green like a spindle top."

Brunson smiled and calmly said, "I think you boys owe me some money."

The three men returned to the clubhouse, click-clacking their way into the locker room in their golf spikes, Stuey still muttering profanities. They sat down by the lockers.

"Ah, don't worry about it, Stuey," Straus said. "We'll get it back."

Stuey stared ahead numbly, and began removing his shoes. Straus opened up his locker and realized that something was very wrong.

"Stuey, where's our money?" Straus asked.

"Huh? I-I-I don't know. I thought you had it, Jack."

Straus dug through his clothes looking for the brown paper bag filled with money that he had brought to the club. The bag contained $50,000—the sum of his and Stuey's combined bankrolls for the golf match.

"I sure hope you boys haven't misplaced my money," Brunson said.

Straus went from locker to locker, opening and slamming shut the metal doors, each empty locker raising the level of his panic. Nothing. No bag, no money.

"Wait a minute, did you check your locker? Which one is yours?" Straus asked Stuey.

Stuey shrugged. He went over to the corner and held up a finger, considering. "I think this is it."

"The one without the lock?"

Stuey nodded and swung open the door. There, sitting at the bottom, was a plain brown grocery sack.

Straus was flabbergasted. "You left the money in there without locking it?"

"Look at this damn door," Stuey said. "It's broken. It won't even shut. Can you believe it?"

Stuey reached in and pulled out the paper bag. It had been there for four hours, with the door half open. Miraculously, no one had touched it.

Straus and Stuey handed the bundles of money to Brunson. They promised to pay him the balance later. Brunson didn't use a paper sack; he had a vinyl gym bag. He put the money in, zipped it up, and slung the bag over his shoulder.

What would we have done if the money hadn't shown up? After crying a little we would have just said fuck it and moved on. We lost that one and would have to come up with a couple of hundred thousand somewhere else.

Jack and I would have gone to our box and gotten together some money and then played in a poker game and got it back that way. I always had good recuperative powers.

All those guys I used to hang out with, we really loved each other. We were like brothers. But when we got to gambling, we took off the gloves. It was like a fistfight. We hated each other, we all wanted to win so bad.

One time Puggy [Pearson] and I were playing backgammon. I beat him so bad he wanted to hit me. They had to grab him so he wouldn't strike me. See, when I play against a person, I have to find something I don't like about them. With Puggy, it's arrogance. He can really set you off. He really gets under your skin. He'll beat you out of a pot, then look at you like he's fucking Einstein, like he really outplayed you in the hand, when the fact is anyone would have played the hand the exact same way. Like, one time, he got pocket aces and I had pocket kings. The aces held up and he gave me that look like what a fucking idiot you are. That little smart-assed smile used to drive me crazy.

Stuey and his group of gamblers were caught in a permanent state of adolescence, always trying to one-up one another with some new hustle or proposition. Whether it was shooting hoops against Amarillo Slim in a $500-a-shot game of H-O-R-S-E or betting a grand on whose suitcase would come off the conveyor belt first at the airport baggage claim, Stuey was always in search of a new challenge, a new kick.

Backgammon became a craze in the early 1980s, and though Stuey had played only a few times, against amateurs, he arranged a match when he heard that Roger Low, one of the top three backgammon players in the world, was in town.

They played at a suite in Caesars Palace, and though Low won, he said afterward, "I was amazed at how good Ungar became. As we were playing, he got better and better, game by game, hour by hour. It was one

NOLAN DALLA AND PETER ALSON

of the most amazing things I've ever seen in backgammon. Ungar was just a natural at anything to do with numbers or progressions."

In 1984, Stuey went to the Bicycle Club, a new card room that had just opened in the L.A. warehouse district, Bell Gardens. Card clubs were becoming big business in L.A. They had first sprung up in Gardena. Then, as municipalities struggled for tax revenues, card clubs spread to other communities, including Commerce, Inglewood, Compton, and Bell Gardens. At the time, "the Bike," as it was called by patrons, was the premier card club. It had more than a hundred poker tables in a clean, well-appointed room.

Stuey, upon hearing that the big games were happening in California, took the forty-five-minute flight from Las Vegas to LAX, but on his way to the Bike's poker tables, he noticed a game called pan that he had not seen before. It was one of the so-called Asian games (later called California games to avoid the racial connotation) that were gaining some popularity among a segment of the gambling population. Pan was a casino game that was a variation of rummy, in which players had to form melds. Never mind that the odds favored the house in every situation, Stuey was intrigued by it, and certain that he could beat the game.

The first night, he played for four hours and lost $10,000.

The next day, he returned and won $17,000. One of the floor men had watched the turnaround and asked Stuey how he managed to reverse his luck and actually win money at a game that supposedly wasn't beatable.

Stuey responded by saying that he had gone back to his hotel room the night before and stayed up all night dealing to himself, hand after hand, absorbing the intricacies of the game and trying to determine an edge. He returned with much greater knowledge, was blessed with a good run of cards, and managed to cut into the house edge.

Mastering games of chance was easy for Stuey. Coping with the other elements of life would prove far more difficult.

12.

CARDS IN THE AIR

Madeline and Stuey had twin Jaguars. They lived in a beautiful home, had two children (two-year-old Stefanie and thirteen-year-old Richie) and seemingly every material comfort that a couple barely into their thirties could want. Inside the house on Coventry Lane, however, things were less happy than they appeared from the outside.

By 1984, Stuey and Madeline were fighting constantly. His disappearances and infidelities, his utter lack of consideration, and his financial irresponsibility made him nearly impossible to live with, even for Madeline, who well understood, and had a high level of tolerance for, the man she had married. The strain of making constant allowances for Stuey just began to take a toll.

The more we fought, the better the relationship was in some ways. Sexually, anyway. I was very jealous with Madeline. I always wanted her to be there for me. But I wasn't there for her very often.

. . .

As the marriage crumbled, Stuey took to crashing in the apartments of friends and associates or staying in hotels. Most of the time, he was impossible to reach. Still, he would drop by at the house on occasion to spend time with Stefanie and Richie, before disappearing again for days on end.

Eventually, he rented a town house apartment at the Las Vegas Country Club, a gated community of condos and McMansions in the shadow of the Hilton. He warned Madeline not to be surprised if she called and a girl picked up the phone. At first, despite such indignities, Madeline weathered the separation with resolve, but after the house on Coventry Lane was broken into by robbers wearing ski masks one night while she was alone in her bedroom, she fell apart.

Coventry Lane was in one of the nicer sections of town, but Las Vegas was notorious for its high crime rate, and Madeline had actually been fortunate: during the course of the break-in Richie had returned from a run to 7-Eleven, and with the help of a neighbor scared off the robbers before they could get to the bedroom where Stefanie was sleeping. Even so, the incident was traumatic. Madeline had been bound with duct tape and terrorized, and she suffered what she realized, in retrospect, was something of a nervous breakdown. "I never went back in that bedroom again," she said. "I slept on the couch after that, with a bottle of vodka next to me to knock myself out."

Stuey got sick to his stomach when he heard about the break-in, but it didn't change things for him. He didn't move back. In a way, all of Madeline's feelings of loss were funneled into the fear and paranoia brought on by the robbery. It took her a year or more to get past the trauma—and she was able to do so only after being commanded to "get over it" by her mother. "That was what I needed to hear," Madeline recalled.

Underlying the split was the unalterable fact that Stuey's first and only true love would always be gambling—and because of that, the people closest to him would wind up taking a backseat.

By the time Madeline filed for divorce on July 18, 1986, she and Stuey had been separated for nearly two years, and the rawness of the initial split had healed to a great extent. They had always been great friends and cared about each other. As Stefanie would reflect many years later about her mother and father, "They were like brother and sister. It was a different kind of relationship."

The day of the divorce, which was not contested, Stuey and Madeline went into the office of their lawyer, Steve Stein, holding hands. Since children and possessions were involved, it was up to the judge to render a decision about custody and child support payments. Surprisingly, Stuey was awarded the house on Coventry Lane. The judge ruled that since Stuey had purchased the house by his own means before the marriage, it belonged to him, and would remain in his possession, although he would have to give Madeline a cash settlement for it. Despite the ruling, Stuey agreed to let Madeline continue living in the house; he was fine where he was for the time being. The two remained close and continued to have contact; their lives were entwined by their feelings for each other and their love for Richie and Stefanie.

In 1984, Stuey had shown up for his fifth World Series of Poker. He rarely played the early, smaller buy-in events at tournaments. They usually didn't interest him, as he considered them a less than worthwhile use of his time. But in 1984, he entered the $1,000 buy-in seven-card-stud event against 124 other competitors and finished second to Ken "Skyhawk" Flaton. The next day, in only the seventh WSOP event he'd ever played, a $5,000 buy-in seven-card-stud contest, he went on a tear and won it, collecting $110,000 and his third gold bracelet.

This was to be his last major tournament win for three years. After a phenomenal run between 1980 and 1984, in which he won two world titles, three bracelets, and several smaller majors, Stuey ran into a cold spell in tournament poker, largely the result of playing so few events combined with his obsessive indulgence in other gambling pursuits, like golf, sports betting, blackjack, and backgammon. Although Stuey continued to make money in side games, his tournament record—for a player of his talent—did not measure up to expectations.

Sports betting took up the bulk of Stuey's time. On any given day, it was common for him to bet every single game on the board. Whether it was a dozen baseball games in the middle of the week or the entire NFL slate on a Sunday, Stuey sometimes had as much as $10,000 riding on every major sporting event of the day. His obsession—there is no other word for it—had him spending countless hours each day running back and forth between betting windows and television screens, and kept him out of card rooms for extended periods. In a sense, playing cards had become a grind, a chore that demanded too much energy, time, and concentration. Beating the bookies was more of a challenge for him: he had less control, and therefore he found it more exciting.

Before he and Madeline separated, Stuey had spent a lot of time watching games at their house, along with Richie. He had one room that was set up like a sportsbook, with five television sets and a satellite dish. He'd sleep late, then put on his bathrobe, eat a bowl of Sugar Pops, and tune in to five different games that he had bet on, Richie right there beside him.

Watching a sporting event with Stuey was an experience. Every base hit or fumble took on galactic significance. Screams of "fuck" and "goddamnit" were commonplace, and people tended to give him a wide berth when he was in a casino sportsbook. But because Stuey's business was so desirable, complaints by other patrons fell on deaf ears. Management was always going to cater to its best customer.

"When President Reagan was shot in 1981," said Mike Sexton, "it happened to coincide with the day of the NCAA basketball finals between Indiana and Louisville. While even the most degenerate gamblers wanted to get the latest news about Reagan, Stuey insisted that the televisions be kept tuned to the game. So they were."

I have no control when I'm betting on a game. I'm like a prisoner trapped in front of the TV. It really brings the emotion out. When I see somebody do something in a game that costs me $50,000, I get pretty bad sometimes. I really don't like it when people are around and I'm in action. It ain't a pretty sight. Doyle once said I was the biggest steamer. I am—if he means steaming in the sportsbook. Nobody can steam there like me.

Madeline had seen him at his worst when they were living together. She said, "He had a terrible temper. One time in New York, he threw all of Richie's toys out the window after he lost. He was really apologetic afterward. He bought him a bunch of new toys, but for half an hour after losing a game, he would be ranting and raving, talking about the game, how this guy should have done this, or that guy should have done that, and then half an hour later he'd be over it. Really over it. But you didn't want to be around him for that first half hour."

Stuey, like all sports bettors, got eaten up by the vig—the 10 percent commission that bookies charged on all losing bets. So he and Doyle Brunson, who was also a big sports bettor, figured out a way around the juice: they decided to book each other's action.

A daily ritual began in which Stuey would call Doyle and they would go down the day's betting lines and make picks. During the baseball season, Doyle would get the early lines and write them down on his line sheet; then, when Stuey called, they'd take turns picking a side. For instance, Stuey would take the Padres against the Dodgers—leaving Doyle, regardless of whether he actually liked the Dodgers or not, stuck with them. In turn, Doyle would get the pick on the next game, leaving Stuey with the other side. They'd cover all the games and routinely bet $10,000 a game, occasionally even $15,000 or $20,000.

Astoundingly, Stuey wasn't betting just with Brunson. He would also go and bet the same games at the sportsbooks, particularly if he didn't like his side in his bets with Brunson. Stuey's betting relationship with Brunson was complicated, because Brunson and Chip Reese also occasionally let Stuey in on a particularly strong play. Brunson and Reese used computer models to pick games, and later became partners with another poker player and big-time sports gambler, Dewey Tomko, to form a sports betting operation called Linemovers that actually moved and manipulated betting lines.

"One afternoon," Brunson said, "Stuey and I were playing golf. I gave him some games I liked a lot and he put everything he had on them. He scattered bets all over town. When it was over, Stuey collected close to $700,000. That was one of his biggest paydays. Of course, some of that money was also from other bets that we'd made with each other."

When Stuey won big, he'd meet Doyle at the bank, and Doyle would pay his debt in cash—a couple of hundred grand or more in a paper grocery sack. One time, Stuey took a taxi home after one of these exchanges. The driver asked him if he'd been to the grocery store. "Yeah," Stuey said. "I got lots of milk and eggs."

The transfer of astronomical sums of money posed obvious logistical difficulties—at least when it involved a casino rather than one of Stuey's buddies. By law, all cash transactions over $10,000 had to be reported to the IRS, but Stuey figured a way around this by taking his wins in sport chips, large-denomination chips used specifically for wagering. Instead of dealing with large, bulky bundles of cash, not to mention having to fill out financial reports, Stuey would simply pocket a handful of $5,000 clay chips. A person could easily walk around with $100,000 in one pocket that way. Since Stuey knew he was going to put the money back into play the next day anyway, there was no point in getting involved in the paperwork that an actual cash transaction would necessitate. The sport chips were like Monopoly money.

The other way Stuey would get around IRS rules was by spreading his wagers around town. Three thousand at Caesars; $4,000 at the Stardust; $5,000 at the Hilton. Then, if he really liked a game and Doyle wasn't around to take his action, he'd take another whirl around town, betting on the same team again, catching taxi rides from casino to casino.*

The betting merry-go-round presented Stuey with some interesting opportunities to wager on middles. A middle is created when a betting line moves sufficiently to allow a bettor to take both sides of a bet with a chance to win both bets. For example, if the Rams started out as six-point favorites but were subsequently bet up to seven-and-a-half-point favorites, an early bet on the Rams, matched by a later bet against them, would create a middle whereby, if the Rams won the game by seven points, a bettor would win both sides of the bet with only a minimal risk on his part, since all he could lose is the 10 percent vig if the game didn't land on seven. Stuey would often go back to a casino where he made a bet in the morning to find that by afternoon, the line had moved enough for him to play a middle. More than a few times, he played this angle and made large wins. While his wagers were sometimes reckless and based on nothing more than a whim, there were also times when he looked for savvy opportunities to exploit a weakness in the betting lines.

---

* Even though Stuey owned several expensive cars, he didn't like to drive and almost always took taxis. Since an average taxi ride from downtown to the Strip cost about $20, the fares could add up in a hurry. "Stuey's taxi bills alone were probably higher than what most people make in a year," Mike Sexton said.

During the mid-1980s, Stuey's fortunes fluctuated wildly. He won and lost huge sums of money, and went broke a number of times. Even when he was broke, it was common for him to have bundles of cash at his disposal, although the situation was different from what it had been when he was a stake horse for the mob. With Victor Romano and Tony Spilotro dead, he could no longer count on them for backing. It was true that Philly Brush continued to manage some of Stuey's affairs, and he remained a trusted adviser to Stuey, but Philly wasn't around as much as he had been. He was married and had his own life.

Instead, Stuey became increasingly reliant on other gamblers, particularly other poker players, to help keep him in action when he was tapped out. There was no shortage of people eager to back him, since he was always a favorite to win. It took little more than a phone call on Stuey's part to find someone willing to put up $20,000 or more in return for an agreed-upon percentage of his profits. In tournaments, Stuey would be on a "free roll"—meaning that he was playing for half of the win, without having to risk any of his own money. He was doing the heavy lifting, after all, so it was only fair for his backer to assume the financial risk and absorb any losses.

Fred "Sarge" Ferris backed Stuey several times, as did Doyle Brunson and Chip Reese. But it was Billy Baxter who gradually assumed the role of Stuey's main backer. The two had met at the Dunes in the mid-1970s. Although they were both gamblers, Stuey and Baxter were nearly polar opposites in their approach to risk. Baxter was an investor, who pursued gambling the way an astute financier buys stock or bonds. Baxter, who comes from Augusta, Georgia, and is the consummate southern gentleman, approached gambling propositions carefully and methodically, like any good businessman.

Baxter himself was an accomplished poker player, whose résumé would grow to include six gold bracelets in the WSOP, most of them coming from his dominance in the ace-to-five lowball events. Baxter's

Alongside Doyle Brunson (left) and
Jack Binion (right), Stuey smiles for
the cameras in 1980 following his first
World Series of Poker championship.

Stuey, with Jack Straus and two
showgirls, after winning the Jack
Straus Heads-Up Championships at
the Frontier Casino in 1983.

"Amarillo Slim" Preston (left) and Stuey, with two Caesars Palace employees, after Stuey's third win at Amarillo Slim's Super Bowl of Poker, Caesars Palace, Las Vegas, 1989.

Stuey checks the odds of the day's sporting events, at home on Coventry Lane, 1980.

The Ungar family's home on the cul-de-sac on Coventry Lane in East Las Vegas.

Richie (age twelve) holds his baby sister, Stefanie (three months), Christmas 1982.

Madeline Ungar at Caesars Palace, 1986.

Stefanie and Stuey celebrate her eighth birthday in Florida, November 1990.

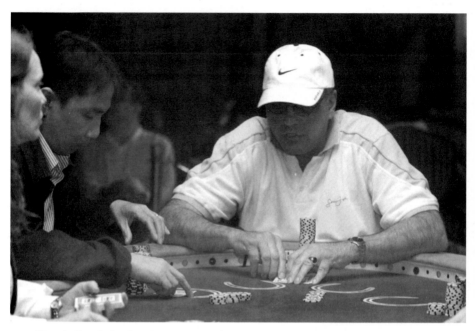

"Baseball Mike" Salem became one of Stuey's closest pals in the mid-1980s. The decadelong friendship was cemented by countless days and nights betting, watching sports, and living in the fast lane.

Part mystic, part genius, part eccentric philosopher, and poker obsessed, Phil "Doc" Earle was one of many friends who tried to intervene and motivate Stuey to get help.

Stuey's most loyal backer, Billy Baxter, also a high-stakes poker player with several major tournament wins.

Richie Ungar on the night of his high school prom. He committed suicide shortly after this photograph was taken.

Stuey with Stefanie, relaxing at home during the summer of 1990.

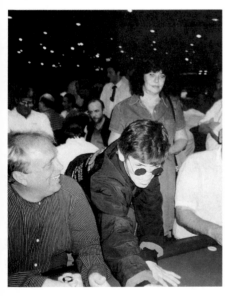

Stuey receives best wishes from Chip Reese (left) and Marsha Wagonner (standing) in the high-limit section of the Horseshoe poker room on the eve of his third World Series of Poker victory.

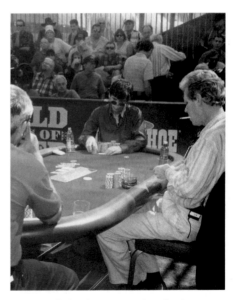

Mel Judah (back to camera), John Strzemp (right), and Stuey (center), the final three players at the 1997 WSOP championship. (Note the glass shield placed on top of the flop cards; strong gusts of wind made it necessary to hold down the cards.)

Jack Binion and Stuey pose for photographers after Stuey's third win in 1997 at the WSOP.

After several dental procedures, the star patient poses with his dentist, Dr. Ray Warchaizer, in 1995 (note Stuey's ill-fitting pants and shirt).

Stuey and W. C. "Puggy" Pearson in October 1998. Stuey holds up a photo of the two old friends. (Incidentally, Stuey borrowed $500 from Pearson moments after this photograph was taken.)

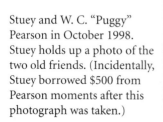

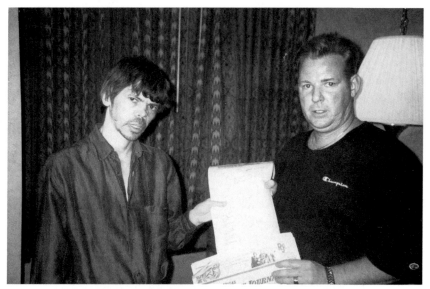

A down-and-out Stuey Ungar, with coauthor Nolan Dalla, inside Stuey's hotel room at the Gold Coast, August 1998. He agrees to a tell-all autobiography and holds up their contract agreement.

The 1998 photograph from *Icon* magazine that Stuey detested.

The last photograph taken of Stuey shows him with (left to right) Nolan Dalla, Puggy Pearson, and Mike Sexton, October 1998.

Stefanie and Madeline Ungar today in Las Vegas.

Stuey's gravestone in Las Vegas.

typical day started at 6:00 A.M., when he ate breakfast while poring over the morning lines on the day's ball games. He would then call his contacts on the East Coast and get the early word on the hot games. After another dozen phone calls to people across the country, he would make his final assessments and book his bets—but only on games where he felt his information was good and he had an edge.

"I gamble for a living," Baxter said. "I don't gamble to try and impress anybody. I'm here for one reason and one reason only—to make money. I have a wife and family. I have responsibilities. When I come to play or I make a bet, I'm there to get the money."

Baxter regarded Stuey as a friend and was happy to give him support, but only if it made good business sense. In 1985, he backed Stuey for $30,000 in a big no-limit side game during the America's Cup tournament at Bob Stupak's Vegas World. Within twenty minutes of sitting down, Stuey had lost half of his stake.

At that point, a hand came up in which Stuey was bluffed out of a pot by an unknown. Typically, when a player makes a bet and his opponent folds, he throws his hand facedown into the muck. Sometimes, though, a player will want to show his hand to send a message to his beaten opponent. In this case, Stuey's adversary knew that by turning his hand up, he might rattle the two-time world champion. The idea worked. Stuey seethed when he saw the bluff and realized he'd been outplayed. Poker is a delicate psychological game. "You have to know your reads are correct," Stuey said. "If you can't trust your instincts, you have no chance at the table. No chance whatsoever."

Down to his last $4,000 in a game where the other stacks were $50,000 and higher, Stuey somehow clawed his way back over the next couple of hours, working his stack back up to $20,000. Then he misplayed a hand and lost part of what he had salvaged. Baxter, who was watching, had seen enough.

"All right, Stuey, rack 'em up. Let's call it a night," he said.

"No, no, I'm okay. We're doing okay here."

"I said rack 'em up," Baxter barked forcefully.

"How can we leave this game?" Stuey asked. "I'm just getting started here."

With all the seriousness that he could muster, Baxter uttered a line in his deep Georgia drawl that has since become legendary in poker circles: "Stuey," he said, "poker is like pool. Some days you make every shot; other days you hit nothing but the rail. Tonight, you're hitting nothing but rail. Now, rack 'em up and let's go."

It was a slap in the face, but Baxter had made a hard assessment that only very disciplined gamblers can make: sometimes accepting a small loss saves you from a bigger loss. For Stuey, having a backer like Baxter ultimately resulted in making him a more disciplined player.

I have no respect for my own money, so in some ways playing for a backer makes me play better. The worst feeling in the world is telling your backer that you lost. That's much worse than losing your own money.

Over the years, Stuey's backers were satisfied more often than not by his results. It would be hard to calculate how much he won for his backers over the years, but the figure is in the millions. He took great pride in those results. There are some backed players who have succumbed to the temptation to "dump"—that is, to purposely lose the backer's money to a confederate in order to split it up later. Minnesota Fats, the great pool hustler, had a reputation for this kind of dumping. Stuey certainly had the opportunity and incentive to engage in it, and in other forms of dumping, particularly when he was broke, but no one has ever come forward to suggest that he did.

• • •

I had a guy offer me a couple of hundred thousand once. All I had to do was dump several games of gin. You know what? I wouldn't do it. At the time, I was busted. So the money would have meant something to me. The guy was going to bet half a million against me. Everybody in town would have jumped on the other side, so he'd have no trouble getting action. Fact is, they'd all think he was a sucker. I'd have a dozen guys in here and at least a million in cash if I told some guy I was going to play the game straight. The guy told me he'd split the money with me. Chop it up right down the middle and hand me a quarter mil.

But you think I'm gonna go around and let some guy brag that he beat the best gin player in the world, when I knew it wasn't true? That would tear my insides out. I mean, I couldn't live with myself if I did that. No one's gonna go around bragging they beat Stu Ungar in a gin game. That's not going to happen. Anybody tells you that, they're lying. Nobody ever beat me. Not ever.

That's the thing about having a backer. See, I'm the most loyal person in the world. Anyone that has faith enough to bet on me is going to get a fair shake. I'm not talking about doing drugs—that's nothing compared to throwing a game. I could never look myself in the mirror again if I intentionally threw a game.

The decade that had started with Stuey on top of the world saw him, by its midpoint, beginning to career out of control both in his personal life and in gambling.

Doyle Brunson—a skilled handicapper and a former bookmaker—began to get the best of Stuey in their daily betting ritual. During one particularly bad week, Stuey lost nearly $500,000 to Brunson. Even though Brunson knew and understood Stuey's penchant for action, as well as his chaotic personal finances, he assumed that Stuey would raise the money and pay his debt. Brunson had always been honorable, and he expected no less in return. But even after the two gamblers flew to Nashville together and hustled some rich high rollers out of several hundred thousand on the golf course, Stuey paid Brunson only a portion of his winnings.

"Two or three days later, I heard that he lost the rest in the sportsbooks and on horse races," Brunson said. "So, after that, we had a falling-out."

It's difficult to know how much Stuey's use of drugs affected these events, but there was no question that his usage had gone beyond the purely recreational.

One time I bought a full kilo: two-point-two pounds of blow. We had a party in a hotel room. People came in that I didn't even know. Girls. Party types. They went through that blow like a pack of jackals tearing through a carcass. After that happened I said I wasn't going to buy twenty thousand dollars' worth of blow and see it wasted like that. So I started doing it by myself, in private.

When Brunson cut Stuey off, that in turn severed Stuey's relationship with Chip Reese. Several of his backers were becoming reluctant to bankroll Stuey unless he was at a tournament and they knew they'd be able to collar him right afterward, as he was cashing out.

Amarillo Slim remembers being stunned at how reckless Stuey was with his money. "Stu musta won a jillion dollars in my tournaments," Slim said. "He always did very well up in Reno and later at Caesars in Las

Vegas. Then, if I saw him three weeks later, he couldn't rub two nickels together.

"See, I always resented that. I didn't understand how a man could have so much natural talent, but had no control over his life. When I was into poker, I always hung around with good people—and Stuey wasn't one of them. He would be a good person, but then he would get on drugs. He was like Frankenstein's monster. I saw what drugs could do to a person. Back in Texas, me and Doyle were partners with Sailor Roberts, who was one of the best men I ever knew. There was a boy who had the biggest heart and was the best son of a bitch that ever walked down the turnpike. When Sailor got into drugs, he started to mistreat everyone in the world. I'm not on a crusade here, but everybody that ever messed with that stuff just ended up a loser. I mean, what is it if ya do somethin' good and you don't have nothin' to show for it?

"And those boys were always wantin' to borrow money. They'd come to me and ask me for five or ten thousand and they'd say they were good for it. And I'd answer, 'Well, if you're good for it, why don't you get it from some those fellas that live here in Vegas, those fellas you see every day and know you better than I do?' I live twelve hundred miles away from here. Why do they need to get it from me?

"See, to me, a gambler's word is his honor. I have to do what I say I'm gonna do. If I don't do what I say I'm gonna do, the whole world's gonna hear about it in a week. And with some guys in Vegas, when you got a loan, it got to be like making a score. It wasn't a loan, it was a score. So Stuey never bothered asking me for money after I turned him down once."

In 1987 Billy Baxter put up Stuey's $10,000 entry in the no-limit hold'em championship in the America's Cup tournament, which turned out to be the last major poker tournament played at Bob Stupak's Vegas World before it was torn down to make way for the

Stratosphere. Stuey made it down to the final two players, facing off against Don Williams, a grind-it-out pro who was described as "the best unknown player in the world." Williams held a chip lead of $70,000 to $40,000 at one point, as the two vied for the $110,000 first prize. But in a key hand that turned things around, Stuey was dealt two aces to Williams's two kings, and a few minutes later the end came for Williams. After a three-year drought, Stuey beamed for photographers, holding up a trophy and the $110,000 in cash. The moment and the money were fleeting, however. Most of the cash quickly found its way to the betting windows and sportsbooks, and what was left was eaten up by Stuey's increasingly expensive drug habit.

13.

THE HAND OF DEATH
AND THE SPORT OF KINGS

The day Madeline and Stuey were divorced, Stuey told their lawyer, Steve Stein, that he wanted to legally adopt fifteen-year-old Richie. Many people would consider that strange, but Stuey loved Richie as much as he loved Stefanie, his own daughter, and he thought it was important to convey those feelings in a dramatic way. "I thought it was a beautiful thing," Madeline said.

Richie's real father had never come through for him in any way, and Stuey wanted to make up for some of that hurt. Stein took care of filing the proper papers, and the adoption became a reality. Though Stuey had showered Richie with gifts when he was growing up, it hadn't really been enough to fill the void left by an absentee father. "Richie had his own demons that nobody could help him with," Madeline said.

After the divorce, Stuey made regular visits to see Stefanie and Richie, but in 1988 matters took a turn when Madeline moved to Florida for a year with Stefanie to see if she could make a life for herself away from the ex-husband to whom she was still so deeply connected. The move proved to be difficult for all of them. Richie didn't want to go, so he stayed with Stuey, who had moved back to the house on Coventry

Lane. And Madeline and Stefanie, after a year in Florida away from the two most important men in their lives, decided to move back to Las Vegas.

Stuey was probably not the ideal role model for a kid, but during the year Richie lived with him he did his best to be parental. Of course, it wasn't surprising that an impressionable kid, watching an adoptive father who happened to be a top professional gambler and world champion poker player, might develop an interest in gambling himself—not that Stuey ever sat down and tutored him.

"Nobody was ever taught anything by Stuey," said Madeline. "Stuey didn't have the patience to teach anybody. If Richie learned anything about gambling from him, it was by watching him. And he did learn by watching. They would go over the sports section together and talk about sports. Richie had a pretty good eye when it came to odds-making. He used to study the newspaper like crazy, and he had a knack for handicapping, how to analyze everything. He made a long-shot bet on a football team at the beginning of the season, and won a few thousand dollars when they made it to the Super Bowl. He used the money to buy himself a used Porsche—his first car. It was a big thing."

But the divorce remained difficult for Richie. According to Madeline, Stuey didn't help things by some of his behavior. "Even after the divorce, Stuey was extremely jealous," she said. "I had moved back into the house with him and the kids for a couple of months, but then I found a place at the Las Vegas Country Club, and I moved there with Stefanie. He used Richie to find out what I was doing. He always wanted to know where I was. Stuey would tell him, 'Richie, find out what your mother is doing. Find out who she's seeing'—that kind of thing. And it was hard on him. That's something a child shouldn't have to do. He was confused as it was, and that didn't help things."

When Richie turned eighteen, he dropped out of high school just short of graduating. That was upsetting to both Stuey and Madeline, though Stuey could hardly start preaching about the importance of education—since he himself hadn't graduated from high school. Instead, Stuey told Richie that if he wasn't going to pursue his education, he had better get a job. To help him out, Stuey talked Jack Binion into giving his adopted son a job at the Horseshoe as a busboy. Stuey thought the job might teach Richie a little bit of responsibility. But Richie hated it and stayed for only a few weeks before quitting. It wasn't easy having a father figure who was larger than life. It created grandiose expectations that were difficult to live up to. Richie was struggling mightily to figure out who he was and what he wanted to be.

Stuey tried again to help him out, calling in a favor with Bob Stupack this time, who gave Richie at job at Vegas World shortly before it closed. But again the job proved too menial for the boy. He was impatient. He wanted a position of some importance, where he could be somebody.

Things got even more difficult when Richie broke up with Jennifer, his steady girlfriend of two years. Jennifer was the one bright spot in his life. The two were always together and "seemed very much in love," according to Stuey. But her parents didn't approve, and as the relationship got more serious, they let their daughter know their feelings. Not only did they not like Richie, but they also thought he came from a bad family and wasn't a good match for her. Most people who were established in Las Vegas society knew about Stuey Ungar, and had heard about his reckless gambling habits and rumored drug use.

Under increasing pressure from her parents, Jennifer ended the relationship.

As if that weren't bad enough, Richie wrecked his beloved Porsche shortly thereafter. "Totaled it," according to Madeline. "He was very lucky he wasn't hurt."

Without a job, a car, or a girl, Richie started to sink into a funk, drinking too much beer, watching too much television, and sleeping late.

"Stuey was getting very upset with him," said Madeline. "He said, 'I am not going to give you any more money unless you go to work.' "

Richie was living at the house with Stuey at the time, but after that Madeline told him to come and live with her at the country club. "He came and stayed with me about a month. I knew he wasn't happy, but I guess I didn't realize how bad it was. One night, he said he was going to go out for the evening. But it was odd; before he left, several of his friends called, but he didn't want to talk to them. Then he just left.

"It started getting later and later, and he still hadn't come home. I went into Stefanie's room to watch some TV with her, but the TV didn't work. Something was wrong with the cable. So, I went to sleep. Then, in the middle of the night, the phone rang. I thought it was Richie, but it wasn't. It was a hang-up."

In fact, it had been Stuey, calling to check up on her. Now, at six the next morning, he received a visitor, someone from the coroner's office, whose job it was to impart the terrible news that Stuey's adopted son, Richie, was dead.

It took a few moments for Stuey to absorb what he was being told—that Richie had taken his own life. Even then, the factual answers to the questions Stuey asked explained nothing. He learned that Richie had unhooked a cable cord from a television, taken it over to the construction site of the new Hilton parking garage, and slung it over one of the iron support beams. It was there where some workers had found him that morning, hanging from the cord.

Stuey went over to Madeline's home to tell her. One can only imagine how he must have been feeling. Not surprisingly, Madeline was "just wrecked" by the news.

"Stuey was, too," Madeline said, "but he was also a real comfort to me."

Madeline couldn't bear to tell Stefanie, so Stuey tried. Stefanie was only six years old, and she had a hard time understanding. After Stuey tried to explain it, she said, "Well, can I go out and play?" He had to explain it a number of times, but she still didn't really understand.

Losing a child is devastating under any circumstances. But in Madeline and Stuey's case, in the crazy back-and-forth of their difficult love, the timing was particularly cruel. They had been planning to make another go of it. "If Richie hadn't died," Madeline said, "we were going to move back in together." Ultimately, his death made that too painful.

For Stuey, losing his mother and father and Victor had been tough. But with Richie's death, his grief was far worse because it was mixed with guilt. At the funeral, Stuey wept. It was the only time in his life anyone ever remembered seeing him cry. He described the period afterward like "being in a fog." He was scarcely seen in public for the next two months. "I could tell that he was doing more drugs," Madeline said. "He was staying home, not going out to play cards. That's what happens when you do drugs. You don't want to be around people."

When my dad died, when my mom died, I never cried. I have this thing that I will not show tears in public. I'm not bragging about it. That's just me. But I cried myself to sleep many times thinking about Richie. I kept on asking myself, "Why? Why did it happen?"

Stuey eventually resurfaced, but his bankroll and psyche were seriously depleted. Still, gambling was the only positive way he could think of to distract himself.

On September 14, 1989, there was a huge carryover in the Pick Six at Santa Anita. The Pick Six is an exotic wager that requires the bettor to pick the winners of six consecutive horse races correctly, commonly the third through the eighth races of the day. The challenge of correctly picking six straight winners is magnified because the races often involve maidens and other less predictable horses, essentially turning the Pick Six into the track's longest shot—as well as its biggest payday. When no one correctly picks the six races of a Pick Six, the prize pool carries over to the next day, and the pool can often exceed $1 million.

On this September day, the pool, with carryover, was more than $4 million. The races were being run at Santa Anita. Stuey wasn't there, however; he was ensconced at one of the VIP tables at the Caesars race and sportsbook, staring up at the hundreds of television screens and the digital out-of-town scoreboard that made the place look like mission control during a space launch. That morning, he had received from his handicapper, Richie Buller, who was acknowledged as one of the best horse-race men in Las Vegas, a small slip of paper containing the combinations that Buller liked for the Pick Six races. Buller's skill in making Pick Six selections was not so much in picking winners as in eliminating horses that he felt had little or no chance of winning.

Stuey went up to the betting counter, and, following Buller's picks (for which Buller would be paid with a cut of the profits, if there were any), bet on an extensive array of different configurations and combinations. By the time his complex bet was processed, he had to fork over $40,000 to pay for it—money that he had won in a cash game in the poker room at the Dunes. In return, he was handed a thick stack of betting tickets.

After the first three races, Stuey was still alive, with several combinations intact. In the sixth race, in addition to his Pick Six wager, Stuey had bet $10,000 to win on the number four horse, Wipper Stand, which was one of Buller's picks. Stuey wasn't content to shoot for just $1 million;

he needed more action on top. The impulse paid off when Wipper Stand cruised by two lengths, going off at 3–2, for a $25,000 return.

The seventh race was the toughest of the day: maiden fillies. Stuey had three horses in the race, and he watched in delight as one of them, Ranking Mom, won by a neck. That brought him up to the eighth and final race. He still had a number of live tickets, and he sorted frantically through the stack in his hands, trying to find the ones that were still in play.

As the eighth race at Santa Anita got under way, Stuey was practically jumping out of his skin. He screamed at the television screen, urging his horses on. When an undersize gelding named Robby Don crossed the finish line six lengths ahead of the field, Stuey started running around the red-carpeted floor of the racebook like a maniac. He couldn't believe it. While thousands of dead tickets were hitting the floor at the racetrack and at sportsbooks throughout Las Vegas, Stuey again started riffling through his stack, looking for the right match that he knew was there.

Of the eight live tickets that were paid that day, Stuey had two. Each one paid a whopping $887,411.60. But interestingly, by the time he got to the window, he was already feeling a sense of letdown. "I don't know how to describe it," he said. "I guess reality kinda set in, that the money really wasn't that big a deal."

On the other hand, it was a bigger win than he'd ever had at poker, gin, or any other gambling venture—and a bigger win than he ever would have again. He walked away from the racebook window with nearly $1.8 million, escorted to a safe-deposit box at the cage by two beefy security guards. After the casino took out withholding taxes, he was still able to fill up two safe-deposit boxes. The rest Stuey took with him in cash.

He and Richie Buller went out to celebrate that night. They invited along Philly Brush, Mike Sexton, and a few other sports gamblers, and headed for the Olympic Gardens—or O.G., as it was called—one of Las Vegas's premier gentlemen's clubs.

A night on the town with Stuey Ungar when he was in the chips was like a night out with Diamond Jim Brady. Everything was done up in style, with cost no object. Regardless of who accompanied him, Stuey paid for everything, throwing around twenties, fifties, and hundreds like someone handing out business cards at a networking party. Doormen, coat-check girls, maître d's, waiters, busboys, valet parking attendants, here you go, this is for you, thanks a lot. *Thank you, sir!*

At O.G., Stuey was recognized less for his stature as a cardplayer than for his reputation as a big tipper. Many of the girls knew him on a first-name basis. The host, on the other hand, called him Mr. Ungar.

"Welcome back, Mr. Ungar, we're glad to see you," said the host. "We have a special area in the back if you'd like some privacy."

"Sure, bring us back your best girls," Stuey commanded.

While the regulars sat in the front with loud rock music blasting, Stuey and his gang were ushered into the VIP lounge in the back. They got comfortable around a small stage, and Stuey immediately ordered three bottles of Cristal champagne.

"Sir, Cristal is $280 a bottle," the pretty but unapprised waitress informed Stuey, unsure if he knew how pricey it was.

"Then bring us four bottles—and put another four on ice."

A few barbacks scrambled around in the rear of the O.G. and brought six frosted glasses and ice buckets laden with the most expensive champagne—bottles that were usually reserved for special occasions such as New Year's eve. Word quickly spread through the O.G. that six high rollers were sitting in the back, fronted by a little guy in a tan Members Only jacket with a curly brown perm who looked as if he should have been stopped at the door for being underage. The girls flocked back to Stuey like swallows to Capistrano.

He sat slumped down in his chair, laughing as the girls performed for him. "Do a dance for my friends," he yelled above the pulsating disco music. "I want you all to do a dance for my friends." Stuey pulled out a wad of cash and tipped each dancer $100. The other members of Stuey's party were as surprised as the girls by his largesse.

"The rest of us just looked at each other," Sexton recalled. "I mean, we were screwed and we knew it. There was Stuey tipping hundred-dollar bills on the very first dance. Normally, those girls would be happy if you tipped them a couple of dollars and bought them a draft beer. Stuey was tipping C-notes and pouring Cristal! These girls were drinking it like it was fucking tap water. I mean, how were we supposed to compete with that?"

Meanwhile, out front, the dancers were abandoning ship, leaving the stage in mid-dance to get some gelt from the high rollers in back before the party was over. While the dollar tippers drinking longnecks sat around the empty stage in front, scratching their heads in annoyance, the little stage in the VIP lounge had women jockeying for a piece of the action as if they were at a 90 percent-off sale of Gucci handbags. Stuey nearly disappeared from sight amid the naked tits and big hair, his smirking face reemerging every so often to shout out an order for more champagne.

An hour later, seven empty bottles of Cristal sitting on the table, Stuey demanded to know why another bottle hadn't yet arrived.

The club manager approached and leaned in close. "I'm sorry, Mr. Ungar, we're out of Cristal. That was the last bottle. May we offer you and your guests Dom Pérignon instead?"

"What do you mean you're out of Cristal?" Stuey asked incredulously.

"We had seven bottles. But nobody in the history of the club has ever ordered so many bottles at once . . ."

Stuey went berserk, putting on a real show for his friends.

"You're out of Cristal? You're out? I can't believe it! I've got all my good friends here and you're going to embarrass me like this?"

"I'm sorry, Mr. Ungar. If it wasn't so late, we'd send a runner out to get some more."

"I guess we'll just have to slum it and drink your Dom. Bring two more bottles. I still can't believe you're going to embarrass me like this."

The night's final bill came to $8,800.

Over the course of the next few days, Stuey went on a shopping spree with his winnings. He bought himself a new Jaguar. He bought Philly a new Cadillac. He paid off the loan he had taken out against the mortgage of his house. He even paid off some of the people he owed money to—including Doyle Brunson, who was paid a portion of the remaining $300,000 of his debt.

With a healthy bankroll again, Stuey decided to blow town for a few days. He arranged a golf trip with Mike Sexton and some others to the La Costa Country Club in Carlsbad, California. Stuey had not been to La Costa in over a year, so he expected that no one would know or remember him. As soon as he and his group drove up to the hotel, the valet opened the door for him.

"Hello, Mr. Ungar!" the valet said.

Stuey tipped him $20, along with everyone else at the valet stand. He then handed out $20 bills to every hotel employee he encountered on his way in. Even two maintenance men working out of a storeroom got $20 apiece.

Later, Stuey and his entourage went to dinner at the country club, in the executive dining area. Normally, it required reservations, but Stuey never scheduled anything. He knew a generous tip was the easiest way to secure a last-second table at a crowded restaurant.

"Stuey always let Benjamin Franklin make his reservations," Sexton said.

While their table was being readied, Stuey and Sexton waited in the bar. Sexton ordered a Budweiser, and Stuey, who rarely drank, decided to have one, too.

The bartender took one look at Stuey and demanded to see some identification.

"You don't look eighteen. I need to see proof," the bartender insisted.

"Whaddya talkin' about? I don't carry ID on me," Stuey said.

"Then I can't serve you," the bartender said, turning to walk away.

"Wait! You're tellin' me that if I don't have an ID, you won't serve me?"

"That's right."

"Here—I'll show you some ID."

With that, Stuey dug into his pocket and pulled out a mammoth roll of $100 bills. Everyone in the vicinity gaped.

"There's my ID," Stuey said. "Now, let me ask you, what kind of underage kid carries around a wad of cash like that?"

The bartender looked at Stuey, then at the money. "You've got a point, sir," he said. "What'll you have?"

Stuey had no appreciation for fine dining. Ambience and haute cuisine were wasted on him. His idea of etiquette was wolfing down his food in big, undiscerning mouthfuls, talking all the while, often spewing particles of food onto himself or any unfortunate soul who happened to be in range. Eating was basically a bodily function for him, like taking a crap or sleeping, something to be gotten out of the way so that he could get back into action.

"He had a hard time sitting through a meal," Sexton recalled. "He'd invite everybody to be his guest and pick up the whole tab. Then, when nobody else was even halfway through their meal, he'd announce, 'I'm done, let's go.'"

As he was leaving La Costa, Stuey called another friend, Mike Salem, who lived nearby in Los Angeles. "Mike, I hit a couple of tickets. Get on a plane and meet me in Las Vegas. I'm headed back to the race and sportsbook at the Caesars. When you get there, you're on a fifteen-percent free roll."

A few hours later, Salem met Stuey at the Caesars. A successful poker player, Salem was known among cardplayers as "Baseball Mike" for his ability to handicap major league baseball games. He was a rangy six-foot-six and built like a pro athlete, with large hands and a strong, intimidating jawline that silently said, "Don't fuck with me." Just as he had in grade school, Stuey had befriended one of the big guys.

The first thing Stuey did was hand Salem $5,000 in cash.

"Put this in your pocket," Stuey said. "It's walking-around money."

Salem pocketed the money a bit sheepishly, embarrassed by his friend's generosity. They went to the Caesars race and sportsbook and took a seat in the VIP section. Strangers were constantly coming up to Stuey, whispering in his ear, then walking away. Finally, Salem's curiosity got the best of him.

"Stuey, what do you got going on here?" Salem had grown up in Boston and had the accent to go along with it.

"I'm in action."

"What?"

"I've got side action going with five other guys."

In addition to the bets Stuey was placing at the windows, he was also making bets with other gamblers, the same way he had done with Brunson, to avoid the 10 percent vig.

"What are you betting on?" Salem asked. "What games?"

"Everything. Dogs, trotters, horses, and baseball."

"Jesus, how are you keeping it all straight?"

"Hey, I got the best trotter man in the country, and you're the best baseball man I know. I don't keep it straight; you're the one who's going to keep it straight. That's why I flew you here. I need you!"

After his big win, Caesars had given Stuey a free suite for as long as he wanted. "Even though I only lived two miles away, I set up shop there," Stuey said. "For the next three months I never left the fucking hotel. Just went between my room and the sportsbook." He played the horses every day, but the losses mounted. Within weeks, he was down to a few hundred thousand and in danger of losing it all.

He turned to baseball. As the 1989 season came to a close, the play-offs began. Reese and Brunson were partners and were betting on baseball heavily. In the play-offs, the Toronto Blue Jays faced the Oakland A's for the American League pennant. The A's were strong favorites, and Reese made a large wager on Toronto at an attractive price, getting nearly 2–1 on his money. A victory by Toronto would have returned nearly $200,000 in profit.

Salem was strongly opposed to the bet on Toronto. Since Brunson and Reese paid Salem to give them baseball picks, Baseball Mike thought he had an obligation to talk Reese out of a wager on the Blue Jays. He started listing the reasons that Toronto had no chance against the A's.

"I just think the price on Toronto makes them too good a play," Reese countered.

"Who cares what price they're getting if they have no chance to win?" Salem said.

Just before game one began, Brunson decided that Salem was right and overruled his partner. He placed $200,000 on the A's to win $100,000, thereby voiding their previous bet (except for the juice). Sure enough, Salem was right. Oakland won the series four games to one.

In what became known as the "earthquake series," after tremors at La Prada rocked the Bay area, Oakland took on its cross-bay rivals, the San Francisco Giants, for the world championship. Reese was stubborn and remained convinced that the A's weren't as good as many believed. As he had done with Toronto, he again made a large wager against the

NOLAN DALLA AND PETER ALSON

A's. And as before, Salem again tried to talk him out of it. Oakland had the superior pitching, hitting, and bullpen, as well as experience in the play-offs. But Reese wasn't impressed. Neither was Brunson. Inexplicably, Stuey also went against his friend's advice, and bet a large share of his bankroll on the Giants.

Unfortunately for all of them, Salem was proved right again, as Oakland swept the World Series. Salem couldn't believe that they hadn't followed him. He had done his job, picked the winner—yet they hadn't listened. He felt entitled to a share of the money they should have made. Brunson agreed with him, but Reese resisted, insisting that Salem should be paid only if the duo collected on a bet. Since they lost big, he didn't feel they had to pay Salem a thing.

The hard feelings that resulted soured Salem's relationship with Reese and Brunson. At the same time, his relationship with Stuey blossomed. "After the 'eighty-nine Series, Stuey thought I walked on water," Salem said.

It wasn't just Salem's prowess at handicapping. Stuey needed the company—to keep him busy, to keep him from being alone, to keep him from thinking about Richie.

Madeline was in a bad way as Thanksgiving 1989 approached. "I didn't know which way I was going," she said. "I was more dependent than ever on Stuey, and it wasn't healthy. I would go to the cemetery just about every day and lie on the ground by Richie. Stefanie didn't understand what I was doing. All she knew was, okay, it's time to go with Mommy and lie on the ground and watch her cry. Finally, I just decided that I needed to see how I could put my life and my daughter's life back together. As my mom said, 'You have a daughter. She didn't die; your son did. You have to take care of your daughter.' So I made arrangements to get a job in Florida. I got it lined up and I packed up everything, and we just got on a plane and left."

Stuey's sense of loss was certainly deepened by Madeline's decision to move to Florida again with their daughter. For the first time in his life, he was truly alone. There had always been a parent, guardian, or wife around to play the role of supporter and protector. Now, there was no one to say no or motivate him to stay straight. There was no one to help him manage his life and keep him solvent. The nights were longer, the pain of his loneliness was deeper, and the wins and losses of gambling were somehow inconsequential by comparison.

The world around him was different, too. Steve Wynn's Mirage Hotel and Casino opened on November 22, 1989, a twenty-nine-story, 3,049-room, $630 million deluxe resort with white tigers, a rain forest, and an active volcano. On Christmas day, only one month later, Benny Binion, the man who had invented the World Series of Poker, died at age eighty-five.

The Vegas Stuey knew was changing, shifting around him like the desert sands.

14.

GET UP, STAND UP

By the early spring of 1990, Stuey had gambled away almost all of his big racetrack score. Emotionally, he was still riding out the storm of Richie's suicide, trying to keep himself distracted—but in a sense he had been doing that in one form or another for most of his life.

On March 17, he and Mike Salem attended the long-anticipated fight between Julio Cesar Chavez and Meldrick Taylor at the Las Vegas Hilton Center. Stuey had loved boxing ever since he was a kid and his father had taken him to the Friday night fight cards at the old Madison Square Garden. The light welterweight bout between the WBC champion Chavez, who had a record of sixty-eight wins, including fifty-six knockouts, and Taylor, the IBF light-welterweight champ and former Olympic champion, whose record was twenty-five wins, no losses, and one tie, with fourteen knockouts, promised to be an epic event. One of the two 139-pounders would emerge from the twelve-round bout as the best pound-for-pound fighter in the world.

There's probably nothing more exciting and excruciating for an action junkie than the high of betting on a big-time prizefight. At any moment, one big punch can kayo your bankroll. Stuey often told friends that this was his ultimate thrill in gambling.

The wiseguys all had the Chavez-Taylor match handicapped as a draw. Both fighters were tough. Both had tremendous stamina. Both could dole out and take a great deal of punishment. The best bet, it seemed, was that the fight would go the distance.

Mike Salem didn't feel strongly enough about the fight to risk his own money, but Stuey offered to give Salem a 10 percent free roll on his own action, just for the sake of camaraderie. Stuey and Salem spent the afternoon of the fight going around town to various sportsbooks. They went to the Mirage and bet $20,000, laying −110 that the fight would go the distance (meaning that a $22,000 bet would return them $20,000 in profit). They went to Caesars and found a better line at −105, and bet another $15,000. Then they went to the Hilton, where the line was also −110, and took that for another $22,000. Just before the fight started, Stuey decided to lay what he had left in his pocket on the same bet. He went to the betting counter and dug out his last $11,400, just about all the money he had left from his Pick Six win, and the last of his bankroll.

All told, Stuey had almost $70,000 riding on the fight. As he and Salem settled into their ringside seats, Salem asked Stuey if he'd really put all his money on the fight.

"All but three hundred bucks," Stuey said, almost giddily.

Salem could only laugh. His friend was nothing if not true to his character.

The bell rang and the fight began.

Taylor took the lead in the early rounds, but as the fight entered the middle rounds, the pace slowed, and both fighters seemed content to try to score points rather than take a chance and go for a knockout. It had all the earmarks of a fight destined to go the distance.

In their ringside seats, Stuey and Salem could hear the gloves slap and the fighters grunt, could hear the blows as they landed. Stuey had been ringside at other fights where sweat—and even blood—had landed on him. The crowd's cheering ebbed and flowed with the subtly shifting tides of momentum.

As the last rounds got under way, Stuey was concerned about only one thing—the time clock. He watched as it wound down through one three-minute round after another, and he breathed a huge sigh of relief each time the bell sounded and both fighters were able to walk back to their corners.

By the twelfth and final round, Chavez was way behind on all the score-cards. Of course, we didn't care who won the fight. The only thing I cared about is that it would go the distance. Chavez had no chance to catch Taylor on points. The only way he could win was to knock him out. Which was the only thing I was worried about.

Now you gotta know that this fight was promoted by Don King. And the referee, Richard Steele, was King's boy. And Chavez was Don King's fighter.

So, the last round started, and Taylor, instead of keeping his distance—and he was a lock to win as long as he didn't get knocked out—was actually tangling with Chavez. Baseball Mike was next to me, counting down the round on his watch.

Two minutes went by. Then two minutes and thirty seconds. I was thirty seconds away from payday.

In the last half minute of the fight, Chavez seemed to realize that only a superhuman effort could save him. He attacked Taylor like a Tasmanian devil, swinging left-handed and right-handed haymakers, many of them missing, but many landing on Taylor's face and body. The crowd was going wild as Chavez desperately tried to get the knockout. There were only twelve seconds to go when a huge left hook caught Taylor below the chin. His head snapped back and his knees buckled, and then he crashed facedown on the canvas in what seemed like slow motion. Just as his body hit the canvas, the red light in the corner came on, signaling the final ten seconds of the round.

Richard Steele, the ref, started the count immediately.

One. Two. Three.

"Get up!" Stuey screamed. "Get up!"

Taylor somehow managed to sit up. All he needed to do was get back to his feet, and the fight was over.

Four. Five. Six. Steele's fingers counted off the seconds.

"God, please, let him get up! Get up!" Stuey pleaded.

Taylor struggled to his knees.

Seven. Eight.

Taylor straightened up. He was standing! His eyes were glassy and his mouth was bleeding, but he was up. Steele approached him, and immediately waved his arms in the air like windshield wipers, signaling that the fight was over.

"The fight's over! The fight's over!" Stuey screamed, thinking he had won. But a moment later, he realized that it wasn't over—it had been stopped. "No! No!"

Taylor was still standing. Chavez thrust his gloves into the air, victoriously, as if he needed to snatch the moment before anything changed it. Spectators flooded the ring. The trainers and members of the fight camps rushed in to protect their fighters. Several brawls broke out. It was bedlam.

Officially, the fight was stopped at 2:58 of the twelfth and final round. Had Steele not called it, with two seconds to go, Meldrick Taylor would have won the fight on points, despite the last-minute pounding he'd received.

Taylor certainly looked like the loser. Chavez had busted him up badly. After the fight, it was revealed that Chavez had broken Taylor's orbital bone (the bone right under the eye), and that Taylor had swallowed a pint of blood from a split lip. He was never the same afterward, though he fought on for years.

Richard Steele. That's a name I won't forget. I know a lot of poker players talk about bad beats, but to me that was the worst beat I ever took in gambling. Two seconds. Two fucking seconds. I don't know how long I sat there. It might have been five minutes. It might have been an hour. I don't remember, really. I just sat there looking straight ahead.

Mike respected my silence. He didn't say anything. He was on a ten percent free roll. I liked to do that with my friends, give them something to cheer for. So he was upset, too.

Neither of us spoke for a long time. There were no words to say that could make the shock go away. The crowd filed out, the lights were dimmed, and still I sat there. We were still there when the cleaning crew came and started sweeping up, moving up and down the rows of empty seats.

"Stuey, that's it. Let's go," Salem said. "We lost. There's nothing we can do about it."

"Can you fucking believe we lost that way?" I said.

"Yeah, but it's over. The money's gone. Come on."

We finally left, and walked outside. As we walked along the Strip, we barely spoke. I took a cab home and Mike went back to his hotel. The night was over.

If we had won, I'm sure we would have gone out partying all night and probably would have spent the next several days betting sports. As it was, I was out of action. Busted except for the three hundred dollars left in my pocket. I stayed home for a while after that. When I was burned out and depressed like that, I would just go off and be by myself.

• • •

Eventually, Stuey returned to the poker rooms and replenished his bankroll. But he promptly went broke again betting on sports and the races. As 1990 rolled on, Stuey's fortunes continued to go up and down in what had become a fairly predictable pattern—win at poker and the occasional gin match; lose at other things. If anything was different, it was that there now seemed to be a more aggressive purposefulness to the swings—what psychologists who categorize mood disorders describe as "rapid cycling."

Despite the fact that he had not done particularly well in the World Series of Poker since his back-to-back wins in the early 1980s, Stuey had dominated the other big poker tournaments of the time. He won Amarillo Slim's Super Bowl of Poker three times in seven years, and would have won it a fourth time if Jack Keller hadn't made a flush on the river against him when the field was down to three players. "No one else had ever won that tournament more than once," Stuey said. "Talk about making a shambles out of an event!"

It seemed that no matter what else was going on in Stuey's life, when he focused his attention on poker, there was nobody else in his league. Jim Boyd, a pro from West Virginia, who enjoyed much success at tournaments during the 1980s and played against Stuey frequently, attributed the Kid's success to the fact that "he thought quicker, played faster, and was generally three moves ahead of any player at the table. Many of the pots he won by sheer ability and guts. He moved players off winning hands when he sensed weakness, and he wasn't afraid to give players free cards so he could trap them on later betting rounds. Stuey didn't need cards to win. He had the ability to size up his opponents very quickly and read their holdings with uncanny accuracy. He was just a cut or two above everybody else."

Most other top players agreed with that assessment. Erik Seidel, a lanky former stock trader turned poker pro, who is one of tournament poker's all-time leading money winners, first heard about Stuey when he was back in New York, learning the game at the underground Mayfair club. "Stuey was like a poker God," Seidel said.

The first time Seidel went out to Vegas, he was at the Stardust and got a chance to watch some of the world-class players he knew only by reputation. He was studious by nature, and there was one player he wanted to watch above all the others: Stuey Ungar.

"I didn't really know the game at the time," Seidel said. "But I got to sit right behind him and watch. It was a very special thing to be sitting there, watching maybe the best player in the world. I got to see his cards and see how he played. How many people get an education like that? I didn't always understand what was going on, but it made a big impression on me. It made me really curious about the game, and a short time later I started playing tournaments." (It might be added that not everyone picks up on things as quickly as Seidel. The first time he played in the main event of the WSOP, he came within a hand of upsetting Johnny Chan for the championship, a confrontation that was immortalized in 1998 in the movie *Rounders*.)

When it comes to skill, there's nothing like gin or poker. In cards, the luck always balances out. The good players are going to win. I really love it when a player kinda knows what he's doing. Those are the best players to play against. Because they know just enough to get themselves into trouble, but they don't know how to get out. That's how I make my money. Any player that thinks card playing is a game of luck—I'll show you a fool. That's what the losers always say. I got unlucky, or he got lucky. The winners don't worry about the short term; we play for the long run.

Jim Albrecht, who directed the World Series of Poker for many years, until his death in 2003, echoed the consensus about Stuey's skills. He recalled, in particular, a hand where Stuey made what Albrecht considered an incredible call to win a large pot.

"It was in a side game during the 1984 WSOP and I was the day shift supervisor at the time. I was doing the table drop on the hour when I came to a no-limit hold'em game where I knew all the players. The pot was down to Doyle Brunson and Stu Ungar. Doyle had made a monster bet at the pot and Stu was thinking long and hard. He lifted his cards for another look, and I saw his hand: two deuces. The board showed five over cards, including two face cards. Stu called Brunson's bet—which had been a stone bluff. The two deuces were good for a pot big enough to buy a house Wayne Newton would be happy with. That was my introduction to a player I followed throughout my career. I honestly do not believe I have ever seen a more talented no-limit player or a more disturbed life, all contained in one person."

In some ways, Stuey's demons and the erratic behavior they produced only added to his legend. In 1989, to get to the Super Bowl of Poker, which had moved the previous year from Lake Tahoe to Caesars Palace in Las Vegas, Stuey decided to drive to the casino in his Jaguar instead of taking his usual cab. Coming off the I-15 freeway ramp at Flamingo, he smashed into the back of another car. It wasn't just any car—it was a police cruiser. The damage to the cruiser was minimal; Stuey's Jag definitely got the worst of it. But the real problem—as if smashing into a police car weren't bad enough—was that Stuey had no driver's license.

Fortunately, the police officer happened to be a small-stakes poker player who idolized Stuey. When Stuey explained that he was late for the start of the Super Bowl's main event, the officer let him go without even writing a ticket. Where else but Vegas would such an excuse fly?

To cap off the saga, Stuey ran into Caesars Palace, took his seat in the tournament, which was already under way, and went on to win it for his second consecutive year and his third time overall, collecting $205,000.

There were other memorable moments. After the Mirage opened in 1989, its card room quickly became the center of the poker universe, featuring the highest limits and the best games. One night, Stuey walked in but found to his annoyance that there was a long list for the high-limit game. Not wanting to sit there and wait, he decided to kill some time by taking a seat in a $10- to $20-limit hold'em. The sight of a high roller and former world champion sitting in on a low-limit hold'em game made up of amateurs, tourists, and semipros was certainly a novelty. Before long, it became obvious that Stuey wasn't taking the game very seriously. He kept raising no matter what cards he was dealt. As he lost hand after hand, one of the players rolled his eyes and said, "You're the kid who won all those tournaments?"

"Yeah. I raise," Stuey shot back.

"I was in every pot," Stuey said. "Raise, raise, raise, raise. I'm probably the only player in history to lose $5,000 in a $10 to $20 game."

On another occasion, at a major tournament, Stuey was at a table with Phil Hellmuth Jr., Ken "Skyhawk" Flaton, Jim Boyd, and a cantankerous South Carolinian turned Las Vegas professional, Sam Grizzle.

"The action was hot and heavy with that lineup," recalled Jim Boyd. "Sam and Stu got into a big pot and Sam won it, knocking Stuey out of the tournament. As Stu was getting ready to muck his hand, Sam asked to see Stu's cards."

Phil "Doc" Earle, who was sitting at the next table, picked up the story from there: "I guess Stuey was fed up with Grizzle and decided to really let him get a peek at those cards," he said. "It's bad etiquette to ask to see a losing man's hand, and Stuey practically bitch-slapped Grizzle with those cards." Earle wound up having to physically separate the two men.

In 1990, as the World Series of Poker rolled around, Stuey was broke and strung out on cocaine. His habit was now costing him $1,200 a week, forcing him to borrow money from other poker players. For the first time, he was lying to his backers, telling them the money was for poker but using it instead to buy drugs.

The morning of May 12, the first day of the championship, Stuey was little more than a railbird (a derogatory term used to describe the brokesters who watch the action from behind the barriers surrounding the tables). Seeing what he deemed a good business opportunity, long-time backer Billy Baxter agreed to put up the $10,000 entry fee for Stuey in exchange for half his profits.

By the end of the first day of the tournament, Stuey had built up his stack to over $70,000, good enough to put him among the leaders. Stuey was always at his best when he could exert pressure. As Mike Sexton said, "He's so far above everybody else in the world when he's got chips that it isn't funny."

"Go back and look at all the World Series tournaments I played in," Stuey agreed. "As soon as they reached the level where antes began, when the blinds first went to one and two hundred, within an hour I had just about every single twenty-five-dollar chip on the table. I went after the antes so much, they had to go into my stack to make change."

After the first-day chip count was completed and verified, Stuey returned to his room across the street at the Golden Nugget, the most elegant hotel in downtown Las Vegas. Baxter was happy to pay for Stuey's hotel room during the tournament week. He wanted his horse to be rested and happy.

Midway through the second day, I had the tournament won. I had pocket tens, the flop came ace, ten, rag. I flopped three tens. The other guy pushed in all his chips on a gut-shot straight draw. I called him in a heartbeat. He had a king and a jack. On the river a queen came. He hit the gutter ball. If I had won that pot, I would have had five hundred thousand in chips early in

the tournament! It would have been all over. I mean, over. Done! No one
else would even have had two hundred thousand. There was no way I'd lose
if I won that pot. But those are the bad beats you have to take.

Even with that misfortune, Stuey remained among the chip leaders, in a
good position to make it to the final table. As he had done the night before, he returned to his hotel room at the Golden Nugget. Since no one
saw him during the remainder of the night, it was assumed that he had
gone to bed to prepare himself for play on day three.

A few minutes past noon the next day, Billy Baxter received an ur-
gent call at his palatial home in Las Vegas's southern highlands from one
of the tournament directors, Jack McClelland. "Stuey's not here,"
McClelland said.

"He's not there? How could he not be there? He's one of the chip
leaders in the goddamn World Series of Poker!"

All the more baffling was the fact that Stuey's hotel was right across
the street from Binion's. Where the hell could he be? Baxter stormed out
of his house and hauled ass over to the Horseshoe poker room.

When he got there, Stuey still hadn't shown up. Baxter grabbed a
house phone and had the hotel operator ring Stuey's room at the
Golden Nugget. The phone rang and rang. No answer. Baxter slammed
down the phone and called hotel security immediately. Then he ran
across Fremont Street and went up to the Nugget's front desk, telling the
management that it was an emergency, something was wrong, and he
had to get into Stuey's room.

A security officer escorted him to room 341. The hallway was eerily
quiet except for the slight hum of the air-conditioning and the soft pad
of their footsteps on the thick carpet. The security officer knocked on
the door, and when there was no answer, used his passkey to gain entry.
As he stepped into the room, he gasped.

Stuey was sprawled across the floor, in his underwear, unconscious and barely breathing.

As Baxter knelt down beside him, the security officer barked into his walkie-talkie, "Room three-forty-one, code ten-zero-five-four. Call Medical. We have an emergency."

While the rest of the world's best poker players were across the street in the Horseshoe, betting and raising and playing their way down to the final table and the $1 million top prize, Stuey, unconscious, was being strapped to a gurney and raced to a service elevator, then through a series of interior passageways, out of sight of the hotel's guests, to a back door where an ambulance was waiting.

Six minutes later, Stuey was wheeled into the emergency room at University Medical Center on West Charleston. Baxter followed the ambulance to the hospital in his car, and once there, informed the doctor on call about Stuey's drug problems.

The doctor, taking a cursory look at Stuey, assumed he was a minor.

"Are you his father?" he asked Baxter.

"What?"

"Are you the patient's father? We'll need his medical history."

"Hell no! I'm not his father! That man right there is almost forty years old. What's wrong with him?"

"He's forty?"

"I don't know exactly, but close to it."

Stuey was in fact thirty-six, although he had no identification to prove it. He also lacked insurance and medical records. Baxter tried his best to explain the odd predicament they were in and why it was important that they proceed quickly, but when the doctor asked who was responsible for Stuey, the flustered Baxter said he didn't know. So, Stuey was treated as indigent. The prodigy who had won tens of millions of dollars was, in the eyes of University Medical emergency room, no different from a homeless man who had been wheeled in off the streets.

They moved him into a curtained alcove, and Baxter followed. Stuey lay motionless on the gurney, breathing with the support of a respirator that an orderly had hooked up. An IV ran from his arm up to a clear bag suspended from a hanger.

Baxter leaned over his unconscious friend.

"Stuey, wake up!" he ordered. "Stuey!"

A nurse walked in and looked at Baxter as if he were crazy. "Can I help you?" she asked.

"Yeah. This is a friend of mine. How long is he going to be like this?"

"Look, I'm afraid you're going to have to go out to the waiting room," the nurse snapped.

Baxter did a slow burn. She didn't understand. Of course, he was concerned about his friend, but he was just as worried about what was happening over at Binion's Horseshoe. Round by round, hand by hand, Stuey's chips were being anted off. Missing a few hours was still something that Stuey could recover from, but as the time continued to tick by, Baxter's investment was slowly but surely going down the tubes.

"This man is going to be here for a while," the nurse said, as Baxter lingered. "He probably won't be released for a day or so."

"You mean to tell me that there's no chance of him getting up and walking out of here?"

"That's right," the nurse said. "Now if you don't mind . . ."

Shaking his head, Baxter retreated. His dream of banking Stuey to his third world championship had been crushed.

Baxter drove back to the Horseshoe. When he entered the poker room, he saw that a number of players had already been eliminated. The field was already down to two tables.

"Where's Stuey?" he was asked.

"In the hospital," Baxter said through clenched teeth.

No further explanation was necessary. Baxter's surly attitude spoke volumes.

As Baxter drew closer to the two remaining tournament tables, he saw that Stuey's vacant seat still had a substantial stack of chips in front of it. His initial $70,000 had been blinded down to $53,000.

Baxter watched the action for a while. He even asked Jack Binion if he could play Stuey's chips. The answer, of course, was that he couldn't. The dealer continued to push two cards to Stuey's empty seat each hand, mucking the cards when it would have been Stuey's turn to act. All the while he kept plucking the appropriate antes and blinds from the missing man's slowly dwindling stack. It was torture to watch, hard not to imagine that at any moment Stuey would burst through the door and take his seat. At last, Baxter grew too frustrated to continue watching. He walked outside in the hot desert air, fuming that his friend's weakness had cost him—and them—this golden opportunity. It was one thing to get into an accident or have a health problem, but there was no excuse for what Stuey had done. As Baxter drove home, he seriously doubted he would ever back the Kid again.

Incredibly, even though Stuey missed the final two days of this World Series of Poker, his rudderless stack of chips earned him a ninth-place finish and $20,050. Billy Baxter, despite his justifiable disappointment and anger, still managed to make 50 percent profit on his $10,000 investment.

The $1 million first prize and the gold bracelet ended up being captured by an Iranian expatriate from London named Mansour Matloubi, in what was arguably the most exciting final table ever. One can only speculate what might have happened and how poker history might have changed if Stuey had shown up on day three, head screwed on and ready to play.

15.

HEART OF A CHAMP

The World Series of Poker of 1990 left Stuey feeling humiliated and embarrassed, though he wouldn't say as much. He was angry with himself. He'd had a shot at making history and at really setting himself apart from all the other great poker players. He might have been the dominant tournament poker player through the 1980s, but it had been nine years since the high of winning in 1980 and 1981. And that was a high no drug had been able to match.

Nothing motivated Stuey more than competition. As Teddy Price, his friend and erstwhile opponent at gin, once said, "the cheapest commodity in his life was always money." Stuey lived to win. That was why he'd never been able to hustle anyone. He hated losing too much. So, after the 1990 World Series, when Stuey saw the attention and acclaim Mansour Matloubi was receiving, he couldn't help thinking that he should have been the winner. Even worse, some people were talking about Matloubi, who had come to the United States with a reputation for being a fearless player with a superaggressive style, as the new Stuey Ungar. So Stuey, after procuring backing, issued a challenge to the current world champ to play a heads-up, winner-take-all no-limit freeze-out match for $50,000. Matloubi wasn't one to back down, and he accepted the offer happily.

The contest took place downtown, across the street from the Horseshoe, at the Four Queens Hotel, during the Four Queens Poker Classic of 1991. The sight of two of poker's biggest names at the same table, going mano a mano, drew several dozen spectators, who pressed in close. Each player put up $50,000 in cash, which was stacked up on the table, just as it was in the World Series of Poker during the heads-up end game. The two would play until one of them had all the chips.

Matloubi had a lot of gamble in him, and he wasn't intimidated by Stuey's reputation. He took an early lead, riding a string of good cards and pressing the action. It seemed that the contest might end rather quickly. But Stuey then made a series of reraises that forced Matloubi to fold, and after forty-five minutes he had pulled slightly ahead. Phil Hellmuth Jr., the 1989 world champion, described what happened next:

Stuey opened for $1,600 in the small blind, and Mansour called with 4-5 offsuit. After a flop of 3-3-7 rainbow, Stuey bet $6,000—he started the hand with $60,000 to Mansour's $40,000—and Mansour called the $6,000 bet. On fourth street, a K came off and both players checked. On the river a Q came off to make a board of 3-3-7-K-Q, and Mansour, smelling weakness in Stuey, bet his last $32,000 or so. Stuey looked "right through" Mansour, and within ten seconds he said, "You have 4-5 or 5-6; I'm gonna call you with this."

Stuey then flipped up 10-9, and called the $32,000 bet with merely ten-high! Wow, what an unbelievable call! Stuey can't even beat a jack-high bluff with his hand, never mind any pair. In fact, Stuey could only beat 4-5, 4-6 or 5-6 in this scenario.

Give Mansour some credit. He did read Stuey right and made a great bluff. But Stuey deserves even more credit. He not only read Mansour right, he then made an amazing call. After Stuey called, Mansour looked up at the ceiling thinking, "I feel so crushed. It's almost like a bulldozer just ran over me. I still love Stuey, but what the heck is going on!"

Mansour tells me now, "When a guy makes a call like that against you, you just give up. It's like he's taken all the wind out of your sails. I decided that I couldn't play any more heads-up no-limit hold'em, at least on that day, if not forever."

Indeed, it proved to be the last hand that Mansour ever played with Stuey heads-up.*

For Stuey, the conquest of Matloubi was a sweet vindication, especially because his nearly otherwordly skills were displayed so dramatically in front of a crowd. As the $10,000 main event of the Queens Poker Classic tournament got under way at the Four Queens Hotel, he was feeling munificent and put up the entry fee for his friend Mike Sexton in exchange for 50 percent of Sexton's winnings.

Midway through the event, Sexton got involved in a big pot in which all the money went in before the flop. "The three of us were all-in," Sexton recounted, "and somebody said, 'Let's turn 'em faceup' [today, most tournaments require players to turn up their cards when everyone is all-in, but back then it was not a rule], so we turned our hands over."

Sexton had two queens and was delighted to see his opponents flip over identical hands—pocket tens—which meant that they were practically drawing dead. He was a 97 percent favorite to win the pot.

Doyle Brunson was sitting at the table and shouted across the room to Stuey, who was seated at another table, "Hey, Stu, your man's all-in!"

---

* From *Cardplayer* magazine, by permission of Phil Hellmuth.

Stuey jumped from his seat and raced over to watch the hand unfold.

"Whatta we got? Whatta we got?" he asked Sexton.

"We're getting ready to triple through," Sexton said, excitedly.

"All right! All right!"

The flop came J-9-2 of three different suits.

The turn brought a seven, and the two players with pocket tens, who had begun to get up from their seats and collect their belongings, now hesitated. The seven had actually given them a glimmer of hope. There was a possible inside-straight draw. It meant that they would have to catch an eight on the river. It was still 11–1 against, but at least they weren't drawing dead.

Sexton, who had been certain of tripling up, now felt the slightest jolt of queasiness. Luck couldn't be that cruel, could it?

The river card was dealt, and even though the thought had entered his mind, when the dealer actually flipped over an eight, Sexton's whole body recoiled, literally moved back from the table. Everyone who was looking on gasped audibly.

The players with the pocket tens let out a cheer that was heard in the slot pits on the other side of the casino. Doyle Brunson shook his head in disbelief. "I've been playing poker for thirty years," he said, "and I've never seen that happen."

Stuey stood there for a moment but didn't say a word. His investment in Sexton was gone, lost in about as bad a beat as one could imagine. He knew better than to say anything; instead, he walked quickly back to his own table to catch the next hand being dealt. His horse had been knocked out of the race, but he still had chips of his own.

Six hours later, Stuey was playing for the Four Queens no-limit hold'em championship and the $250,000 first prize. At the final table, in a little over an hour, he broke every single player including the final one, a twenty-two-year-old dropout from Caltech named Huck Seed, who a few years later would become world champion.

What made the feat all the more remarkable was that Stuey was playing while in the grip of unbelievable physical pain. Earlier in the day, he had begun to get a toothache. By midafternoon, the swelling and pain was so severe that he couldn't talk. Had he not been involved in a major poker tournament his abscessed tooth would have required emergency dental surgery. As it was, Stuey hung tough despite the fact that the inside of his head was throbbing like the dance floor in a disco. It took a staggering sense of focus to block out the pain. "I had a hundred-four-degree fever," he said later. "But I didn't know it at the time."

The victory marked the ninth occasion that Stuey had made it to a no-limit final table. On eight of those occasions, he won. As he was presented with the gold trophy and the $250,000 in cash, no one inside the Four Queens grand ballroom could have possibly predicted the long hard road that was to follow. It would be his last win in a major tournament for six years.

With no family in Las Vegas, Stuey started playing poker regularly at both the Bicycle Club and the Commerce Casino in Los Angeles. He often stayed, while he was there, at Mike Salem's house in Sherman Oaks, which was within a twenty-minute drive of both card clubs. Stuey and Salem would go to the Hollywood Park or Santa Anita racetrack during the day, depending upon which was running, and then play poker at night.

Stuey's visits to California were motivated by more than just the need to get out of Las Vegas. He had met someone, a waitress at the Commerce Casino named Marcella Ortiz.

• • •

Marcella was an angel, as beautiful on the inside as on the outside. I heard she was running around with Rod Peate [a professional poker player in the L.A. area]. But I made up my mind I was getting her, and that was it.

I took her to the racetrack several times and eventually won her over. She even came to Vegas with me. Stefanie met her on a visit from Florida, and liked her a lot. They really got along great. Marcella had a son, a boy named Reuben. I met him, her sisters, her parents. We all got along really great. Marcella wasn't into money. She told Stefanie that she'd marry a cripple if she loved him. That's all that mattered to her—love. So that made it special between us. She wasn't into the money part of it. She really loved me as a person.

Despite their blossoming love, Stuey knew that if he was going to make things work he would have to clean up his act a little. He was thirty-eight years old, he had a drug habit, and he dressed like a man twice his age.

"Stuey always wore these Members Only jackets and double-knit pants," Mike Salem recalled. "I don't think I ever saw Stuey in a pair of blue jeans. Not even once."

Salem constantly ribbed Stuey about his old-school attire, especially since Stuey had the financial means to dress better. He persuaded Stuey to visit an upscale men's store in Los Angeles called Politics. Stuey bought a dozen pairs of pants and several expensive shirts, which were specially tailored for his small frame. On the way out the door, he noticed a $1,500 Christian Dior suit, which he added to his bill. The suit was Stuey at his most impulsive; it ended up crumpled in the bottom of his closet, never to be worn.

Stuey's new look—the snappy clothes and modern style—had a profound impact on the way he carried himself in public. At poker tournaments, where the mostly older men wore ragged baseball caps and cheap windbreakers, Stuey now stood out for reasons beyond mere youthfulness. He wore a white mohair sweater on one occasion, a blue haute-couture shirt on another, and a gold silk jacket at the World Series of Poker. But his new, flashier appearance didn't seem to translate into success at poker. As good as he looked, his game was unfocused, and the results reflected it.

For the first time in his life, Stuey considered the effects of his behavior in terms of how other people related to him. He wanted Marcella to like him, and he was concerned that aspects of his personality would grate on her or annoy her. New clothes were a start, but they did not alter his basic deficiencies in the kind of commonly accepted social behavior that most people took for granted. To help Stuey in his quest, Mike Salem's wife, Gail, agreed to help teach him some manners and etiquette. There was a comic sweetness to it all. The charm school convened at the Salem residence whenever Stuey was in town. Gail would sit down with Stuey and quietly explain the ways of the civilized world, teaching him how to hold a knife and fork, how to place a napkin in his lap, generally educating him as if she were Emily Post.

"His table manners were atrocious," Baseball Mike said. "When he ate, he used his knife and fork like a shovel. He'd talk with his mouth full. It was like watching a wild animal eat."

Gail constantly had to remind Stuey to chew his food before swallowing it. Correcting thirty-eight years of bad habits was a task that took immense patience, but the hard work paid off. He improved.

During most of 1991, Stuey spent so much time flying back and forth between Las Vegas and Burbank that the flight attendants on US Airways not only came to recognize him, they knew him by name.

Stuey hoped that his new look and improved manners would earn Marcella's affection. He was also incredibly generous with her, buying her a new car and helping her get out of credit-card debt by paying off her bill in one lump sum.

Coinciding with this new love in his life was Stuey's reconnection with his daughter. His relationship with Stefanie had been difficult after the divorce. But when she moved to Florida with her mother, things actually got better.

"During the summer I was seven or eight, it all started to change," Stefanie said. "I was sent to Las Vegas to see him, and that was when I started to get to know him on my own, and I got to see that he wasn't so bad of a guy as long as my mom wasn't around and they weren't fighting. I saw how much he loved me and I started to soften. We got really close."

Stefanie would spend holidays and part of the summer in Las Vegas with her father and his new girlfriend, whom Stuey had begun referring to as his "fiancée." When Stefanie or Marcella was in town, Stuey was a different person. He stayed around the house, hanging out with them by the pool in his backyard. He rarely went to the casinos. For a time, he even stopped snorting coke.

For Stefanie, the vacations with her father became something she looked forward to with great anticipation. She liked Marcella enormously, thought she was really beautiful and good for Stuey. "You could just see she loved my dad so much," Stefanie said. "And she was so good to me, and she was a good mom to her son, and just a good person, period." As for her father, well, the truth was that Stuey spoiled Stefanie rotten. It is not uncommon for a parent to try to make up for previous failings by overcompensating, and Stuey desperately wanted and needed this connection with his daughter.

"I would go home every summer with a new wardrobe," Stefanie remembered. "Anything I wanted, he gave me. He totally spoiled me. I couldn't ever do anything wrong. The only time he ever punished me, I was ten years old, at the end of the vacation, about to go back to Florida. My mom asked me on the phone if I'd been to Richie's grave, and I hadn't, and she was like, 'Well, I think you should.' And I was like, 'Okay.' So that night I had the bright idea to steal my dad's car, his Maserati. I took it when he was sleeping. I was only ten, and I didn't even know which pedal was the gas and which was the brake, and I drove it down the street to my friend's house. She was older than me, and I knew as long as I got to her house, she could take over and drive it to the grave."

The two girls planned it all out, even putting on makeup and putting up their hair so they'd look older, in case the cops saw them. Like her father, Stefanie was fearless. The two girls made it to the grave, with her friend driving, and then they drove back to Stuey's and went up to Stefanie's bedroom.

A few minutes later, Stefanie recalled, Stuey's next-door neighbor and friend, Dr. Ray Warchaizer, rang the front doorbell, and when Stuey answered, she overheard Warchaizer saying, "Stuey, I was going to come over earlier, but I thought you were out."

"What made you think that?"

"Your car wasn't there."

"What are you talking about? I've been home all night."

"When Dr. Ray left," Stefanie remembered, "my father went outside with him. That was when he realized that the car was parked in a different spot than he'd left it in. He came storming up to my room, and my friend and I were there, and he got so mad at us. He was like, 'You stole my car? You stole my car?' And I was like, 'Well, I didn't drive it that much. I let her drive it.' So she was sitting right there about to pee her pants, and he was like, 'You're older than she is. You didn't think there was anything wrong with this?' He was yelling at her and saying he was going to tell her parents. He was furious. He made her go home, and he told me I had to stay in my room. But an hour later, he came and knocked on my door and said, 'I'm sorry, honey. I can't punish you. I just can't do it. I know it's the right thing to do, but I just can't do it. It breaks my heart.' And I was thinking, 'Okay! This is so much easier than my mom.' 'Cause she was the hard one and he was just a softy. I was totally daddy's little girl."

When Stefanie was staying at the house, Stuey and Marcella had an interesting arrangement: Marcella would never spend the night. Stuey was old-fashioned. Although he was a womanizer and a chauvinist, he didn't want to set a bad example for Stefanie.

"He was very respectful of how it might affect me," his daughter said. "I didn't know it at the time, but looking back I think he was trying to protect me."

As if Stuey's domestic arrangements weren't complicated enough, Philly Brush, whose wife had recently died, was also staying on and off at the house on Coventry Lane. Stuey had a number of friends, but Philly was his oldest and dearest, and also his only tie to his old days back in New York. "He trusted Philly more than anyone else in the world," Stefanie said. Fortunately, the large house had plenty of room for this odd, disparate family.

The one other regular member of the household was the housekeeper, Jeanie. Stuey had absolutely no clue about maintaining a home, so Jeanie was indispensable. Her duties included cleaning, shopping for food, cooking, and paying bills. Jeanie was also—perhaps appropriately, given the character of her employer—a degenerate bingo player. Stuey was sympathetic and often gave her money when she was feeling a pinch.

With a large gathering at home around him, Stuey spent very little time inside the sportsbooks or the poker rooms. He had installed two satellite dishes in the backyard, so he could now tune in to virtually any game he wanted. When Stefanie was around, Stuey always made his bets at the casino through a runner. Sometimes Philly, if he was available, would run and make Stuey's bets for him. Stuey also used local bookies, who were plentiful in Las Vegas despite legalized sports gambling.

In the fall of 1992, with Stefanie back at school in Florida, Marcella moved in with Stuey, and Philly moved out and got his own place. Marcella was determined to get married. But Stuey dragged it out. He would later say, "The chase is the best thing about a relationship. After the chase is over, I lose interest." Now that Stuey finally had Marcella, his interest in her waned.

When she gave him an ultimatum—get married or else—and he still couldn't pull the trigger, she moved back to Los Angeles.

Once she was gone, Stuey started missing her, and the chase was on again. After several months of back-and-forth emotional torture, Stuey called her one day, and knew immediately from the inflection of her voice that something had changed.

"Are you seeing someone else?" he asked.

"Why do you say that?" she replied.

"I thought you might be seeing someone else."

There was an awkward pause.

"I am," she said at last, sounding upset. "How did you know?"

"I could tell," Stuey said. "It was your voice. I could tell by the tone of your voice."

"Do you hate me?" Marcella asked softly.

"No, not at all," Stuey said. "Have a nice life."

It might have sounded to her as if he were kidding. But he wasn't. After that conversation, Stuey never saw or spoke to Marcella again. "I always respected her," he said. "But I didn't love her anymore."

Even without Marcella in his life, Stuey continued to make frequent visits to Los Angeles. But now, without any reason to modify his behavior, he began using drugs with a vengeance. He was staying at the Ramada Inn, a $45-a-night motel across the street from the Bicycle Club. Late one night, after suffering a particularly bad session at the tables, he returned to his room alone and depressed. In need of some kind of consolation, he went overboard.

Mike Salem was the one to find him. He got into Stuey's room later that night, just as Billy Baxter had done at the Golden Nugget two years

NOLAN DALLA AND PETER ALSON

earlier, and found his friend lying on the floor, unconscious. He called 911, and an ambulance arrived within minutes.

Stuey was rushed to the Community Hospital of Huntington Park, about three miles away. In the emergency room, a doctor stuck a needle into Stuey's arm. To Salem's horror, Stuey didn't even flinch. He was completely unconscious. The next step the doctor took was to pump Stuey's stomach. That was the bulk of the treatment.

Amazingly, just a day later, Stuey got up from his bed and left the hospital without even checking out. That night, he was seen back at the Bicycle Club playing $200–$400 stud, still wearing the hospital ID tag on his left wrist.

On another night at the Bike, Stuey sat in on a huge poker game that had been built around Roger King, one of the brothers who owned King World, the syndicators of popular television shows like *Jeopardy!* and *Wheel of Fortune*. King was superrich and loved to gamble. He was what casino executives referred to as a "whale." To get his business, casinos would cater to his every whim. So would high-stakes poker players.

Aside from Stuey, the other participants in the game that night included Doyle Brunson, Chip Reese, and Johnny Chan. With such a tough lineup, the results were predictable. Roger King threw a party. A mediocre player when sober, King was even worse when he was drinking. After several hours, and numerous visits from the cocktail waitress, King had lost all the money he had on him. He might have been worth millions, but late at night even a rich gambler may need cash. According to Stuey, King borrowed a large sum of money from Johnny Chan and promptly lost it. King then turned to Stuey, who was only too happy to oblige King with a loan of—reportedly—$150,000.

King continued to hemorrhage money. Early the next morning, as the sun came up, he finally left the game, having swelled the bankrolls of at least four of the world's best poker players. That evening, it was time to collect. Stuey took Mike Salem with him, and they went to visit King in his hotel suite at the deluxe Westwood Marquis on Hilgard Avenue near the UCLA campus. The elevator took them straight up to King's suite, which was the top-floor penthouse. King answered the door, wearing a bathrobe.

"What do you want?" King asked.

"I want my money," Stuey said.

"You guys really fucked me last night," King said. "You got me drunk and really took advantage of the situation."

By this time, Stuey and Salem had made their way into the suite. Stuey sat on a large ottoman next to an even larger couch. "I'm here to collect my money, Roger," he stated matter-of-factly.

"You've been cheating me," King said.

"What the fuck? Now w-w-wait a minute," Stuey stammered, angered by the prospect that he wasn't going to get the money. Stuey turned to Salem and asked him to leave the room. Salem was only too happy to get out of there; he went into the hallway and waited.

"You gonna fuck me on this, Roger?" Stuey asked.

"Here's what we're going to do," King said. "I'm going to write you a check for seventy-five thousand and we're going to call it even." It was an old gambler's move, trying to strike a deal for a lesser amount.

"I don't think so," said Stuey. "I want my money. You owe me one-fifty, not seventy-five."

"I'm going to give you a check for seventy-five and next time I'll owe you. Take it or leave it," King said, writing out a check and holding it up in the air.

Convinced that he wasn't going to get the full amount, Stuey grabbed the check out of King's hand. As he rode down the elevator with Salem, he slapped his head. He didn't have a driver's license or any other form of ID. The check made out to "Stu Ungar" was hardly worth the paper it was printed on. To make matters worse, the check was drawn on a bank in Boston. Stuey had no bank account, no ID, and no means by which to cash a personal check, especially such a large one.

Stuey went right back up in the elevator. He rapped on the suite door.

"What the fuck?" King said angrily, pulling back the door.

"I need the check made out to Mike Salem."

"What?"

"Just do it."

"Where's the old check?"

"Here, tear it up and write a new one so I can get this cashed."

With the new check in hand, Stuey and Salem immediately drove to a nearby bank and deposited it. With some clever improvising, it cleared only two days later. According to Doyle Brunson, King paid the debt in full a few days later.

Not all their adventures were quite so intense. When Stuey was in town, he and Salem often followed up a day at the track by playing gin with each other in Stuey's motel room. They would play for only $20 a game, so it wasn't about the money. Stuey just needed company.

"We used to stay up and play gin for twelve to fourteen hours straight," Salem said. "We'd stay up all night sometimes. I know Stuey would do some stuff to stay up. I mean, when I was starting to doze off, he'd be ready to deal another game. The thing was, it never seemed to affect his life much at the time. He'd do it, then stop, and everything would be okay. He took it too far a couple of times, but he could always bounce back and be good as new.

"When he had too much, he'd just sleep it off. The next day he'd get up and go play poker or go bet on a game and for a few weeks he wouldn't do it at all. I used to fly into Vegas every weekend. I'd stay at the Mirage. I was giving one of the hosts there baseball games to bet on. In return, he set me up with a suite on the thirtieth floor every weekend. So

Stuey liked to stay with me at the suite most of the time. We'd bet sports all day and crash in the room when we needed to."

At one point, Salem was running bad and mentioned as much to Stuey during the course of a phone conversation.

"What do you need?" Stuey asked.

"Nothing, Stuey. I'll make it."

A few days later, Stuey sent enough money to cover four mortgage payments on Salem's house in Sherman Oaks.

"I didn't even ask for it," Salem said. "He just did it. That was the kind of guy he was. When you needed help and he had money, he'd do anything for you."

16.

CHASING THE DRAGON

I've achieved everything a man could want . . . but I have nothing at all.

Years of neglect and escalating drug consumption were starting to take a serious toll on Stuey's health. Through most of his life he had managed to fend off any major illness, but in 1993, as he approached his fortieth birthday, he started to encounter difficulties with breathing.

The asthmatic condition he developed was unusual for a person of his age, but he insisted quite reasonably that it came from years of sitting next to chain-smoking poker players in poorly ventilated card rooms. After a few asthma attacks left him unable to breathe, he began carrying a prescribed inhaler, which contained Ventolin, a medication for the relief of severe bronchial spasms. It became a common sight to see him at a poker table armed with his little white L-shaped albuterol inhaler, which he kept tucked inside his pocket at all times.

Stuey's other major medical problem stemmed from his teeth, which were in a horrendous state of decay as a result of poor care and inattention. After his win at the Queens Poker Classic in 1991, when he'd had the abscessed tooth, Stuey had begun seeing Dr. Ray Warchaizer, a dentist who was his neighbor in Las Vegas.

"The first impression I had when I saw Stuey was that he looked like a jack-o'-lantern," Warchaizer recalled. "Just about every other tooth was missing. I'd never seen anything like it."

Treatment began immediately, and would ultimately take many sessions of reconstructive surgery over an extended period. Warchaizer's biggest challenge was getting Stuey to cooperate.

"Any dealing with Stuey required tremendous tolerance," Warchaizer said. "He could switch gears at any time. Just because he was sitting in a dentist's chair with his mouth open and shot up with Novocain was hardly enough to separate him from doing what he loved most. He'd scare the other patients, running through the office to the front desk phone with a bib on and God knows what sticking out of his mouth."

Warchaizer, in his fifties, a member of Mensa, found in Stuey someone he understood and could relate to, since he also played poker and was well acquainted with the gamblers' lifestyle. Despite a slight age difference and their having little in common professionally, the two men quickly established rapport. Like many of the caretakers who had helped Stuey through the years, Warchaizer recognized what was special about him and felt a need to protect him.

Stuey was easily his most difficult patient. "Sometimes everything flowed, and other times I was just emotionally wiped out at the end of a session with Stuey, just being able to accomplish whatever the dental task was at the time," Warchaizer said.

It was nearly impossible for Stuey to sit still in the dentist's chair. "Stuey would jerk around, jump up, run to the bathroom, and demand to use the phone to call ScoreLine while undergoing complex dental procedures that required delicate skill. His teeth hardly seemed to matter compared to what was happening on a baseball diamond in Cleveland or Milwaukee." At first, the dentist didn't read anything in particular into Stuey's frequent visits to the bathroom, but he soon came to suspect that Stuey was dealing with his losses by doing a few lines of coke.

Making an appointment for Stuey was pointless. He never adhered to a schedule, didn't wear a watch, and often didn't know what day it was. And of course, he didn't have dental coverage. Like everything else in his life, the dental work was paid for in cash, usually with a tip, which was typical of Stuey. When he had money, he could be counted on to pay his bill in full on the spot. One day, he even showed up at Warchaizer's house with two new bicycles for the dentist's stepsons. "He was very generous," said Warchaizer. "Sometimes he'd just give you something for no reason at all."

When Stuey was tapped out, Warchaizer carried his tab over to the next visit—or the next.

One week, Stuey arrived with a man named Frankie, whom he introduced as his chauffeur. Since Stuey didn't like to drive, the introduction seemed plausible. But on the next visit, he came alone, and when Warchaizer asked him what had happened to Frankie, the look on Stuey's face told the dentist everything he needed to know: a couple of bad weeks of sports betting had made the chauffeur suddenly expendable.

As the friendship between two men began to extend beyond the dentist's chair, they occasionally played gin at Warchaizer's kitchen table. Warchaizer had no chance to win, and Stuey quickly became bored, so he created alternative ways to amuse himself. One time, the two were playing but were interrupted when a call came in for Stuey. While Stuey gabbed on the phone, Warchaizer looked down at his hand. He had gin! He'd been dealt a perfect hand. Warchaizer could hardly contain his excitement as he waited for Stuey to get off the phone. The dentist was practically hyperventilating, but Stuey just kept gabbing away.

"He would look over at me occasionally, and I had to pretend indifference," Warchaizer recalled. "It turned out the son of a gun had done it to me on purpose. He had fixed the deck on me and was having a good time watching me while he talked on the phone. I wanted to gin, but I couldn't. It was agony for me having to sit there while he talked on forever."

As the two men became closer, Warchaizer began to win some of the games, which were played for a few dollars. To this day, he wonders if Stuey was letting him win out of friendship and gratitude. "I still don't know," Warchaizer said. "But I do know that after eight cards were played he could tell me card for card what was in my hand."

By the time all the dental work was completed, every tooth in Stuey's mouth had been replaced or capped. "It was one of my finest works of art," Warchaizer said. To protect what had been accomplished, Warchaizer taught Stuey to care for his teeth properly to avoid future problems. He even took a Water Pik over to Stuey's house and taught him how to use it. "It was like talking to a child," he recalled.

On the surface, Stuey seemed genuinely interested in taking care of himself. He assured Warchaizer that he would protect the work that the dentist had so painstakingly performed. But it proved to be a vow, like most vows in his life, that he would break. Stuey never followed through; the Water Pik wound up under the sink, collecting dust.

During all the dental work, Stuey had been taking the painkillers and antibiotics that Warchaizer had prescribed. He had been given strict instructions on what to take and how often, but he frequently ignored the recommendations on the prescription label, particularly with the painkillers. If his tooth hurt, why just take one or two pills? Why not take a handful?

Before long, Stuey got hooked on the euphoric effects of the prescription painkillers and began taking larger and more frequent doses. When he ran out, he went to Warchaizer and asked for more.

"It was hard to say no to him," Warchaizer recalled. "He was taking so many pills for pain that he built up a tremendous tolerance to whatever he was given. Still, I managed to hold a strong front."

One afternoon, Stuey was playing poker and collapsed on the table from exhaustion and the effects of all the medication. His head slammed face-first onto the edge of the table, breaking off one of the caps on his front teeth and causing massive bleeding. Stuey rushed to Warchaizer's office, where the dentist immediately redid the delicate work.

Warchaizer was able to help Stuey with his dental problems, but like many others, he watched helplessly as his friend's drug problem grew worse. Gone were the days when Stuey just did a few lines of coke to help him stay up through a long night. His psychological dependency on the drug was born of an emotional void so wide and so deep that nothing could fill it for long, no gambling bet, no tournament win, no wife, no girlfriend, no drug—yet he kept trying, gambling higher, pursuing more women, taking more drugs, trapped by compulsions he neither understood nor could control.

Cocaine was both the easiest and the unhealthiest of his addictions. Sometimes, his binges lasted days or weeks at a time. No one would hear from him, neither friends nor family.

He would miss appointments, fail to return calls, or even fail to answer his door. Then, he would magically resurface with no explanation of where he'd been. Madeline, Stefanie, Philly, Salem, Sexton, Warchaizer, and most of his poker-playing friends knew what was going on. It was common knowledge that Stuey had developed "a problem."

According to most sources, he was able to keep his addiction under control for extended periods, appearing, at least on the surface, to have put his problems behind him. Then, often without any explanation or obvious reason, something would trigger a binge and Stuey would vanish again. It was an emotional and physical roller coaster that went on for the rest of his life. As much as he may have wanted to quit and get clean, the temptation was always there—and the drug dealers knew it. Stuey was a cash cow, a dream customer, who always seemed to be able to acquire more money. If Philly was staying over and some shady characters showed up at the door, he chased them away, sometimes violently threatening them. But he wasn't always there, and the dealers were not so easily discouraged.

Doyle Brunson tried to help Stuey by getting him out of an environment where drugs were so easily obtainable. At Brunson's invitation, Stuey went to stay with him, his wife, and his son Todd, at their ranch in El Paso in West Texas. "My wife and I are very religious," Brunson said. "We tried to work with him. He could kick the stuff for a while, but when he had adversity, that's when he went back to it."

The Brunsons' ranch seemed like a perfect healing retreat for Stuey, a place where he could spend time sitting around talking, eating healthy meals, and watching television with people who cared about him and treated him like a member of their own family. And the program seemed to work for several weeks. Unfortunately, it was just a temporary respite, not a cure. Eventually, Stuey got antsy and decided to go back to Las Vegas.

"He wasn't ready to change his life, I guess," Brunson said, with regret in his voice.

In the early 1990s, Stuey had taken out a second mortgage on his house to raise money for gambling. Since he wasn't able to deal directly with the bank (through his entire life he never had a bank account or credit card), a friend of his wound up assuming the loan against the house on Coventry Lane (then valued at $250,000). Predictably, Stuey blew through the mortgage money. He stopped making payments. The friend gave Stuey several chances to make good on the note. But when Stuey didn't, the friend decided that there was no recourse but to foreclose.

Judy Ungar had been alerted by Stuey's ex-housekeeper, Jeanie, as to what was going on. Judy remembered calling Stuey from Puerto Rico and pleading with him not to lose the house. "Stuey, whatever you do," she said, "don't give up that house. That's the only thing you have that's yours, the only thing you have to show for all the money you've won."

Stuey tried to explain that he owed too much money on the note and had no choice. "If I give it up, I'm going to get $35,000 for my part, and that will be the end of it," he told her.

Judy argued that $35,000 wouldn't even last a day with Stuey's habits. A house was forever, a home base, a place he could call his own. The conversation ended with Stuey promising that he'd try his best to keep the house. But just as with his mother's co-op, twenty years earlier, from which all her possessions had been carted off because of his inaction, the house on Coventry was lost.

If Stuey had been in bad shape before losing the house, the period that followed was much, much worse. "I really wouldn't have been surprised to hear that my brother took a bunch of sleeping pills and killed himself," Judy said later, recalling the time. "He never said anything to me, but he told Jeanie at least twice that he wanted to kill himself."

For the first time since he had begun playing in the World Series of Poker in 1980, Stuey missed two tournaments in a row—1994 and 1995. He might have been able to find backers, but he was too strung out to perform well. Also, he'd already tapped most of his friends for money, and they were fed up with him, knowing that money they'd given him to play poker had gone straight up his nose. According to one source, some of his backers insisted that he take a urine test before they'd put him in action; even then, worried that he might have cheated the test, they sat behind him when he played, watching to make sure he didn't pull any funny business.

Stuey had become an anachronism. Barely forty years old, he was living in a city that was changing before his eyes, addicted to a drug that had been trendy years earlier, and down on his luck when the financial boom of the 1990s and a new generation of high rollers were beginning to make his five-figure sports wagers seem pedestrian.

In 1994, a middle-aged Greek immigrant named Archie Karras, who had arrived in America penniless, walked into the Horseshoe with a couple hundred dollars and began shooting craps. Within a few hours he was betting $1,000 a roll. Within a few days he was betting $100,000 a roll at a special table reserved just for him. Karras went on a winning streak that most gamblers could only conceive of in their wildest dreams, reportedly booking consecutive winning sessions of $1.6 million; $900,000; $800,000; $1.3 million; and $4 million. According to Michael Konik, who wrote about Karras's amazing lucky streak in *Cigar Aficionado*, "At one point, he had all of Binion's chocolate-colored $5,000 chips."

Karras claimed that he gambled high on craps because the poker action had "dried up." Karras simply couldn't find any players willing to put up the kind of money he wanted to play for. One who tried, with the backing of Billy Baxter (and reportedly of Reese and Brunson), was Stuey. The other top players had already tried to beat Karras and lost, and since Stuey was universally acknowledged as the best heads-up player ever, the consortium put up his stake, reasoning that even at less than his best, Stuey was still a good bet. Moreover, of all the top players he was the least likely to be affected by the superhigh stakes of the game.

The two forms of poker that Stuey and Karras played were seven-card stud and razz (a game much like stud, except that the best low hand wins) with limits of $5,000 and $10,000.

The late Jim Albrecht was a firsthand witness to the biggest-limit game that had ever been played until that point. "Even if you think you have an edge," he said, "playing at five-thousand and ten-thousand limits is like Russian roulette. If I use a gun with two bullets, and I give you the one with one bullet, you're a big favorite to live longer than me. But are you going to play? It's suicidal."

In six hours, Stuey lost $900,000 to Karras, at which point his backers pulled the plug. The nearly $1 million loss hurt more than Stuey's pride. It made those people who had still been willing to back him gunshy. By 1995, four years had passed since Stuey had last cashed in at a tournament, and the loss to Karras seemed to confirm that it was not a run of bad luck. Reese was the first to say no to Stuey, believing that cutting him off was the only way to motivate him to change his life.

Several other friends suggested that Stuey check into a drug rehabilitation center. Brunson even made the extraordinarily generous offer—after having failed earlier in his attempts to help—to pay for treatment. But Stuey steadfastly refused to seek any assistance. One reason he claimed he didn't want to check into rehab was that he believed drugs were just as available at the treatment centers—thus making the whole exercise pointless. He'd heard from Danny Robison, a recovering addict, that rehab was no guarantee and that some of the rehab personnel were working in tandem with drug pushers. "Hell, it's easier to get drugs in rehab than out on the streets," Robison reportedly told him. "After all, in rehab it's a perfect market. All your customers are right there."

The most visible sign of the physical toll the cocaine use was taking on Stuey could be seen in the damage to his nose. Snorting massive amounts of cocaine had gradually destroyed the central membrane that separated his right and left nostrils, causing his nose to literally cave in on one side. Close up, it looked like a prune. His breathing problems, which were bad already, got worse, particularly when, no longer able to snort cocaine, he began smoking it in the form of crack.

The effects of crack are much more intense and powerful than those of powdered cocaine—as well as shorter in duration and more highly addictive. The physical toll is also harsher; addicts often develop a chronic sore throat and hoarseness, and are vulnerable to emphysema.

In addition to his respiratory problems, which became worse with his use of this new drug, Stuey also developed severe peptic ulcers, the result of poor and inconsistent eating habits. For this new physical ailment, he began taking another prescribed medication, Sucralfate, which forms a pastelike substance that clings to the mucous membranes of the stomach and prevents damage from an excess of acid.

Old and infirm before his time, and perilously close to falling off the grid, Stuey was encouraged by Dr. Phil Earle to get back into playing poker. Doc Earle, as he was called, was part mystic, part genius, part eccentric philosopher—a poker-obsessed practicing medical doctor who had migrated to Texas from Newfoundland, Canada, and learned the game in the tough Texas underground scene. He had become a fixture on the tournament poker circuit and had gotten to know Stuey over the years. Earle believed that if the Kid could somehow refocus his energy on what he did best, he might get back on his feet financially and begin to recover.

In the spring of 1995, Earle backed Stuey in a number of small daily tournaments, just to get him back into the swing of things and keep him occupied. For a former world champion accustomed to playing in the biggest-money games in the known universe, $20 buy-in events at the Gold Coast casino were a huge comedown, but Earle looked on them as therapy.

Earle stressed the positive. Stuey was back in his element. He was taking small steps, but they were in a better direction. By the time the World Series of Poker of 1996 rolled around, Stuey had managed to scrape together enough money from assorted backers to maintain a hotel room at the Four Queens during the five-week tournament. Meanwhile, Earle had a room right across the street at the Horseshoe. One night, according to Earle, he had a nightmare that included Stuey. Panicked by the strange vision, he called Stuey's room at the Four Queens.

Stuey answered, half asleep. "Who is this? Doc? . . . What time is it? . . . What's the matter?"

"Stay there. I'm coming over. I have to talk to you."

Fifteen minutes later, Earle and a now wide-awake Stuey were sitting at a small round table in Stuey's room, talking by the soft glow of a single lamp.

Earle told Stuey about the revelation he'd had in his dream. "The only enemy you have is yourself," Earle said. "You're brilliant. You can do anything. But you're going down the wrong path. Who do you love more than anyone in the world?"

"My daughter," Stuey answered, without a second thought.

"Stuey, you've got loneliness. You've got boredom. You've got insecurity. Whatever you're doing, you're not solving those problems."

Earle tried to explain how loneliness was the most challenging of all personal demons. Being broke or having drug problems was something that was easy to fix. Broke? Get money. Drugs? Stop taking them. But inside the depths of the soul there were more difficult problems that were harder to diagnose. "When the problem is invisible," Earle said, "it's much more of a challenge."

Stuey said that he had tried to quit drugs many times. He knew the destruction his habit was causing.

"No, you haven't tried," Earle shot back, unwilling to let Stuey off the hook so easily. "You haven't tried hard enough. When you look at yourself in the mirror, look at yourself really close. I mean really close. Let me tell you something—a miracle happens. When you look at your deepest problems that way and aren't afraid to face them, they dissolve by themselves. You don't have to find an answer for yourself. It's not the end result, it's the attempt that matters."

They talked back and forth about the psychological addiction of drugs, Stuey saying that he could stay away for a while, but at moments of weakness, all it took was one slipup and he was back into it. The nightlong conversation left both men physically and emotionally drained. Earle hoped that the challenges he had laid out would have a profound effect on the way Stuey lived.

The truth is that this was a conversation Stuey had already had and would have again, in different forms, with friends like Mike Sexton and Billy Baxter, with Doyle and Todd Brunson a few years earlier, with Madeline and Stefanie and Marcella and Ray Warchaizer and everyone else who cared about him. And it always ended up the same way, with the same promises repeated over and over, that Stuey would try his best to change and grow. No matter how sincerely they were made, these promises could never be fulfilled.

Once the friend or group of friends was gone, once Stuey was left alone in the room with himself, with no one to talk to and nothing to do, the void would open up, the wound he could not heal or even identify. And then it felt as if his only salvation was to distract himself from it, with a phone call, or on a street corner, or in a crack house.

From the Four Queens it was a ten-minute walk along Fremont, past the tawdry souvenir stores and the pawnshops to a dingy motel room on Sixth Street that was open twenty-four hours a day, servicing the city's most desperate addicts.

By the start of the championship event, Stuey was clearly in no shape to play, "spaced out and high as a kite," according to one witness. But Billy Baxter, who had sworn never to back Stuey again after he had missed the third day of the main event in 1990, took pity on his friend and put up the $10,000. Baxter hoped it would help give Stuey confidence to conquer his other problems if he knew that someone still believed in him and thought the impossible was possible.

It may have been a good thought, but it was wasted. Stuey got knocked out of the tournament within the first thirty minutes, his quickest exit ever. Those who observed his play noted that he did not seem mentally alert, and he demonstrated none of the cutthroat characteristics that had served him so well in the past. The aggressive minia-ture pit bull who taunted his opponents and made extrasensory reads was nowhere in evidence.

It was painful for Stuey, having to stand up and walk out of that room before he'd barely even settled into his seat. As he wove his way through the maze of tables, he heard a few shouts—"Hey, look, Stuey's out!"—and felt a burning sense of shame. He vowed never again to show up in such an altered state.

17.

THE COMEBACK KID

The months following passed in what Stuey himself described as a drug-addled haze. He survived, as usual, with the help of friends, who lent him money and gave him a place to stay when he was thrown out of hotels for nonpayment of rent. Eventually, he moved in with Don McNamee, whom he'd met and become friendly with in and around various poker rooms. McNamee was a strong, robust man of fifty, who'd moved to Las Vegas from the oil-rich town of Valdez, Alaska, a decade earlier. He himself had beaten nasty drug and alcohol problems, so he understood what Stuey was going through.

McNamee was a Teamster working in the convention business. With the money he made doing that work and playing poker semiprofessionally, he'd been able to buy a nice four-bedroom home away from the Strip. Stuey was welcome to use one of the bedrooms free of rent, provided he stayed clean.

"I was there for Stuey for one reason," McNamee said. "I was his friend. I wasn't his mother. I couldn't look after him every second. But he was good company, and if I could help him in some way, I did it. He was an extraordinary person, without one bit of malice in his body—if you really got to know him, you saw and understood that. His main problem was that he always needed instant gratification. That was the whole deal with the drugs. Instant gratification. I'll tell you a funny story that Stuey told me that really gives you some insight into that side of him. When he was back in New York, he decided he wanted to become a jockey. You know, he loved horse racing. Just loved it. And in New York in those days he didn't have any trouble getting anything he wanted. So they [he and Victor Romano] go down to the racetrack, and he meets the trainer, and the guy hands him a shovel, and Stuey says, 'What's that for?' and the trainer says, 'Well, I gotta get you used to the horses.' And Stuey says, 'Fuck you. I just want to be a jockey.' He didn't care that he'd never ridden a horse. He was fearless. 'Just put me on the horse! Put me on the horse!' That was Stuey. That was who he was. 'Put me on the horse!' "

During one of Stuey's worst drug binges, Madeline and Stefanie grew concerned because they hadn't heard from him, so they took a trip to Vegas for a week, staying at the MGM Grand. After asking around, they were put in touch with Don McNamee. "He was a really good guy," Madeline said. "He told Stefanie, 'I am helping your father out and I want you to talk to him.' So we did, we got together, but I could tell that Stuey was still far away. He wasn't happy to see me. It was just like, 'Oh, well.' "

The three of them had dinner together, and Madeline told Stuey that he couldn't just disappear without a trace. She let him know in strong terms that he had a daughter to think of, and he hadn't talked to her or seen her or paid any support. Stuey got defensive. It wasn't as if he didn't want to take care of his daughter; he just didn't have any money. He even accused Madeline of wanting money from him for herself, not Stefanie.

It wasn't the smoothest reunion, to say the least, but McNamee told Madeline and Stefanie to be patient with Stuey. He was doing better, give it time. At least they now had a way to contact him and stay in touch.

On St. Patrick's Day, in March 1997, McNamee, who'd been doing all the cooking, decided that the time had come for his boarder to don the toque for a change. McNamee wanted traditional Irish corned beef and cabbage.

Stuey had never so much as boiled water, so he treated the challenge the way one might have expected—he freaked out.

"Stuey got more worked up than if he had bet fifty grand on a ball game," his host said.

After McNamee told him what to do, Stuey put the beef into a pot of boiling water and covered it.

"What do I do now?" Stuey asked.

"Every twenty minutes, you check it to see how it's doing."

Five minutes later, the nervous chef asked if he should take a look.

"You just put it in, Stu."

"But maybe it's done. I better check it. You think I should check it? I'm going to check it." This went on, with Stuey asking McNamee questions incessantly and running into the kitchen every couple of minutes to take a look.

When they finally sat down at the kitchen table, Stuey was thrilled with himself. "Is it good? Tell me, is it good? It's pretty good, isn't it?" He was desperate for approval, any kind of approval, even for something as trivial as boiling corned beef.

McNamee was sure Stuey was on the path to change, as if the adherence to the spartan lifestyle he'd set out was what Stuey had needed all along. "He was coming out of this self-destructive place to a place where life was going to make sense to him," McNamee said.

In 1997, however, just before the World Series of Poker, Stuey moved out McNamee's house, and McNamee lost contact with him. "It worried me," McNamee said. "Because I knew that whenever Stuey started using again he didn't want to be around me. At least initially. When he got really down and out and wanted to try and stop, well, then I'd get a call from him."

• • •

At 7:30 in the morning on May 16, 1997, five hours before the world championship was to begin, Doc Earle was sitting in the coffee shop at Binion's, finishing an early breakfast. He was surprised to see Stuey walk in. Gone were the fast gait and the manic enthusiasm that had always seemed to be such an essential part of Stuey's persona. Just by looking at him, Earle could tell that he had been up all night, trying to raise a stake. Stuey looked strung-out and beat. He joined the doctor in his booth and immediately wolfed down two pieces of dry wheat toast that had been sitting on the edge of Earle's plate.

"Stuey, you're in no shape to enter this tournament," Earle said. "Why don't you pack it in and get some sleep?"

Stuey forced his eyes open wider, to seem better off than he looked.

"Doc, you gotta put me in the tournament. It'll be the best money you ever spent. I'm in great shape. I know I don't look it, but I'm ready."

Earle didn't have the $10,000 entry fee to spare, but Stuey was so adamant that he persuaded Earle to give him $600, which, added to the $500 he had already managed to scrounge from some other players, was enough to pay his way into one of the last single-table satellites.

Stuey grabbed the six $100 bills out of Earle's hand gratefully, and raced out of the coffee shop, upstairs, and through a secret passageway that connected the old Horseshoe to the newer west side, at what used to be the Mint Hotel.

As he entered the poker room, a floor man was just calling a $1,050 buy-in satellite. "One seat left," he announced. "Single-table ten-thousand-dollar satellite!"

Stuey raced over to the table and grabbed the last facedown card on the table, securing his seat. He handed over the money and sat down.

Earle had followed Stuey from the coffee shop, and he now pulled up a chair behind him to watch—and protect the $600 investment.

One by one, players were eliminated. Nearly an hour into the satellite, it was down to the last two survivors—Stuey and a player from Houston named Herman Zewalski. With a $10,000 seat in the World Series of Poker at stake, Stuey made a modest raise with A-Q. When Zewalski reraised all-in, Stuey immediately called. Zewalski's jaw dropped. "You could see right away that Herman was dejected," Earle said. "I knew Stuey had him beat."

In fact, Zewalski was drawing to a three outer. He had Q-7, which meant that only one of the three sevens left in the deck could win for him.

The flop came without a seven. Stuey was two cards away from his seat in the World Series.

The turn was another blank. One more card to go.

Zewalski stood up, ready to shake Stuey's hand and congratulate him.

And then it came, a seven on the river, like a spike through Stuey's heart.

Oddly, he didn't scream or swear, as one might have expected. He just stood up slowly and walked away without saying a word.

For most, that would have been the final blow. But there were twenty minutes still to go before the tournament started, twenty minutes to raise $10,000.

Stuey picked up the house phone and tried calling Billy Baxter. He let it ring and ring, but there was no answer. At last, he hung up, looking around the room frantically. Where was the guy? He knew Baxter was playing in the Big One. He'd seen Baxter win the seat the night before. So where the hell was he?

When a quick walk around the room failed to locate Baxter, Stuey headed toward the door and the harsh sunshine outside. Baxter had been his last hope. Just before he got to the exit, he passed another house phone and decided to try one last time.

Billy Baxter was on his way over to the Horseshoe, driving north on I-15, when he heard his cell phone ring. He fished it out of the well underneath the dashboard and pulled up the antenna with his teeth.

"Hallo," Baxter shouted in his Georgia drawl.

"Billy, I been trying to find you everywhere."

"Oh, hey there, Stuey," Baxter answered guardedly.

"Billy, I can't get into the tournament unless you put me in. You gotta put me in," Stuey pleaded, seemingly oblivious of the fact that Baxter and everyone else had lost all faith in him.

There was a long pause, as Baxter considered the desperation in his friend's voice and how he felt about it. "I knew Stuey was having problems and wasn't in great shape," Baxter said. "But he was always hard to say no to. It just seemed from his tone that he wanted to play in that tournament more than anything, and in the end I didn't have the heart to tell him he couldn't. What the hell—I done worse things with my money."

A poker pro named Tommy Fisher was standing by the big board in the tournament area when Stuey's name was added to the list, the last player registered in a field of 312, the largest in the World Series' history. "That's wasted money," Fisher thought to himself.

Stuey certainly didn't look like the same player who had once struck fear into anyone unlucky enough to be seated at his table. He was perilously gaunt, with his belt cinched tight. His bangs were ragged; his hair was salted with gray. His caved-in nose was partially hidden behind cobalt-blue sunglasses, the kind that John Lennon had worn in his post-*Sgt. Pepper* days.

Stuey took his seat, along with the rest of the players, at a few minutes before one o'clock. He hadn't slept in nearly two days.

"I was looking across the room, and I could see Stuey," said Doc Earle. "Every once in a while, he'd start falling off his chair, swaying to the left, then swaying to the right, his elbow slipping off his knee. He was nodding off in the middle of the tournament!"

When Baxter walked in and saw Stuey's condition, he was furious. He leaned in close and hissed, "You son of a bitch, don't you fall asleep!"

At the first break, Stuey bumped into Mike Sexton on his way to the restroom. "Mike, I don't think I'm going to make it through this. I'm dying. I'm just not going to make it."

"He wasn't himself the first day," Sexton remembered. "He just wasn't totally there. But he got better and more comfortable as time went on."

Though Stuey was playing with only a fraction of his abilities, his natural aggression and fearlessness still gave him a big advantage over the field. In the early stages of the tournament, almost everyone played tight. Stuey, on the other hand, seemed not to care if he went bust, and as a consequence he was able to double his chips by the first break, and then again soon after, simply by bullying the fainthearted out of pots. But he came precariously close to elimination during the fifth hour of play.

The first day was always the toughest part for me. Once I got my hands on fifty thousand in chips, going after the other three million was easy. That's why I busted out early so many years. I never busted out in the middle. I was either out at the beginning or went on to win it.

The most important hand I played on day one was when I made O'Neil Longson lay down three sevens. I raised him on the river when the board paired the sevens. I bet out, he raised me holding a third seven in his hand, and I reraised enough to put him all-in. I knew what he had, but I also knew that he would lay that hand down if I raised him back. He's got to give me credit for the full house. It was an impossible call to make. It would have taken a kamikaze pilot to call with his hand. That was the key play for me. If I had lost that pot, I would have been down to twenty-five hundred and probably would have been knocked out of the tournament.

When you know what a guy has, he's got to know that you know what he has. And when you reraise him, you freeze him. I mean, you completely fucking freeze him. That's what great poker is all about. Taking a shit hand and outplaying somebody just by using your head.

The first day ended with Stuey at $41,175, seventh in chips among the seventy-seven remaining players. On Monday night, he went to a hotel room on the eighteenth floor of the Horseshoe that Baxter and Sexton had arranged for him. He didn't say a word to anyone and went to bed around midnight.

He was up and out of the room the next morning by 9:00. Doc Earle was sitting in a booth in Binion's coffee shop just as he had been the previous day. Twenty-four hours earlier, Stuey had looked terrible—eyelids drooping, a walking zombie. Now, he bounced into the place looking fresh and full of life. The doctor could hardly believe the transformation.

"He looked like a different person," Earle said. "He was shaved and all cleaned up and he looked terrific. He sat down with me, ate a full breakfast that a lumberjack couldn't have finished, and was just bubbling. Right then, I knew he was going to win it."

"Goddamn, Stuey, what happened?" Earle asked.

"I'll tell you, Doc, I got a full night's sleep."

"You what? How could you sleep? You're right up there with the chip lead."

"When my head hit the pillow, I was out."

Most participants in the WSOP complain about fatigue. It's not just the strain of the event, the energy required to sustain a high level of concentration over many hours and a number of days; it's also the lack of sleep. Many players get so wired up that sleeping becomes nearly impossible. In their hotel rooms, they toss and turn in bed, replaying the key hands of the day, and thinking about calls they made or didn't make, raises they should have made, and unlucky rivers that cost them precious chips. But somehow Stuey tuned it out and slept like a baby. He started the second day fresh and alert.

Play on Tuesday lasted ten long hours, and at the end of it, there were twenty-seven survivors who had made it into the money. Stuey was second in chips, with $232,000, behind a popular pro in Las Vegas, Ron "the Carolina Express" Stanley, who had $401,500. At the very least, Billy Baxter was guaranteed a small profit on his $10,000 investment. Day three would determine the six finalists who would play in front of the television cameras for the $1 million first prize.

On Wednesday morning, Stuey again joined Earle in Binion's coffee shop. Earle watched his friend devour a Benny's Special as they talked about the upcoming day. Stuey was excited and extremely confident. One of the topics they discussed was the reconfigured seating assignments that had Stuey sitting at the same table as his good friend and financial backer Billy Baxter. Remarkably, both men had made it into the money.

There have been instances of "soft-playing" and "chip dumping" in tournaments when two players with a shared financial interest are assigned to the same table; however, there is nothing to indicate that Baxter and Stuey did anything but play hard and square against each other.

Their table that day was arguably one of the toughest lineups ever assembled. "Stuey was on my right," Baxter said. "Phil Hellmuth was on my left, and Doyle Brunson was straight across from me. Chris 'Jesus' Ferguson [who would go on to become world champion three years later, in 2000] was also at the table. One of these assassins would jam the pot full of chips and the next one would re-pop it. I was sitting there in the middle of it like I was watching a Ping-Pong match. I mean, you raised at your own risk. I got to watching Hellmuth and Stuey. Finally, Hellmuth quit raising. Stuey was driving him crazy coming over the top."

Hellmuth would later say, "Stu's very good at looking at a player and knowing what he has. That's one of his strengths. I know because I personally bluffed off two hundred thousand to the guy during the tournament. In fact, my bluffing him so many times kept him going strong and knocked me out."

Hellmuth, Ferguson, Brunson, and Baxter (who finished twenty-second) were all eliminated during the course of the day. And Hellmuth was right: Stuey was in top form, with his reads of his opponents as good as they had ever been. In one hand, for example, a player named David Roepke opened the betting for $20,000 with a suited K-10. Stuey called with a suited K-Q. The flop came 7-6-2 offsuit, and Roepke moved in with the rest of his chips, nearly $50,000. Stuey called in a flash, confident that Roepke had neither an ace nor a pair. The turn and the river failed to produce a ten, and Roepke was eliminated. "No other player at the table would have called in that spot," Stuey bragged. "No one."

By the day's end, he had taken a commanding chip lead with $1,066,000 to Ron Stanley's $694,000 and Bob Walker's $612,000. The remaining three players—Mel Judah, a former hairdresser from London; Peter Bao, a $10- to $20-limit player; and John Strzemp, a recreational player who also happened to be the president of the Treasure Island casino—were all at $300,000 or below.

Gabe Kaplan, who was anchoring the telecast for ESPN that year, interviewed Stuey on the eve of the final. Kaplan had known Stuey for years, had played with him many times, and had obvious respect and affection for him, as Stuey did for Kaplan. Like everyone in the poker world, Kaplan was acutely aware of the rough times Stuey had been through, the problems that were still there, and the significance of his presence at the final table.

"How's it feel, Stuey," Kaplan asked, "leading the World Series of Poker going into the final day? Does it bring back a lot of memories?"

"Oh, it's great, Gabe," Stuey said. "It really is." He appeared relaxed, with the camera and lights on him. "You know, I haven't done well in this tournament since 'eighty-one, and I really forgot how great it is to be on TV, everybody shaking your hand and asking you how you're doing."

"Your life's been like a roller-coaster ride, Stuey," Kaplan continued, choosing his words carefully. "You've had some highs, some lows, some personal tragedies in your life. It must feel really good to get back in here and be competing, be in front, final day, World Series of Poker. What's gonna be your strategy tomorrow?"

"I'm gonna be a little more disciplined," Stuey said. "I'm not gonna tell you my strategy right now, but I'm gonna try and have half the chips and get down to heads-up with someone else—because I pretty much don't think that anyone can beat me two-handed."

Later that night, Billy Baxter and Mike Sexton visited Stuey in his hotel room upstairs at the Horseshoe. The memory of 1990, when Stuey had failed to show up for day three, was still vivid for Baxter, and he wasn't taking any chances this time.

"Stuey, if you don't show up tomorrow, I'm going to kill your ass," he said, only half jokingly.

Stuey looked down and shuffled his feet a bit. The shame of 1990 was something he still felt. "Of course, I'm going to show up. Are you crazy?"

Baxter understood how fragile Stuey was, and how much he needed encouragement.

"Anyway, it's over," Baxter said.

"It's over? What are you talking about?"

"Tomorrow. It's all over. The rest of them—they're playing for second place."

The effect of Baxter's words was more powerful than a hit of cocaine. Instantly, Stuey stood up and started bouncing around the room, like a boxer showing off his moves, as if fully realizing how close he was to doing something no other player in history had ever done—winning three world championships.*

"I did that to get him psyched up," Baxter said. "I knew that if I did that, letting him know how much confidence I had, it would elevate his mind to another level. And that's exactly what happened."

Local bookmakers had slated Stuey as the –140 favorite over the rest of the field, meaning that to win $100 on Stuey, one would have to bet $140. Incredible as it may seem, the oddsmakers were saying that Stuey was a favorite over the rest of the five players combined. That's how much respect they had for his talents. Baxter told Stuey he was betting every penny he could on Stu, even at those odds, and Sexton said he was, too.

Sexton underscored the importance of Baxter's remark and actions. "You have to appreciate the beauty of what Billy did for Stuey that night," he said. "If you knew Stuey, you knew that would pump him up—that here's a man willing to go out on a limb, and tell everybody that he's laying every dollar he can on Stuey. I mean, Stuey was so fragile at the time; that comment was just the perfect boost to get him ready and keep him straight."

On the fourth day, Stuey changed his daily ritual of meeting Earle in the coffee shop. Instead, he ordered from room service, not wanting any

---

* Johnny Moss also "won" three, but the first one, in 1970, was by vote. The following year, 1971, the tournament adopted the competitive freeze-out format that has been used ever since.

distractions. He didn't arrive at the final table until just moments before play started.

For the first and only time in the history of the tournament, the final was played outside. Bleachers had been set up around the table under the giant canopy of the Fremont Street Experience, the multimillion-dollar overhead laser light show that the Downtown Association had built in the early 1990s in a futile attempt to compete with the casinos on the Strip. With misters spraying clouds of moisture in the air to humidify and cool the ninety-eight-degree desert heat and an ESPN crew filming with eight-camera coverage, the players took their seats.

Stuey wore a frayed green long-sleeved, button-down shirt and a pair of too-large faded blue jeans. He also had on the blue-tinted granny glasses* that had become his trademark in the tournament. Ron Stanley wore a dramatic but impractical tailored black tuxedo, topped off with a baseball cap, which did not look like the wisest choice under the conditions. But it was difficult not to consider that Stuey Ungar, with twice as many chips, posed a bigger problem for Stanley than the nuclear heat.

You know what people get caught up in? The crowd. It's the crowd that really gets to you at the final table. You hear that "Ohhhhh!" You hear everybody that's talking, what they're saying. Every sense you have is going a hundred miles an hour; you just pick up on everything. It gets into your head.

Some players get lost at the final table. I mean they don't have a clue. Even some of the people that have won it.

I was dead broke at the time. But if I would have finished second, even

---

* Stuey explained later that he wore the unusual glasses to conceal the damage to his nose, an aim which they seemed to accomplish.

though the money would have been good, I would have been in a state of
depression you can't imagine. I would have killed myself if I had lost that
tournament. In my mind, I had no concept that I could lose. There was no
question about it. I was going to win. You have to understand that there
were a lot of people who were saying that Billy was crazy to put up the
money to get me in the tournament. So I had something to prove. I think
that motivated me more than anything.

Early on in the play, with the blinds at $5,000 and $10,000, Ron Stanley
opened the betting for $35,000 from early position. Stuey called on the
button, and John Strzemp called from one of the blinds. All three
checked the dangerous-looking A-K-6 flop. The turn produced a seven,
and this time, after Strzemp checked again, Stanley bet $45,000. Stuey
thought for a while, then called, while Strzemp folded.

A three came on the river, and this time Stanley checked. Stuey's call
had clearly scared him.

Without wasting much time, Stuey cut off ten red $10,000 chips and
slid them forward. Stanley, perhaps feeling the need to demonstrate at
the beginning of the day that he wasn't going to be pushed around,
called with A-J. When Stuey showed him an ace and a queen, he sighed,
nodded, and mucked his hand.

Phil Hellmuth, doing the commentary on ESPN along with Gabe
Kaplan, was moved at that point to say, "I see this tournament as a battle
for second place."

Kaplan, however, was quick to point out that Hellmuth had made
a similar pronouncement in a tournament where, from a chip position similar to Stuey's, Hellmuth had ultimately finished third. "Let's
not award it to him yet," Kaplan said. "There's a lot of playing left yet."

A round later, Stuey got involved in a hand with John Strzemp. An
earlier all-in move by Strzemp had prompted Bob Walker, the victim of

the raise, to comment that "it must be nice to have a job. You can play with no fear." And it seemed to be true. Strzemp, who bore an uncanny resemblance to the actor Gary Busey, seemed to have some of Busey's attitude at the table, too—which is to say that he was unpredictable and dangerous.

Now, on a flop of A-K-3, he checked. Stuey, as in the earlier hand, checked behind him. When a small spade came on the turn, putting two spades on the board, Strzemp bet out $45,000, and Stuey flat-called behind him. All this was very similar to the hand that Stuey had just played against Ron Stanley.

The river card was another low spade. Strzemp grimaced slightly, then bet $70,000. Stuey stacked and unstacked his chips, as he often did when weighing a move. Finally, he plucked seven red chips from a stack and flicked them into the pot.

Strzemp turned over a king and a ten of spades. The nut flush.

The crowd and the commentators murmured in surprise. Stuey himself seemed nonplussed.

Moments later the players reached a break, and as Stuey got up from the table, Gabe Kaplan collared him, calling him over to the broadcast table.

"Why did you make that call on the river?" Kaplan asked Stuey.

Stuey shrugged. "I knew he didn't have an ace, and I didn't think he got running spades. The guy could have been betting second pair and thinking it was good." It was a weak rationalization for what had amounted to a misread, and Kaplan felt entitled to tease Stuey about it. "What do you know about poker, anyway?" Kaplan said.

Stuey shrugged again. "The guy's an owner of a hotel," he said, implying that Strzemp was the kind of player likely to have anything.

"Ahh, take a walk," Kaplan ribbed him. "Go back to New York."

Stuey's main competition at the table still appeared to be Ron Stanley, who had recovered from the earlier hand against him, and built his stack up to a level at which he trailed by only a couple of hundred thousand.

Thirty-six hands into play, the two big stacks got involved in small blind–big blind confrontation, with Stuey having position on Stanley. Both players checked the flop of A-9-6, but when an eight of spades came on the turn, putting two spades on the board, Stanley bet $25,000.

Stuey again went into his stack-chopping routine, breaking the stacks down, shuffling chips between his long bony fingers, pondering, and finally raising $60,000. It was a semibluff. Stuey was holding Q-10. The eight on the turn had given him a gut-shot straight draw, nothing more. Most players would have folded in his spot and moved on to the next hand, but he had raised instead, putting Stanley to the test.

Gabe Kaplan discussed the hand with Phil Hellmuth as it was unfolding. "Having played a lot with Stuey," he said, "I would say either he's got the straight already, or he's drawing to it."

Stanley seemed to decide it was the latter and called the $60,000.

The final card, a king, made neither a straight nor a flush.

Stanley checked.

Now, Stuey bet $220,000.

"Stuey's got either ten-seven, five-seven, ten-jack, or ten-queen," Kaplan said. "One of those four hands." Two of them were the nuts and second nuts, and two of them were air.

"If Ron Stanley were to call and lose this pot," Hellmuth pointed out, "Stu would have an absolutely huge chip lead."

Hellmuth's remark divined the real power of Stuey's bet. Whether consciously or unconsciously, Stuey understood that the size of Stanley's stack would force him to the conclusion that calling and being wrong would be a disaster for him; whereas folding and being wrong would be only a serious mishap. You could see the gears spinning in Stanley's mind. Something about Stuey's bet smelled fishy, but in the end it was too risky a call. Stanley showed his 9-7—a pair of nines, in other words—and mucked. At this point, Stuey, turning the screw, flipped over his cards, revealing his bluff.

Both Stanley and the crowd were stunned as Stuey raked in the healthy pot, stacking his chips greedily.

A while later, Stanley opened up a hand for $35,000 with pocket kings, and was only too happy to call when John Strzemp moved in behind him. Strzemp turned over pocket tens, and when Mel Judah announced that he had folded a ten, Strzemp realized he was drawing to a one-outer.

The flop and the turn brought no help, but just as Strzemp's day seemed to be leading him back to valet parking, a miraculous ten on the river had Stanley looking like a man in need of a good antacid.

Stanley's horrendous luck in the hand with Strzemp, combined with his earlier mistake in laying down his nines against Stuey, caused him to come unglued. Not long after, he made a $60,000 bet on the button with J-8, and Strzemp (again!) called him from the big blind. On a flop of K-7-2, Strzemp, as he so frequently had in the tournament, led out with a bet, $80,000 this time; and Stanley moved in, over the top, for the rest of his chips, on what was a stone-cold bluff. His timing and his read could not have been worse. Strzemp had pocket aces. Adios, Ron Stanley.

Mel Judah was the next one out, overplaying a middle pair against Stuey, whom he mistakenly put on a draw. Suddenly John Strzemp was all that lay between Stuey and his third world championship.

Strzemp had about $900,000 to Stuey's $2.1 million, a substantial deficit; but of all the players Stuey had faced on the day, Strzemp seemed to be the only one he had failed to figure out.

As was the long-standing tradition, when the tournament got down to the final two players, there was a break in the action so the money could be brought out from the Horseshoe's vault. Several heavily armed security guards accompanied an executive who was carrying a cardboard Chiffon toilet paper box that now held $1 million in cash, in banded $10,000 bricks. It was typical no-frills Binion style to bring out the money that way—like Mike Tyson coming into the ring for the heavyweight championship wearing a towel with a hole cut in it instead of a fancy silk robe.

The money was stacked up at one end of the table, with the coveted gold bracelet laid on top like a glittering bow. Then, with the bounty in place, the combatants, who had stood up to stretch, took their seats once again, as did the spectators.

There was no slow build in the confrontation between Stuey and John Strzemp, no feeling out, no parrying and thrusting. As soon as the cards were back in play, they got into it.

The very first hand, Stuey raised Strzemp's big blind $40,000, and Strzemp, now wearing a pair of corded reading glasses, quickly called.

The flop came A-3-5.

The desert wind had picked up as the afternoon had worn on, and the dealer laid a clear piece of Plexiglas atop the cards to keep them from blowing away. Strzemp examined the board for a moment, then bet out—as he had so many times when first to act. One hundred twenty thousand.

Stuey started his chip-riffling routine, peering at Strzemp over the tops of his blue lenses. Uncharacteristically, as he shuffled the chips, the slippery disks slid out of his fingers and spilled across the felt. Was it nerves? He picked them up and began shuffling them again, continuing to stare down the casino executive.

Finally, he made his decision.

"I raise," he said. He moved five stacks of red chips toward the pot like a general deploying troops on a war map.

It was an $800,000 raise—all of Strzemp's money, in other words.

Strzemp wasted no time in contemplation. "I call," he said. He flipped over his cards defiantly. An ace and an eight.

Stuey cocked his head, as if surprised, and turned up his own hand. An ace and a four. Once again, he'd misread the amateur. He was trailing and needed help.

The turn card was dealt. Another three, pairing the one onboard, meaning that if the final card was a six, seven, or eight, Strzemp would win the $1.8 million pot and take a three-to-two chip lead. If, on the other hand, the final card was a four or a deuce, Stuey would win the tournament.

Any other card would produce a tie and a split hand, keeping things going.

The blond female dealer thumped the table softly and turned the final card.

A deuce!

Stuey clapped his hands triumphantly. John Strzemp blinked at the board as if not, for a moment, wanting to accept what his own eyes were telling him.

The crowd began hollering and cheering. It was over. Stuey had done it. He was champion again, for the third time.

Fans and players alike jumped over the rail and mobbed the little man. The television cameramen pushed forward trying to reach him. When Gabe Kaplan pulled him aside, finally, for a wrap-up interview, Stuey was emotional. He showed Kaplan a picture of Stefanie. "I did it for her," he said. "I called her up last night and she said to me, 'Daddy, I'm going to disown you if you don't win the tournament,' and I said, 'Stefanie, I love you too much for you to disown me. I'm going to win.'"

"Stuey, let me ask you a personal question," Kaplan began, speaking loudly to be heard above the buzz, "and I think I know you well enough to ask you this question—"

"You do, Gabe, you do," Stuey said.

"In nineteen-eighty and 'eighty-one, you won the world champi- onship, but you weren't smart with the money after that, your life didn't go a hundred percent in the right course. Now you're older, you're wiser, you're forty-three years old. You think you're gonna do things differ- ently?"

"Well, I hope so, Gabe. You know, I've neglected my kid. I've done a lot of stupid things to myself, but I want to tell you something for a fact: there's nobody who ever beat me playing cards. The only one who ever beat me was myself, my bad habits. But when I get to playing the way I was, when I'm on stroke the way I was in this tournament, I really be- lieve that no one can play with me."

Just before the cameras broke away, Kaplan delivered his final comic dig to the man who had just won a cool million in cash: "Stu, you think I can get that three hundred you borrowed from me about six years ago?"

In fact, Stu still had the empty pockets he had arrived with five days earlier. The $1 million in cash had already been carried back to the vault. When such a large sum is won, Binion's normally gives the winner a re- ceipt for the money; after that, a cashier's check is issued. Stuey was eager to split up the money with Baxter and take his share out the door in cash.

Jack Binion gave each of them a W-2 form to fill out, but just as he had done years earlier, Stuey ran into a snag when he was told that he needed valid identification, to be photocopied along with the com- pleted forms, before he could receive his share of the prize money. He no longer had valid ID. Moreover, the problem couldn't be resolved so quickly this time.

"I've got to have some walking-around money," Stuey said.

"How much do you need?" Baxter asked, ready to give him what he needed from his share of the winnings.

"Fifty thousand."

"Fifty thousand! For one night?" Baxter was incredulous. "How about five thousand?"

"No, I need fifty."

On this momentous occasion, it seemed impossible to refuse Stuey. Baxter counted out five packets and handed them to Stuey, who somehow managed to stuff the money into the pockets of his jeans. The remainder of the cash was locked inside the vault to be collected a few days later when Stuey returned with identification.

That night, Binion's held a catered banquet in Stuey's honor out on Fremont Street, in an area that was roped off. The guests included local celebrities, other players, friends, and members of the press. Stuey showed up wearing the same clothes he had worn in the tournament. He grabbed a chicken drumstick from the buffet and sat down at a small café table with Jack Binion, devouring the chicken leg like a man who hadn't eaten in days. Smacking his lips, gesturing wildly with the drumstick, and talking with his mouth full, Stuey hadn't changed one bit.

Yet for all the satisfaction he took in winning, something was missing. There were hundreds of people around him, players with wives and girlfriends, and there was Stuey, alone, flashing his Warchaizer-made smile at Binion.

After thirty minutes, Stuey shuffled back into the casino, moving through the door without looking up, so as to avoid eye contact with anyone. He went upstairs to his room. Later that night, he went out, but no one knows where.

18.

STUCK

Both major newspapers in Las Vegas—the *Sun* and the *Review-Journal*—put Stuey on the front page the next day, calling him "the Comeback Kid." It wasn't just the fact that he had won his third world championship—sixteen years after the previous one—that captured the public's imagination; it was the idea that a man who had been destitute and on the verge of homelessness had managed to win $1 million and redeem himself.

"That's when everyone decided—no matter what his personal problems were—this son of a bitch is the best damn poker player there is," Billy Baxter said.

Flushed with his victory, Stuey flew Madeline and Stefanie out to Vegas and put them up in the Mirage for a week. Stefanie was now fourteen, a beautiful young woman, and Stuey loved taking her around to the casinos on the Strip and going shopping with her and eating in the best restaurants. "He was on cloud nine because of winning," Madeline said. "And he was so proud of her. He wanted to show her off to everyone. They hadn't seen each other in at least six months at that point, maybe longer, and that week was really about the two of them."

Stuey's relationship with Madeline had often been stormy, but she was always there for him when he needed her most, and because of the good feelings that abounded during that week, he sat her down one night at the Mirage, looked in her eyes, and said, "Would you like to move back here?"

It wasn't a romantic appeal, at least not in a clear-cut way. It was more like "Let's be in the same city and be friends again because there is this connection that we share that includes our daughter." Stuey swore up and down that he was off drugs, and Madeline believed him. She told Stuey that if he'd help, and pay all the back child support he owed, she'd consider it. But when they told Stefanie, who was in high school in Florida and had all her friends there, "she flipped out at first," according to Madeline. So they backed off.

By the time Madeline and Stefanie returned to Florida, the publicity from the World Series of Poker had died down and the phone calls from reporters had stopped. But there was another group of people who had not stopped trying to contact Stuey: all the people he owed money to, a long line of creditors that included fellow poker players, sports bettors, bookies, and even some drug dealers. By the time these debts were paid (and many were not), along with back child support, Stuey was left with less than $200,000 out of his $500,000 winnings.

Still, it was a bankroll, and he was a player again, in more ways than one. He renewed a relationship with an attractive younger woman named Kim Carl, with whom he had been involved on and off for a few years. Kim was a tall, springy-haired blonde with a nice figure, who worked at the race and sportsbook at the Golden Nugget. She was bright and funny, with a quick sarcastic wit—and also, as it turned out, a serious drinking problem. According to Stefanie, who met her later, Stuey "liked her because he liked challenges, and I could tell that she was a challenge for him." Stuey crashed at Kim's apartment for several weeks, basking in the glow of his renewed fame. For years, he had walked the streets and entered the casinos of Las Vegas without drawing much attention. Now, he was a local celebrity again, as recognizable as gambling moguls like Steve Wynn, Bob Stupak, and Jack Binion.

His new status as reigning poker champ figured to bring other fringe benefits as well. Some of the high-profile players like Amarillo Slim and Johnny Chan were regularly issued invitations by wealthy businesspeople and rich amateurs who fancied the idea of playing against a champ. Stuey was a bit gun-shy, having been burned once by Roger King, but he let it be known that he was open to the opportunity should it arise. However, with only about $200,000 in his bankroll, he would need backing for really high-stakes games.

One such invitation came his way through David Rabbi, a well-known high-limit player. There was a rich amateur who had played the previous year's winner, Huck Seed, and he told Rabbi that he wanted to play Stuey in a no-limit hold'em freeze-out.

Rabbi contacted Doc Earle, who relayed the invitation to Stuey.

"Set it up for a minimum of $25,000," Stuey instructed Earle. "If you bring it off, I'll give you and Rabbi twenty percent of what I win."

Word got back to the wealthy eccentric that Stuey was amenable. But for some reason, when actually presented with the opportunity he'd sought out, he got cold feet and backed out of the deal.

Stuey then tried to get an invitation to Larry Flynt's private game, but he was unsuccessful in that, as well. Nobody—at least no easy marks—wanted to play him in either gin or poker.

During his most strung-out period, Stuey had lost touch with almost everyone, including Phil Tartaglia. Now, Stuey used some of his windfall to buy Philly a new Cadillac. He also gave Philly his gold Neiman Marcus WSOP bracelet. Even when Stuey was at his lowest, he always knew he could count on Philly—at least for a few dollars, a place to stay, or a word of advice—and he wanted to show his appreciation.

As with so many of his romantic entanglements, Stuey's relationship with Kim Carl blew hot and cold. Although he sometimes stayed at her apartment, she threw him out whenever they had a fight, and in midsummer 1997, during a period when they were on the outs, Stuey revisited with Madeline the idea of her and Stefanie moving back to Las Vegas. This time, Stefanie was less resistant, and mother and daughter began making plans for the move. "I was thinking that Stuey was whistle-clean and that everything was good, good as could be," Madeline said, "and that we could have a nice friendship, a regular friendship."

Madeline should have realized from the moment she and Stefanie arrived and moved into an apartment at the Las Vegas Country Club that her ex-husband was a long way from having licked his problems. "We got off the plane, took a taxi to this apartment that we had arranged for, and tried to reach Stuey," Madeline said. "For three days, we were sitting in an empty apartment, no furniture, no car, and we couldn't reach him. I didn't even know where he was living. We finally reached him, and Stefanie said, 'Daddy, we're here.' He said, 'Where?' And she said, 'Here. Here in Las Vegas. We moved here.' "

Madeline, to this day, claims that even after the initial strangeness following their arrival, she didn't suspect that he was using drugs again. "I really believed he was cleaning himself up," she said. "What else was I going to do?"

When he came to see them, she asked him for money to buy furniture.

"Here's five thousand," Stuey said.

"That's not enough to furnish an apartment," Madeline said.

The two finally compromised on $6,000, which Stuey took from his pants pocket and handed to her. Ray Warchaizer happened to be there that day, and on the way back to his apartment, he said to Stuey, "Instead of just throwing money at them, why don't you give them what they really want—your time and attention?"

Stuey looked stunned, as if he'd never really considered what it was they wanted from him. But he of all people should have known. After all, he treated money with more disdain than anyone else.

When Stefanie's school started in late August, Stuey drove her home most days, and the two of them also talked frequently on the phone. But even with his daughter around, he couldn't seem to find the strength to fight off his demons. As the glow of his victory faded, Stuey found himself faced with the same old emptiness. Nothing was ever enough, or lasted long enough. It was a vicious circle. The weakness in himself, the urges he couldn't fight off, filled him with self-loathing. The self-loathing, in turn, made him want to punish himself, which he did by giving in to the weakness.

He began bingeing again, taking dangerous amounts of crack. He started to develop a severe paranoia, which is common in the later stages of heavy abuse. Ray Warchaizer was with Stuey at Kim Carl's apartment one night, watching a baseball game, and saw him undergo a transformation after a trip to the bathroom.

"He came out," Warchaizer said, "and it was like nothing I'd ever seen before. He was like a lunatic. He was having flashbacks to the early days in New York, worried that people from decades earlier were out to get him. He was totally incoherent and lost all interest in the game we were watching, that he was betting on, and just kept raving in this scary, paranoid way. I sat there and said to myself, 'Jesus, I have to get out of here!'"

By any gambler's standard—even after buying the car for Philly and furniture and other things for his ex-wife and daughter, and blowing money on drugs—Stuey had a sizable bankroll, well over $100,000. But for him that was dangerously close to the felt. Unsure of what direction his life should take, he decided to return to the blackjack tables. He browsed around the downtown casinos looking for a single-deck game, which he found at the Lady Luck.

Even though he had paid six months' rent at Kim Carl's place, he decided to book a suite at the Lady Luck so he would have easy access to the tables. He assured the managers that he would give them a fair amount of action in the pit in exchange for a full comp, including room, food, and beverage. It was agreed that Stuey would play blackjack with a spread limit of $2,500 to $7,500, which would neutralize his ability to count cards by preventing him from plunking down a much larger bet when the deck was favorable to him. The casino would, however, allow him to play five spots at a time; this meant that he could conceivably bet as much as $37,500 on any single deal—or upwards of 30 percent of his bankroll.

In spite of Stuey's skill at card counting, it was a recipe for disaster. On the first night of the arrangement, he sat down at a blackjack table and asked for purple chips. The sight of him playing $500 chips in a low-rent downtown joint like the Lady Luck, which was more accustomed to nickel slots and $5 tables, was like seeing Jack Nicklaus swing a Big Bertha on a miniature golf course. Stuey was risking more money on a single hand than all the rest of the gamblers in the casino, combined, were betting. The first night, he lost $50,000, half of his entire stake. The second night, he rebounded with a $200,000 win.

Surveillance cameras recorded Stuey's every move. A pit boss approached him at one point and said, "Congratulations, Mr. Ungar. The crew upstairs said you're playing with ninety-eight percent accuracy."

After the second night, Stuey went downstairs to talk to the casino host. He had given the Lady Luck plenty of action and could ask for virtually anything he wanted.

"I need another suite," Stuey said.

"But Mr. Ungar, we've already got you comped in the nicest suite in the hotel. Why do you need a second room?" the host asked, curiosity piqued.

"Hey, I lost fifty the other night and didn't ask for a thing. Now I've got it back and more. If you want my action, get me another suite. But make sure it's not right next door."

A second suite was arranged. While Kim Carl was asleep in the original deluxe suite, Stuey sneaked down the hall to the new one. A short time later, a girl from an escort service rapped on the door. Stuey ushered her in. There he was, ever the risk taker, partaking of his high-roller perks while his unsuspecting girlfriend was snoozing a hundred feet away.

Stuey ended his six-week stay at the Lady Luck by losing most of his six-figure bankroll. He was able to build his winnings up to over $300,000 at one point, but he then lost steadily over the next week and was back to even. After taking a few days off, he went back to the tables and ran the bankroll up to $175,000; then he lost nearly half of that betting on sports. Daily six-figure swings were common. It was inevitable that with so little margin for error, the odds would catch up to him. All it took was three big losing days in a row to bust him back to nothing, to where he'd started before the World Series of 1997.

As the World Series of 1998 drew closer, the inspiring comeback of a year earlier, and all the hope that it had engendered in Stuey's friends and supporters, seemed like nothing more than a cruel tease. Not that he was in precisely the same spot he had been in. He might be broke again, but this time he would have no problem getting Billy Baxter's backing. In fact, there would be dozens of people willing to put up money for Stuey if Billy changed his mind.

As was the custom at Binion's, Stuey, as the defending champion, was given a fully comped room for the length of the tournament, plus all expenses. He checked into a twelfth-floor suite three weeks before the main event was set to begin. Since he was out of money, he wasn't able to play in the high-stakes side games that were going on down in the poker room twenty-four hours a day. Instead, he stayed up in his room, alone much of the time.

Down below, rumors were flying. Some people speculated that he had adopted a physical regimen to get into shape. Others theorized that Stuey, like another famously eccentric champion, the chess genius Bobby Fischer, was meditating inside his room and wouldn't make an appearance until the main event. Stuey's absence only heightened his mythological status in the gambling world. The longer he stayed away, the wilder the rumors got.

The truth was predictable and sad. Stuey was getting high, using drugs provided by a runner from the poker room. The few friends who had visited him saw a man in the throes of a crack binge.

"I never could understand how Stuey couldn't stay straight for just that one week of the World Series," Mike Sexton said. "I mean, go ahead, do drugs the rest of the year, but why he couldn't stay away for that brief period, I'll never understand."

Since he had no money to buy drugs, Stuey was forced to rely on deception and guile. Ray Warchaizer was in the room with Stuey when a drug dealer showed up one night. "Stuey faked a phone call to get credit," Warchaizer said. "He called my house and pretended to have a conversation with me." While Stuey explained to the dealer that his rich dentist friend would back up the loan with cash later, Warchaizer was sitting right there with them, listening to Stuey's line of bullshit. "That was classic Stuey," Warchaizer said. "He was bluffing the drug dealer. And it worked!"

Others who visited Stuey during his three-week stay at the Horseshoe included Phil Earle, Phil Hellmuth, Bob Stupak, and of course Billy Baxter. "I really wanted to be with Stuey in 'ninety-eight," Baxter said. "I kinda thought I was throwing my money away, but everybody knows Stuey's got a knack for these events, so any time Stuey was ready to play, I was ready to back him."

· · ·

At noon on May 11, 352 of the world's best poker players milled around downstairs in the tournament area of the Horseshoe, waiting for the action to commence. Stuey was conspicuously absent from the gathering crowd, and whispers again began to circulate that he might not show up.

Minutes before the final event was set to begin, Baxter picked up the house phone and dialed Stuey's room.

"Where the hell are you?" Baxter barked into the phone. "I've already paid the money. You're in!"

"I'll be down, don't worry," a frazzled Stuey mumbled before the line went dead.

Five minutes later, he had still not appeared. With all the players in their seats, and the tournament director, Jack McClelland, approaching the microphone to start the event, Baxter was steaming.

He marched over to a wall house phone and nearly pulled it from its moorings.

"What the fuck are you doing?" he yelled into the mouthpiece.

"I'm just worn out, Billy. T-t-t-take your money down. I'm not gonna play."

"What?"

"I said, I'm not going to play." The line went dead again.

Baxter was left shaking his head. "Here was a man who told me he needed his rest," Baxter said, "and he rested for three weeks—and then said he was too tired to play! I couldn't believe it."

Baxter went to McClelland and informed him that Stuey would not play. The $10,000 entry fee was refunded, so that wasn't the issue. Baxter just couldn't get his head around the idea that Stuey was so messed up he couldn't even do the thing he loved best. It boggled his mind.

A few moments later, McClelland said, "Shuffle up and deal," and the World Series of Poker of 1998 got under way.

•   •   •

Jack [Binion] was mad I didn't show up. I don't blame him. I was on the front cover of the program. People were counting on me. It was very embarrassing. A humiliating experience. But I still have my pride. I had a choice to make. I didn't look good. I didn't feel good. My mind wasn't right. I showered and got dressed but I looked at myself in the mirror and I looked terrible. So I took the lesser of two evils. I could have shown up looking completely out of it, and people would have pointed at me and laughed. The alternative was not playing at all. So I didn't play. There's not many people that would do that. I was being staked. I walked away from a chance to win half a million. All I had to do was show up and play. It was a million-dollar free roll. There isn't a player in the world that would have walked away like I did. But after it was over, I realized how wrong I was not to show up. I really want to win another world championship. I want to win a fourth world championship because nobody has done that before. That would really separate me from the rest of them. And I guarantee I will win another championship—if I'm alive.

The writer Michael Kaplan (no relation to Gabe) was standing by Stuey's conspicuously empty seat when he heard McClelland announce over the PA system that the Kid would not be defending his title, that he was not feeling well. As the news was greeted with a mix of groans and some laughter, Kaplan made for the nearest phone. He had been trying for three weeks to set up an interview with Stuey. The assignment he'd gotten from *Icon* magazine (now defunct) to profile Stuey suddenly seemed both more intriguing and less likely to happen. To Kaplan's amazement, Stuey answered the phone in his room.

"Stuey, my name is Michael Kaplan, and I flew out here from New York to do a story on you for *Icon* magazine. Do you think I could come up and talk to you for a few minutes?"

"*Icon* magazine? Never heard of it," Stuey said. His voice was hoarse and raspy, like an old man's.

"It's new," Kaplan said. "It's very . . . cool. I'll bring up the current issue. Johnny Depp's on the cover."

"Yeah? They put [Donnie] Brasco on the cover? If they did that, they could put me on the cover."

Kaplan took the elevator up to Stuey's room on the twelfth floor. When he knocked on the door, Stuey opened it but wouldn't let him in. Instead, he stepped out into the hall. He was wearing a T-shirt and a pair of jeans, and, according to Kaplan, he looked dreadful. "It was shocking to meet him," Kaplan said. "I mean, this was a guy who'd won half a million dollars a year earlier, and he looked like a derelict. I've seen drug addicts before, but never anybody who looked as bad as he did. He was tiny, under five-five, and he couldn't have weighed a hundred pounds. His body was just wasting away. On top of that, he was unshaven and missing a couple of front teeth, I guess from where he had a bridge. I mean, if you were going to take action on whether or not he was going to live for another six months, you'd have taken the under."

The journalist and his potential subject talked in the hall for a few minutes, and then Stuey told Kaplan to call him the next day; they'd do the interview then. "I'm going to do it for my daughter," he said. "If I can show her that I was in the same magazine as Johnny Depp, that would impress her. . . . You gotta get me on the cover."

"The next day, I called him, and he put me off," Kaplan said. "I called him dozens of times over the next few days. Either he'd answer or someone else would, but he kept putting me off, and finally I had to leave town."

Five weeks later, the determined reporter flew back for another try. Stuey was no longer at the Horseshoe, and nobody there knew where he was. Kaplan spent a few days trying to track him down, and finally, with the help of Don McNamee, was able to find him.

"When I reached him on the phone, he was so happy," Kaplan said. "He apologized for blowing me off, and said he wasn't himself. He said, 'I knew you were coming back. I told myself, this fucking guy is coming back. This fucking Kaplan is an aggressive guy.'

"We met at Arizona Charlie's, a small-time locals' casino far off the Strip, and he was like a changed person. He'd put on some weight and his hair was neatly combed and he had shaved. He was also wearing nice clothes, a button-down shirt and slacks and an expensive pair of loafers. His whole affect was different. I could see why people liked him. He was fun and funny, an odd combination of a kid, an old-time wiseguy, and somebody who had lived beyond his years."

After Kaplan wrote the story for *Icon,* the magazine wanted to do a photo shoot with Stuey. The editors knew how difficult he was to pin down and thought that Kaplan might be able to help the photographer, Sian Kennedy, by being present for the shoot. But Kaplan didn't want to go. "I thought, 'Let the photographer do his job. That was what he was getting paid for.' "

Sian Kennedy drove from Los Angeles to Las Vegas in his brand-new Saab in August 1998. He got a room at El Cortez downtown, but when he tried to contact Stuey, who was supposed to be staying at the Horseshoe, he couldn't find him. Kaplan told him to get in touch with Puggy Pearson, who might know where Stuey was, and Pearson was, in fact, able to lead Kennedy to Stuey, who was at the Horseshoe but registered under an alias.

Stuey, as he had done with Kaplan the first time, kept putting Kennedy off, telling him "they'd do the shoot the next day." While this was going on, Kaplan, in New York, got a call from Mike Sexton.

"Sexton said he was calling for Stuey. 'He thinks you've done something to Madeline,' he said. 'He's very upset. Madeline's disappeared and

Stuey thinks she's with you.' It was crazy and I told Sexton it was crazy. I was in New York, for Chrissake. What was Stuey talking about? Sexton said he realized it was crazy, that it was probably the drugs talking. He was just humoring Stuey, basically."

That same night, Stuey pounded on the door of Kennedy's hotel room at four in the morning, waking the photographer, who let him in. Stuey stormed into the room, ranting and raving about Madeline, making very little sense. In the middle of it, he collapsed on Kennedy's bed and fell sound asleep. Not knowing what to do, but wanting to make the best of a bizarre situation, Kennedy took some photos of the sleeping former world champion. Finally, he woke Stuey up and told him he had to leave.

The next day, Kennedy called Stuey to say that he was leaving town, at which point Stuey finally agreed to let himself be photographed. The only condition was that he wanted his daughter to be in the photos with him. A couple of hours later, the photographer drove Stuey to Stefanie and Madeline's apartment. On the way there, Stuey said he was hungry and needed to stop and get a hamburger. Kennedy, who just wanted to get the shoot over with before Stuey had a change of heart again, tried to talk him out of it, saying why not get something afterward. Stuey was adamant.

"We just passed a burger place!" he snapped at the photographer.

Kennedy tried to make a U-turn, but as he did, a car in another lane broadsided them, smashing the front end of his Saab. Everyone jumped out of the cars, right in the middle of traffic, and Stuey started screaming at the people in the other car, blaming them for the collision, saying, "I'm Stuey Ungar, the World Series champion; don't you know who I am?"

Soon, the police showed up. While Kennedy was talking to them, trying to straighten things out, he noticed that Stuey was gone. He'd just walked off.

Since Stefanie's place wasn't far away, and not knowing what else to do, Kennedy decided to drive there. Stefanie met him at the door and informed him that Stuey had just left. They'd gotten into a fight because she'd told him she didn't like the way he was living.

Kennedy finally caught up with his subject back at the Horseshoe, and they did the photo shoot there, a series of odd-angled, unflattering shots, including some in which Stuey's collapsed nose was prominent.

When the issue of *Icon* appeared a few months later, the portrait of Stuey that emerged, particularly in the photos, was of a scared, vulnerable, haunted man, who looked and acted like a drug addict.

The photos were deeply troubling to Stuey, probably because they were so close to the truth. He didn't like facing the reality that he was addicted. He loved attention and being in the public eye, but seeing himself illuminated in such a stark way left him feeling frightened and betrayed.

I posed for all the pictures and gave them whatever they wanted. Then they made me out to be a total loser, a freak. I can't stand to even look at it. They told me I could be proud of the story, but I can't even show it to my daughter I'm so ashamed of it. After I saw that picture, I'd never show it. Never! It's a disgrace what they did. Those cocksuckers. I don't trust people anymore. They say one thing and do another.

Stuey might have felt betrayed, but the experiences with Kaplan and Kennedy illustrated the kind of wild mood swings and erratic behavior that those who knew him intimately recognized all too well. He had exhausted the good graces of many of his friends, and others were on the verge of giving up on him.

During the summer of 1998, Stuey once again found himself at a low ebb, depending upon others for handouts and loans, staying first at the Continental Motel, a third-rate gambling hall on South Maryland Avenue, for a month; and then at the Gold Coast for ten weeks, sinking into a miasma of despair in which he rarely left his room, spending most of his time doing drugs, watching television, and sleeping. After ten weeks, his bill at the Gold Coast came to $6,600, at least half of it from the in-hotel movies and room service. Stuey had rented hundreds of movies, mostly soft-core porn, at $7.95 a pop.

Sexton wanted to help Stuey, but he had limited cash resources. He agreed to foot the bill for the hotel, but he wouldn't lend Stuey any cash on top of it, for fear of how the cash would be used. Stuey had to look elsewhere for a stake.

Over the next several months, he borrowed from Ray Warchaizer, Puggy Pearson, Dewey Tomko, and Nolan Dalla, among others. The exchange of money was innocent enough. "Can you help me out?" Stuey would ask, in his ingenuous, tough-to-turn-down way.

If those who lent him money had any doubts about where it was going, they got a pretty clear answer on July 12, when Stuey was arrested for carrying a pipe with a small vial of crack. He was picked up in the Naked City district, just south of downtown. Naked City may have been only a few blocks away from the lights and neon of Glitter Gulch and the downtown casinos, but it was not a place that unsuspecting tourists wanted to wander into, even during the daytime. It was a run-down area of white-frame boardinghouses, dilapidated no-tell motels, porno theaters, and sex shops, its cracked pavement littered with the detritus of such commerce: empty vials, broken bottles and needles, and discarded condoms. At night, travelers, especially those on foot, went there for two reasons: drugs and sex.

The crack houses, of which there were several, were open twenty-four hours a day, seven days a week, even on Christmas and New Year's

Day. Most of the addicts who came there went because they had nowhere else to go, or because they wanted to hide their addiction from family and friends. Some of the houses allowed smoking on the premises, which created an oddly comforting communal atmosphere for those wanting to share in the rituals and mutual understanding of what was otherwise a lonely pastime.

But most houses had a rule against using the drugs on-site, and consequently their clientele could often be found around the sides of the building, or in the back, down some dark alley—a face or maybe two faces, illuminated by the red glow of a burning pipe.

Following his arrest, Stuey was handcuffed, fingerprinted, and jailed on a charge of possession by the Las Vegas police department. The arrest report listed his weight as 110 pounds. He spent the night in jail and was released the next day after his bail was put up by Billy Baxter. A court date was set for October. Baxter drove him back to the Gold Coast, where Stuey mostly stayed in his hotel room for the next six weeks, spending hours on the phone talking to Stefanie to try to make up for the weeks he'd been out of touch. He visited her several times, usually driven by Mike Sexton, although he even rode the transit bus a few times when Sexton was too busy.

As the new school year approached, Stuey was desperate to buy Stefanie some school clothes, his symbolic way of maintaining a degree of parental responsibility. But everyone he asked for money turned him down, fearful that he would use the cash for drugs. On the afternoon of August 29, Stuey picked up his phone in his room at the Gold Coast and called Sexton.

"Mike, I'm begging you to help me out. I just need a couple hundred dollars," Stuey pleaded.

"I can't do it, Stuey," Sexton said. He had learned the hard way after so many lies. "I'll pick up the hotel tab and comp your meals, but I can't give you any cash."

"Mike, please. It really is for school clothes for Stefanie. I swear to you."

Sexton had a daughter himself. He knew what it meant to want to be a responsible parent. He understood that Stuey had failed his daughter in many ways and desperately wanted to make up for it. As he began to think about Stuey's plea, he reasoned that taking pride in providing for Stefanie might be a positive thing. But how could he make sure that Stuey wouldn't blow the money on drugs?

Sexton agreed to give Stuey a credit card from Dillard's, a local department store, and told him he could spend up to $300. He also arranged a car to ferry him and Stefanie to the mall and back.

The following day, Sexton visited Stuey at the Gold Coast, unsure of what to expect. Would Stuey be there? Had he done what he said he was going to do?

Sexton found him sitting up on the bed, watching a movie, in good spirits.

"Mike, I want you to know how much that meant to me," Stuey said, tears coming to his eyes. "For me to be able to do something for Stefanie means more to me than winning a million dollars. You could give me a million right now, and it wouldn't mean as much as what you did for me."

When we were in the mall and I saw Stefanie looking at price tags—that's when it hit me. What did I do? What am I doing? The most beautiful girl in the world, a gem, and she's mine. And she's got to look at price tags? After the money I've gone through and given away? It's disgraceful. Stefanie saw that something was wrong. She said, "What are you worried about, Dad? It's okay." When I heard her say that, it really tore my heart out. I mean, I couldn't even breathe. It was so humiliating. All the money I went through—I tell you, that's an atrocity.

. . .

Yet even Stuey's love for his daughter wasn't enough to enable him to break the cycle of addiction. Stefanie pleaded with him to get help. "I used to tell him, think of all the people that look up to you. If you could beat this, you'd have even more people looking up to you than ever before. You could be an inspiration." He promised her on numerous occasions that he would beat it, and for a while he'd manage to stay clean, but then the phone calls from him would cease for days at a time, and Stefanie would know he'd slipped again.

It was especially painful because when he was not bingeing, they had an exceptionally close connection. "We would talk for hours and hours," Stefanie said, describing conversations in which they would discuss everything, ranging from school and careers to love and religion. "Dad was never impatient with me like he was with other people. He would leave me messages on my answering machine. 'I know you're at school, I just want to say I love you.' Things like that."

In August, however, scared by the way he was looking and acting, and fed up and hurt by his frequent disappearances, Stefanie left a message on his hotel voice mail. She told him that she didn't want to see him again until he was clean. "I got tired of the broken promises. I didn't like being that way, but he'd disappear for three weeks and I needed to talk to him. I didn't want it to go on like that for the rest of our lives. I wanted him to be my dad."

The ultimatum had mixed results. Stuey was devastated and tried to call Stefanie back several times, leaving messages that weren't returned. He sat in his lonely hotel room, caught in a paralyzing internal tug-of-war, in which his longing for his daughter's love and his fear of losing it both pulled him toward sobriety and pushed him away from it at the same time. It didn't help that there were drug dealers coming by his room with "just one more" fix each time he had resolved to stop.

I once asked her if there was someone to completely make me over, would she want me to change. After she thought about it, she said, "Daddy, I love your personality. I love you the way you are. I really don't want you to change. I love you just the way you are." You wanna talk about tearing my heart out?

See, when I'm around my daughter, I don't have any temptations, you know? Getting back into it is the last thing on my mind. . . . Stefanie's sixteenth birthday is coming up. I want to buy her a car when she learns to drive. So, I better start playing again. Gambling can get me out of this. If I can raise a stake, I can get back into action and do what I need to take care of her.

Right now, though, I can't play. I'm stuck in this fucking hotel room. It's three o'clock in the middle of the afternoon, and this is the last place on the face of the earth I want to be. Right this very second, a half mile away, they're playing in the highest-limit poker game in the world. It's at the Mirage, and they're playing $1,000 to $2,000 seven-card stud. Half the people in that game are donkeys. They don't have a fucking clue. It's the rich tourists and big movie producers from L.A. God bless 'em. I can whip every one of them. But instead of being at the Mirage, I'm here, out of action. Broke.

That's right. I've got exactly four cents in my pocket.

A year ago I had a million dollars stacked up in front of me at the Horseshoe and I was drinking Dom with Jack Binion. I fucked it all away.

I've been in this hotel room for a while. A few weeks, I think, but I'm not sure. I've burned a lot of bridges and pissed a lot of people off. I tried staying with a few people, but it didn't work out. So I've had to stay at hotels.

A few days ago, I couldn't take it anymore. The walls were starting to close in on me. I went downstairs and walked through the casino. It really felt good to get out of the room. I didn't have any money on me. I just stood and watched the tourists at the blackjack tables. There they were—betting something like five bucks a shot—splitting face cards and standing on soft seventeen. What were these people thinking? Don't they know basic strategy? It made me want to throw up. I came back upstairs and slept for twelve hours. Then I watched TV all night. When was that? Wednesday? Thursday? Fuck, I don't even remember. The days are all running together now. I can't even tell if it's night or day unless I open the curtains and look for the light.

I'm going fucking crazy in this room right now. This place is a mess. The room smells like shit. I can't even remember the last time I shaved or took a shower. The maid came in last week. She changed the sheets, but I told her to leave everything like it was. I don't want to be disturbed anymore. I put the sign on the door. The only time I open the door is to dump dirty dishes in the hallway from room service.

Being without a stake is a fucking curse. A player's got to have a stake. Otherwise he's nothing. You might as well be Pavarotti without a voice. And that's exactly what I've been trying to work on the last few months— raising enough of a stake to get back in action. It's why I'm here now. Until I get some stew, I can't get back in the game. I figure I need about twenty thousand to get started. But I've betrayed some people, and in gambling that's the one thing you just don't do. You don't fuck people. Especially those people who trust you. That's everything.

There's an old saying in poker that at the table your worst enemy is yourself. I'll tell you one thing: in my case, truer words were never spoken.

19.

THE RIVER CARD

Mike Sexton couldn't carry Stuey's tab at the Gold Coast any longer. He said that Stuey was going to have to find someone else to foot the bill—either that, or find another place to stay. With nowhere else to turn, Stuey called Don McNamee, who'd been such a rock for him in the past. McNamee told Stuey that he was welcome to stay with him, with the same stipulations as before: no calls could be made from the house, and no drugs were allowed on the premises.

"Don was one of my closest friends in the world," Stuey said. "He really helped me a lot. Helped me through times I can't even remember."

By late September 1998, the summer heat of the desert had dissipated. Fall arrived and the nights grew cool. On many nights, a broke and very thin Stuey Ungar was seen hanging around downtown. Too many times, Don McNamee would check Stuey's room and find his bed lying undisturbed. "He would just disappear for a few days at a time," McNamee said wistfully. McNamee knew what those disappearances meant.

At his most strung-out and desperate, Stuey returned to the Horseshoe poker room, the scene of his greatest triumphs, hitting up players who had never seen him before, asking for small loans. The poker room was located right off the street, by a side door, just a short walk from the abyss of Naked City's drug dens.

Stuey stopped in late one night and saw Tony Shelton, supervisor of the graveyard shift. After some back-and-forth banter, Shelton agreed to give Stuey $15, which Stuey promised to pay back within twenty-four hours. The following night, when Stuey showed up again, it wasn't to give Shelton his money back; it was to borrow more money. This time, Shelton refused.

Stuey's next target was O'Neil Longson, a world-class cardplayer known for dry wit and a sometimes surly attitude. Longson hardly seemed an inviting sort for Stuey to cadge a loan from, but the two had played many tournaments together, and Longson was the only man in the room with a fat enough bankroll and some sort of personal link to him.

Longson was playing heads-up $100–$200 Omaha, and winning. He had stacks and stacks of black $100 chips backed up by a huge wad of cash. But Stuey might as well have been talking to a wall.

In desperation, Stuey produced a small piece of colored glass from his pocket, which he tried to palm off as a ruby. Even a cursory glance made it obvious to Longson that the object Stuey held in his hand was nothing more than a piece of broken glass.

"You keep your ruby," Longson said at last, as he reached into a pocket of his houndstooth sports coat and pulled out a folded $10 bill.

This sad transaction took place in the back of the poker room, not twenty feet away from the wall where Stuey's picture hung in the Gallery of Champions. In his photo there, he was smiling and confident, wearing a blue silk jacket, a very different-looking man.

"To see Stuey belittle himself that way so he could get some rock was just about more than I could take," Tony Shelton said.

On another fall night at Binion's, Lou Mingh, a part-time cabdriver and poker player, was sitting in the $15–$30 hold'em game, the biggest game in the room at the time, in the middle of a good run, with a couple of racks of red chips in front of him. When Stuey entered the room, Mingh recognized him and went over to shake hands with him. Seconds after Mingh had introduced himself, Stuey asked for $100, explaining that he was short and needed something for the night. Mingh was only too happy to oblige. He reached into his pocket and handed Stuey two $50 bills, which were gratefully accepted.

Twenty minutes later, as Mingh was cashing out, Tony Shelton walked over. "What did Stuey say to you?" Shelton asked.

"I lent Mr. Ungar a hundred dollars. He said he'll give me back two hundred tomorrow."

"Young man, write that loan off as a tax deduction."

"What do you mean? Mr. Ungar is a champion."

"Mr. Ungar will not bring you anything," Shelton said. "Mr. Ungar has a problem."

"Oh," Mingh said, with a look of disappointment and dismay that seemed to have less to do with the lost $100 than with the disillusionment of seeing an idol fall.

Perhaps the low point came on one of the last nights Stuey was ever seen inside the Horseshoe. It was a particularly slow evening; only three games were in progress. Stuey came in and started working the room, trying to hit up anyone who would listen. By now the regulars at the Horseshoe had seen him a number of times and had learned to look away when he approached.

As Stuey lingered by the podium, where the brush man (slang for casino employee) was stationed with the sign-up sheet, a player who had just been called for one of the games handed the brush man two white $1 chips as a tip. When the phone at the podium rang, the brush man answered and turned away, putting the two white chips on top of his clipboard sheet. He hung up the phone less than a minute later, but when he turned back, the two white chips were gone. So was Stuey.

Stuey's prime supplier in Naked City was in a weekly motel located between Seventh and Eighth streets near Carson Street, east of downtown. That was where he had been just before he was arrested for a third time by police on patrol, who caught him down an alley half a block away, on October 23, with a lit crack pipe. He called his attorney, Steve Stein, from jail.

Without money to post bail, Stein couldn't spring him. The problem was that the bail this time was high, because Stuey had two other recent arrests, and the judge considered him likely to flee. Add to this problem a quickly diminishing list of people who might help him, and it was evident that Stuey was in a jam.

He told Stein to try Chip Reese, who, in addition to being an old friend, was one of many poker players who had offered to back Stuey whenever he wanted—provided he could prove he was straight. When Reese was contacted through Stein's office, however, he declined to help, saying that he didn't want to get involved. He despised drugs and saw no point in peeling off more money for Stuey, whom he considered a lost cause.

Stuey then tried Sexton. But the bail was set at $50,000, which required a cash payment of $5,500, and Sexton needed a couple of days to get the money together. Stuey wasn't willing to wait in jail that long. He called Stein back and instructed him to contact Reese again.

This time when Stein called Reese, it was with a sense of urgency that Reese had never heard before. Reese weighed his response carefully and finally said, "Listen, you tell Stuey I'm gonna do it this one last time.

But tell him to lose my number and not ever call me again. Ever. Is that understood?"

In a parking lot at a shopping center, two late-model cars pulled up side by side. Reese and Stein got out of them and exchanged an awkward handshake.

"Don't call me again," Reese said, reiterating what he'd told Stein earlier. "I don't care if he gets busted and rots in jail. I'm done with it."

He handed Stein fifty-five $100 bills. An hour later, Stuey's bond was posted and he was free, at least temporarily. Before he was released, he discovered that his court date on the previous drug charge was scheduled for the following week. That unnerved Stuey, but there was little he could do but let his attorney mount a defense. Stein discussed with Stuey the possibility of entering a voluntary drug treatment program, which might win the court's favor and allow Stuey to plea-bargain a sentence of probation.

For the first time in his life, Stuey thought seriously about entering rehab. He agreed he would discuss the matter with Stein when the two met again the following week in court. Mike Sexton and Doc Earle jointly decided that it might be good for Stuey to get out of Las Vegas and seek help. They also believed that if Stuey showed signs of trying to help himself, a judge would be more lenient on the charges of drug possession.

Sexton and Earle tried to persuade Stuey to do what must have seemed almost unthinkable: go to Newfoundland and live with Earle for a few months. They figured that Newfoundland was as faraway a place as there could be, and that Stuey would have no temptations there. When apprised of the plan, Stuey agreed that it was a good idea. But he also had misgivings about being cooped up and bored in a place like that, without even the opportunity to get back in action.

Could it be worse than what he was going through now? they asked.

No, he admitted, but he also remembered the failed experiment in El Paso with the Brunsons years before.

Sexton and Earle didn't know what to say. If Stuey didn't make an effort to change, there was nothing they could do.

I'm afraid of going to hell, of being damned.

I pray, but it's always when I feel like dying. You don't have to get on your knees to pray. I don't. I've prayed many times.

God gave me a gift that no one else has. I might not have used it right, but I do know I've been blessed. I'm not a great person, but what I've done that's bad, I've done to myself. Still, I know I've hurt other people along the way. Especially the people who are close to me.

During October, Stuey made repeated calls to Billy Baxter, pleading with Baxter to give him a stake so he could get back in action. Baxter was still simmering over Stuey's no-show six months earlier at the WSOP. His trust had been shaken. Whenever Stuey called, Baxter would turn him down. But the following day the phone would ring again and Baxter would be forced to say no again.

To help justify his refusal, Baxter, who was as big a sports bettor as anyone in Las Vegas, explained to Stuey that he was having a tough year in football. Finally, though, worn down by Stuey's persistence and the incessant phone calls, he threw his old friend a bone: "If I have a really good weekend in football, I'll stake you in the big game at the Bellagio."

Steve Wynn's spectacular Bellagio Hotel and Casino had opened just a week earlier, and within days its ultralavish poker room was boasting the highest-limit games in the world. Stuey was only a few miles from the Bellagio, but he might as well have been a million miles away—at least without Baxter behind him.

Stuey found out Baxter's football plays each Sunday, and watched the games as if his own money were riding on the outcome. When Baxter had consecutive losing weeks at the end of October, Stuey was crushed. He felt as bad about Baxter's losses as he would have if he'd been betting the games himself—in fact, worse.

Then, in early November, Baxter had a terrific week, and Stuey was on the phone immediately.

"I knew I was throwing the money away, but I had given Stuey my word," Baxter said. "So I gave him twenty-five thousand."

On November 11, 1998, Stuey Ungar, forty-five years old, five-foot-five, and weighing barely a hundred pounds, charged across the shining marble floor of the Bellagio's grand entrance with a bounce in his step and a wad of cash in his pocket. It would have been a real stretch to call him the Kid at this point, though from a distance his Beatles haircut and boyish frame still gave the impression of youth. Up close, he looked like what he was: a longtime drug addict whose excesses were now written in his face. The ravaged nose was the most disturbing feature: one side of it was deflated like a flat tire.

Still, Stuey was excited to be making his first foray into Las Vegas's newest and most spectacular hotel. It was a different world from the one he had arrived in thirty years earlier, when the town was mostly run by the mob. But no matter how Vegas was dressed up or presented, no matter how corporate it might have become, or how much like a theme park, the blood that pulsed through its veins was still gambling blood.

Stuey walked into the poker room, where he met up with Mike Sexton. The two of them briefly discussed what game Stuey should play. Sexton knew that Stuey needed to hang on to the money Baxter had given him for a little while if was going to have any chance of getting back on his feet. "Don't blow it all in one big game," Sexton cautioned him. "Start off playing $200–$400 limit."

Even in the shape Stuey was in, his ego prevented him from thinking that small. He wanted to play in the biggest game around.

"What about no-limit?" Sexton offered. "That's your strongest game. What if we got a no-limit game going?"

Stuey agreed that this made sense.

But, as Sexton later recalled, "This was before no-limit was played widely in cash games the way it is today. It was still unusual to get a no-limit cash game going. Plus, as Stuey pointed out, who was going to want to play no-limit with him?"

Erik Seidel, the former stockbroker turned poker pro who had been the runner-up to Johnny Chan in the WSOP of 1988, was sitting across the poker room, playing in what he described as a "very good Omaha game." He got up and walked over to say hello to Stuey. Stuey mentioned that he was interested in playing no-limit, and Seidel said he'd consider playing a $5,000 heads-up freeze-out.

"There's nobody in the world I wouldn't play heads-up against," Stuey said. "But you're one of the few that would give me a tough time. I'll tell you what, I'll give you a hundred bucks to play me."

It was pure, classic bravado on Stuey's part. Seidel laughed, thinking that even though Stuey had lost some of his spark, there was hope. "Like maybe he could give up the drugs. Like maybe he really was back and this could be another chance."

In the end, Seidel decided he didn't want to get up from the game he was in just yet. But as soon as he walked off, Stuey and Sexton looked around and saw Melissa Hayden, one of the strongest women poker players in the world at the time. Sexton said, "You want to play a freeze-out?" and Hayden said, "Sure."

Sexton laughed and said to Stuey, "See, you've been out of action so long you got girls that want to play against you."

The manager of the card room found Stuey and Hayden an empty table and set them up with a dealer and chips. Melissa wanted to start off with a $2,000 freeze-out, but Stuey insisted on $5,000, and she finally agreed.

They sat down in the expensive upholstered swivel chairs and watched the dealer fan the deck across the felt faceup. Stuey reveled in the moment: the nonstop musical chatter of chips being shuffled, bet, and dragged was as soothing to him as the sound of the ocean waves or the wind in the trees. He was back in action.

The game started with $25 and $50 blinds. Hayden, a tall, attractive redhead who had been a professional photographer back in New York before moving to Las Vegas to concentrate on poker, recalled, "Everyone who knew Stuey was concerned about him. There was a feeling of wanting to protect him."

That noble sentiment didn't stop Hayden from trying to beat Stuey's brains in. In fact, forty-five minutes after they began, Hayden had won every chip on the table. Someone from the high-limit table next to them said, "Aw, Stuey, letting a girl beat you."

"When the guy said that," Hayden recalled. "Stuey leaned over and whispered to me, 'Don't let him get to you. Don't ever let them get to you. That guy's a piece of shit.' And he was. He was a guy who was known to have beaten up his girlfriend. I mean, you had to know Stuey to really appreciate what a gentleman he was, and how much he loved women. He was extremely gallant in his way."

By this time, a couple of other players had wandered over, and a non-freeze-out no-limit game began at the table with the same $25–$50 blinds. Erik Seidel got up from his Omaha game and joined in. The painful truth was that Stuey was the "live one" in the game. "Yeah, that game was pretty much built around him," Seidel said.

The members of the poker fraternity might've been rooting for Stuey to get his life back on track, but the sympathy stopped as soon as the cards were dealt.

It was no easy lineup under any circumstances. Aside from Hayden and Seidel, the other players included the Russian poker pro Ralph Perry, the young gun Daniel Negreanu, and Perry Green, the Alaskan fur trader who'd been runner-up to Stuey in the World Series final in 1981.

"It was strange that Perry Green was there," observed Melissa Hayden. "He didn't live in Las Vegas, and it was unusual to see him. It was a little eerie, to tell you the truth, almost like the completion of some kind of circle."

Stuey was far from at the top of his game. Hayden said he seemed "very edgy. His focus and attention weren't good." Playing impatiently and aggressively, he bluffed off most of the $25,000 in a few hours. Hayden said she didn't think that he lost all of it. "I think he probably kept some of it to buy dope."

The game was still going when Stuey got up. As he was leaving the poker room, he saw Mike Sexton again, and the two chatted briefly. Sexton was under the impression that Stuey had not lost everything and interpreted his departure as a positive sign, demonstrating that he had some discipline and patience, and that he would try to find a better spot the next day.

Stuey made his way out of the Bellagio's north side exit. He walked past the fountains. Twelve hundred multicolored jets of water danced in computer-choreographed rhythm high above the quarter-mile-long lake that fronted the hotel. Stuey stopped to watch for a minute, standing with a large crowd of vacationing families, tourists, and convention-goers who stared up in awe at the majestic geysers leaping 240 feet toward the heavens while giant loudspeakers piped out Sarah Brightman and Andrea Bocelli singing "Time to Say Good-Bye."

No one who knew Stuey saw or spoke to him during the next four days. It is reasonable to speculate that he went back to the crack houses of

Naked City, though there is no record that he checked into any hotel in the area until he arrived at the Oasis Motel on November 20.

According to the manager of the Oasis, Peter Napoli, Stuey registered as "Stu Ungar," and paid $58 in cash for one night, listing the poker room at the Mirage as his address. Stuey took room 16, which was on the ground floor, facing the parking lot, and had a king-size double bed and a hot tub.

He slept there Friday night. On Saturday morning, a motel employee unlocked the door of room 16 and saw Stuey lying facedown on his bed. Stuey was shaking, as if cold, and there was vomit on the floor. A porno flick was playing on the seventeen-inch television set. When addressed, Stuey didn't move and could barely speak. He managed to tell the motel employee that there was $60 on the dresser and to take it for another night's stay. Shivering uncontrollably, he asked that the window in the room be closed. The window was already shut.

On Sunday, November 22 (the anniversary of the assassination of John F. Kennedy), the same clerk entered the room again after her knock went unanswered. She found Stuey lying on top of the bed in a tangle of sheets. He had stopped breathing and was cold to the touch. She called the EMTs, but it was too late for medical help. Stuey Ungar was dead.

An autopsy was performed two days later. The coroner's report showed that Stuey had died from a heart attack. Small amounts of cocaine, methadone, and Percodan were found in his system, but not enough to have caused his death. Responding to calls for an investigation, the Clark County coroner, Ron Flud, issued a statement: "The cause is accidental death by coronary atherosclerosis. The heart condition developed over a period of time. The death was brought on by his lifestyle."

No drugs were found in the room or in Stuey's possession. He did have $800 in cash on his person.

• • •

On November 26, 1998, Stuey Ungar was buried at the Palm Mortuary in East Las Vegas. The funeral was attended by about 250 friends and family members. Many of those in attendance had played with Stuey at the tables—among them, Doyle Brunson, Mike Sexton, and Puggy Pearson. Madeline Ungar was present with Stefanie, who delivered an emotional eulogy. During the ceremony, Bob Stupak took up a collection. Stuey had won an estimated $30 million in his lifetime, by some accounts, but he left behind no inheritance and nothing of monetary value.

The collection was used to pay for the funeral.

EPILOGUE

On May 14, 2001, Stuey Ungar was posthumously inducted into the Poker Hall of Fame. A crowd of two hundred of the poker world's luminaries gathered in Binion's Horseshoe to celebrate him. His daughter, Stefanie, who was now seventeen, proudly accepted the honor, which culminated with the unveiling of a portrait of Stuey, nestled on the wall among the framed likenesses of other poker legends such as Johnny Moss and Benny Binion.

Three years after Stuey's induction ceremony, in March 2004, Becky Binion Behnen was forced to sell the Horseshoe, which had fallen on hard times in the wake of an acrimonious estate battle between her and her brother Jack Binion. The Harrah's gaming corporation bought not only the Horseshoe but the rights to the World Series of Poker—just in time for the 2004 event.

A record 2,676 entrants participated in the 2004 world championship; a majority of them had won their seats in satellites or supersatellites contested in cyberspace. For the third year in a row, an amateur won the title, this time a patent lawyer for Pfizer, Greg "Fossilman" Raymer, who took home the first prize of $5 million in cash.

Seven years earlier, when Stuey Ungar had won his record third championship, he had conquered 381 other competitors. In 2005, the winner is going to have to beat out an estimated five thousand or more entrants. All of which is to say that it is unlikely that anyone in the future will ever be able to duplicate Stuey Ungar's feat. The Kid himself would be hard-pressed.

But if he were alive, you can be sure of one thing: he'd show up full of the same swagger and cockiness as always, letting everyone in his path know that no matter what the odds or how many people he had to beat, once the cards were dealt, none of them stood a chance.

ACKNOWLEDGMENTS

No book is a solo effort. In fact, we had help from many sources during the six-year Stu Ungar project: Larry Grossman might not remember the casual conversation we had in May 1997, but it was the creative spark for this undertaking, and for that we wish to thank him.

Mike Sexton is another friend and ally without whom this book would not have happened. He provided the initial link to Stuey as well as serving as the conduit to other important sources who knew our subject well and generously shared their reminiscences.

In addition, we would like to thank Greg Dinkin and Frank R. Scatoni, agents at Venture Literary, who went to extraordinary lengths to keep the momentum of this project moving forward at times when our energy was flagging.

Thanks are due also to Madeline and Stefanie Ungar, extraordinary women both, who shared with us aspects of Stuey's life and character that were warm, funny, and painful, and without which the story would not have been nearly so rich. Thanks as well to James Kimsey for his diligence and support.

At Atria Books, we had the great good luck to have as our editor Wendy Walker, whose enthusiasm, optimism, and wisdom have been irreplaceable. She was always there when we needed her.

We are also indebted to all the other folks at Atria who contributed to and supported this book, particularly our publisher, Judith Curr, and deputy publisher, Karen Mender.

A special thanks to our production editor, Sybil Pincus, and copy editor, Susan Gamer, who made sure our mistakes did not find their way to the printed page.

We also do not want to forget Howard Schwartz at the Gambler's Book Store, who has been a longtime friend, mentor, and guide to the authors.

There are a number of other fine people who shared their time, resources, and memories to help make this book what it is. They are, in no particular order, Pamela Shandel, Michael Kaplan, A. Alvarez, James McManus, Brian Koppelman, David Levien, Anthony Holden, Benny Behnen, "Mad Jack" Wooten, Alan Miller, Howard Burroughs, Tex Whitson, John L. Smith, L. A. Brown, Eric Harkins, Linda Johnson, Erik Seidel, Andy Bellin, Don McNamee, Jan Fisher, Barry Shulman, Jeff Shulman, Steve Radulovich, Mark and Tina Napolitano, Billy Baxter, Dr. Phil Earle, Doyle Brunson, Todd Brunson, Chip Reese, Dr. Ray Warchaizer, Mike Salem, Lou Krieger, Bruce Kramer, Melissa Hayden, "Amarillo Slim" Preston, Phil Hellmuth, Bob Stupak, Bobby Baldwin, Gabe Kaplan, Puggy Pearson, Glenn Abney, Danny Robison, Russell Rosenblum, Jay Heimowitz, Steve Fischman, Peter Secor, David Trinidad, Mitch Kramer, Chuck Weinstock, Larry Peters, Max Shapiro, Kim Scheinberg, Gloria Richmond, Rich Korbin, Dan Goldman, Adam and Debbie Bacharach, Barry and Betty Tanenbaum, Steven Goldman, Mitch Firestone, Paul and Eileen Berkowitz, Arthur Reber, and the late Bill Alan Hafey.

Individually, Nolan Dalla wishes to thank his attorney, Tiger Wyle, for all the legal advice. He also wants to thank various family members, including Paul and Rebecca Glover, Jerry and Nina Dalla, Monta L. Hall, Don Harris, and Ioana Petre.

ACKNOWLEDGMENTS

Peter Alson gratefully acknowledges the support of Larry and Libby Alson, the Mailer family, and his late stepfather, Al Wasserman. He also wants to give an extra special thank-you to his mom, Barbara Wasserman, for always going above and beyond the call of duty.

Finally, we wish to thank our women: Marietta Dalla, Nolan's loving wife of fourteen years, and Peter's bride-to-be, Alice O'Neill.

Madeline Ungar would like to acknowledge Stuey by saying:

Thank you for the journey that we shared together. Thank you for giving me our loving daughter, Stefanie, and for sharing my son, Richie, with me and loving him as much as I did. Stu, you have always been my rock in the hardest times in my life. I guess what I am trying to tell you is that you are a very strong person through tough times. Thank you for the laughs, which were as many as the tears. Our life has included many surprises and disappointments, much giving and taking, and many rewards. One last thing: you always told me what a great mom I was, and I want to tell you what a great dad you were, and still are.

Stefanie Ungar would like to acknowledge Stuey by saying:

Even though the time with my dad was cut short, I still learned so much about life from him. His honesty, loyalty, and compassion for others has left a great impression on my life. I only hope that everyone who reads this book will not only learn about my dad's life and all of his accomplishments, but also learn from his mistakes as well.

SELECTED READING

Alvarez, A. *The Biggest Game in Town.* Boston: Houghton Mifflin, 1983.

Holden, Anthony. *Big Deal.* New York: Viking, 1990.

Reid, Ed, and Ovid Demaris. *The Green Felt Jungle.* Cutchogue, N.Y.: Buccaneer Books, 1963.

Sheehan, Jack, ed. *The Players: The Men Who Made Las Vegas.* Reno: University of Nevada Press, 1997.

INDEX

DiMeglio, "Big" Anthony, 38
dog racing, 60
Downtown Association, Las Vegas,
 253
Drache, Eric, 115, 117, 118, 119
Dreyfuss, Richard, 88
Dunes casino, Las Vegas:
 golf course, 158, 161–62
 hair stylist in, 137
 poker games in, 88–89, 92, 93–95,
  99
 safe-deposit box in, 90, 109
Dunwoody, Charles, 112

Earle, Phil "Doc":
 and golf, 162–63
 nightmare of, 236–38
 and poker, 205, 236, 246, 265
 as Stuey's backer, 236, 244
 and Stuey's comebacks, 248
 and Stuey's drug problem,
  237–38, 270, 287–88
ESPN, 250–51, 253, 254–56

Farny (gangster), 19, 21
FBI wiretaps, 20
Ferguson, Chris "Jesus," 249–50
Ferris, Fred "Sarge," 89, 174
Fischer, Bobby, 35, 124, 270
Fisher, Gene, 126, 128
Fisher, Tommy, 246
Fishman, Steve, 33
"Fixer, the," 55
Flaton, Ken "Skyhawk," 169, 205
Flud, Ron, 293
Flynt, Larry, 88, 265
Four Queens Hotel, Las Vegas, 212,
 213, 236

Four Queens Poker Classic, 212,
 213–15, 227
Fowler, Hal, 109–10
Fox's Corner, 5–7, 9–11
 closed, 22
 Fay working at, 9
 gambling in, 6–7, 14, 36
 police surveillance of, 19–22
 TV and sportsbook in, 6
Frankie (chauffeur), 229
Franks, Harry, 122–23
Frasca, Gus, 56
Fremont Street Experience, Las
 Vegas, 253, 261
Friars Club, Beverly Hills, 81

Gambino family, 38, 42
gambling:
 with a chip and a chair, 157–58
 adolescent nature of, 165
 for gambling's sake, 156, 165
 honor in, 179
 as legitimate profession, 92
Gaughan, Jackie, 113, 121, 130
Genovese family, 19, 36, 37, 40,
 60
gin rummy:
 deals made in, 85
 forms of, 29
 Hollywood, 53
 invention of, 29
 memory needed in, 49
 "schneidered" in, 53n
 standard rules of, 29
 Stuey's enticements to opponents
  in, 77
 Stuey's obsession to win, 78,
  85

poker (*cont.*)
high-stakes games of, 88–89, 90,
110
IRS ruling on, 92*n*
learning the game, 109, 113,
115
live-game players, 103
no-limit Texas Hold'em, 92–94,
95, 106, 107, 108–9, 114, 204,
212–13, 265, 291
Omaha heads-up, 284
Omaha high-low, 107
ORAC computer, 155
playing with another man's
money, 104–6
popularity of, 134
as psychological game, 175
razz, 107, 234
seven-card stud, 59, 88, 90–92,
104–6, 107, 169, 234
side games, 103, 212
Stuey's achievements in, xii,
93–94, 202, 263, 296
"tell" (reading one's opponents)
in, 13
Texans in, 89
tournament players, 103, 106,
109, 110; *see also specific
tournaments*
in Vegas casinos, 88–89
"whales" playing, 222
Poker Hall of Fame, 295
Preston, Amarillo Slim:
first meeting of Stuey and, 77
and golf, 159, 160
and no-limit Texas Hold'em,
92–94
as regular, 89, 90, 265

and Stuey's recklessness, 178–79
and Super Bowl, *see* Amarillo
Slim's Super Bowl of Poker
and WSOP, 76, 89, 110, 122
Price, Teddy, 48, 211

Rabbi, David, 265
Raleigh Hotel, Catskills, 14–15, 18
Ramada Inn, Los Angeles, 221–22
Ranking Mom (horse), 187
Raymer, Greg "Fossilman," 295
Reagan, Ronald, 171
Reese, Chip:
as backer for Stuey, 174, 235, 286
background of, 103
at Bicycle Club game, 222
cutting Stuey off, 178
and Linemovers, 172
and no-limit Texas Hold'em, 94
old guard challenged by, 89–90
and sports betting, 172
sports betting by, 193–94
stamina of, 142–43
as Stuey's mentor, 90–91
and WSOP, 124
Resorts casino, Atlantic City,
145–46, 153
Ripp, Joey, 10–11
Riviera Casino, Las Vegas, 83, 84,
85–86
Robby Don (horse), 187
Roberts, Bryan "Sailor," 89, 110,
179
Robison, Danny:
and drug rehab, 235
and gin, 75–76, 77, 90
as nonstop talker, 91
and poker, 89–90, 91

Ungar, Judith "Judy":
birth and childhood of, 8, 9,
13–14
and drugs, 32, 57, 101, 135, 142
and father's death, 24–27, 32
and Madeline, 135
marriage of, 67, 101, 135
and mother's death, 101
socializing, 18, 21
teen years of, 27, 32, 65
in touch with Stuey, 57, 134–35,
233
Ungar, Madeline Wheeler:
breakup of Stuey and, 167–69
details handled by, 109, 137, 195
divorce of, 169, 181, 182, 185
early years of, *see* Wheeler,
Madeline
in Florida, 181, 195
marriage of Stuey and, 136–37,
167
robbers in home of, 168
son of, *see* Wheeler, Richard
and Stefanie's birth, 137–38
and Stuey's death, 294
and Stuey's drug problem, 238,
242, 264, 266
and Stuey's gambling, 169, 263
and Stuey's infidelities, 140–41,
167
Ungar, Stefanie, 101, 216
birth of, 137–38
childhood of, 167, 185, 194, 218
in Florida, 181, 195, 218, 221,
264
in Las Vegas, 182, 266–67
and parents' divorce, 169, 218
and Stuey's death, 294

Stuey's love for, 138, 181, 218–19,
220, 259, 278–80
as teenager, 263–64, 295
Ungar, Stuart Errol:
achievements of, xii, 39, 93–94,
202, 204, 263, 296
as aggressive player, 94, 110, 111,
112, 247–48
aptitude for numbers, 14, 17–18,
166
in Atlantic City, 145–46
attitude problems of, 31, 33, 34,
39, 53, 63, 76, 85, 86, 91, 106
backers of, 3–4, 174–80, 206–10,
222, 234, 235, 236, 238, 244,
245–47, 248, 249, 251–52, 254,
270–71, 278, 286, 288–90
banks unknown to, 90, 232–33
bar mitzvah of, 19, 36
birth and childhood of, 8–18, 32
and blackjack, 50–51, 72, 151–52,
153–54, 170, 267–68
as borrower, 28, 83, 206, 232, 277,
278–79, 283–89
bubble-gum theft of, 12–13
in California, 81–82, 166
as card savant, 82, 109, 202–4,
212–13, 230, 247–48
and cars, 62–63, 137
in the Catskills, 14–17
childhood poker games of,
16–17
and children, *see* Ungar, Stefanie;
Wheeler, Richard
clothing of, 61–62, 63, 65, 137,
216
comebacks of, 4, 174, 248,
257–58

Discover what "all in" *really* means…

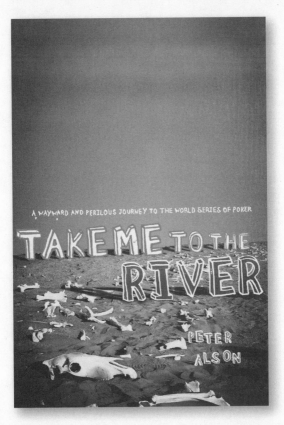

An overeducated underachiever, Peter Alson has spent decades rambling, gambling, and doing his best not to grow up. But at fifty, this tried-and-true bachelor decides it's time to settle down and asks his girlfriend to marry him.

But not before one last hand.

In this hilarious, heartfelt memoir, Alson takes you on a quest for the multi-million-dollar pot, and along the way discovers the true meaning of luck, perseverance, and commitment.

Available July 2006 wherever books are sold or at www.simonsays.com.

ATRIA BOOKS
A Division of Simon & Schuster
A CBS COMPANY

14550